Unraveled and Reconstructed
Steve's Story

Steve Wilhelm

ISBN-13: 978-1541208346
ISBN-10: 154120834X

Cover by Jessica Ozment

Dedicated To

My parents, Dede and George Wilhelm

Acknowledgements to:

Sarah G., my co-worker who was a huge inspiration.

Laura H., for giving me the time to write.

Rob, Steve, Jason and all my friends who I haven't mentioned—you know who you are.

My Bellevue family at the time, for allowing me into your home and lives.

And a special thanks to Heidi B., for always being there for me.

FOREWORD

When I was in the early stages of writing this book, I was asked why I was writing it. At first I said that I wanted to write my own "authorized biography" of my life up until now, so that if I ever became famous, the book would already be written, and penned by me. That way it could be termed "authorized." And so my project, as I called it, started out truly more as a lark, just a whimsical piece. Then, as I began to put words onto "paper" I began to see patterns emerge, just little things in the beginning; my mother had more than a few times told me that from a young age I had a problem with lying. Every time she had mentioned that, however, I had shrugged it off, thinking that it was no more or no less something that anyone else did in their lives that I didn't do it very often and surely it wasn't anything that was a "problem." But as I wrote about my pre-teen and early teenage years, I did notice that there was a commonality to many of the events that I will relate to you. Mom was quite right! However lying isn't the only thing I have been good at. There have also been poor decisions, immaturity, the inability to stand up for myself, i.e.: no backbone… and though I know I have said in the past that I never seem to have been with many women or had a lot of sex, I had undoubtedly forgotten a lot of things…I may have been a late bloomer, but for a period of time, though brief it was, I had my share (but I must not reveal too much too soon!). And what I will have written hasn't been everything that happened in my life, God only knows how long and boring this book would be if I wrote about everything! And some things are just too personal and/or insane that I felt I cannot reveal *every* sordid detail.

I just want to say that I am not a professional writer, and this book will undoubtedly prove that (though as at the time I have gone back through this book and re-edited it for publication as an eBook, I have written and published three works of fiction that can be found on Amazon.com). There may not be cohesiveness in everything you read, one story may be completely out of context and have no relation to the next one or the last one, but as I have been writing, I find that I have learned more about myself (too bad it took more than 47 years (now 56) to learn what I know now). If anything, I hope maybe to shed some insight, possibly impart some words of wisdom to others in the world what can happen to a normal kid, growing up with so much potential in life, who at times takes for granted what there is out there. What can happen when one strays from the norm too much and instead of taking the high road to what could be success, takes roads that for most level-headed people would be clearly marked with *huge yellow caution signs* and doesn't seem to learn from the results of those early journeys. My life has been a long trek up and down so many of those back roads that I am sure most readers will be scratching their heads in wonderment, some maybe laughing hysterically, while others may be wondering why I was not locked up and committed long ago. Believe me; I would be lying if I didn't admit I have had those same thoughts from time to time.

I am not complaining or whining about my life. I have done that in the past. I have lamented, I have cried, I have done the "woe is me" thing and said, "how come I can't get a break!?" "Why do bad things always happen to me?" Well, the more that I write, the more my questions seem to get answered. This is not by any means a Fourth Step project, which is just one of the many steps that I still have not gotten around to completing (I hope that is not too much of a spoiler). This is just a story of my life. Where I have been, what I have done. I have changed many of the names of the people that I write about in my life, as I do not want to portray anyone, my friends or acquaintances in any derogatory light. I will not name actual places of anywhere I have worked, as I am not doing anything other than telling my story. It all is as factual, as best as I can recollect. I may embellish some things unknowingly, as for example the first story regarding my birth. My brain *is* 50 plus years old, and has been affected by alcohol and other things in my life, as you will read, so that very well may have skewed my memory somewhat. But bear with my writing and me and think what you will. Everyone will have his or her own opinion, and that is as it should be. I just hope everyone gets something out of it!

PREPARING FOR THE REAL WORLD

My life began much like anyone else's ... I was born. But that is where the comparison begins to differ a bit: I was adopted. That isn't so strange, however the actual adoption was started and completed before I was actually out of the womb. They call it a "gray market" adoption, where all the paperwork and details are taken care of before the actual birth. I have never had a problem with this, as I love the mother and father who raised me as much if not more than I may have loved the man and woman who actually brought me into the world.

But what I believed to be true for most of my adult life about my birth parents was later told to me to be untrue by Mom. I have always recollected to my friends as I grew up that my biological parents were high school students who were messing around one weekend at the drive-in (yeah, remember those?) or whatever/wherever, and then found out they were pregnant. They were not married and figured out that something needed to be done. Fortunately and thank God that abortion was not in the front of their minds as the decision, or else you would not be reading this book. Regardless of all that, at some point in my life, when talking to Mom or asking about specific details about my birth parents and what year in high school they were in, she looked at me like I didn't know what I was talking about. She said that certainly was not the case and how had I ever come up with that tale. I told her that I was positive that early in my childhood when she had first told me I was adopted, she told me that story. She said I must have made up my own details to make it more entertaining, and she told me it was just a couple of normal people who decided they wouldn't be able to care for me like they wanted to and loved me enough to give me up for adoption. That's all she really knew.

I have an older brother, who was also adopted in the same way. Mom and Dad were told that they would not able to conceive and since they wanted children, they did what they did. My younger brother happened to come along normally, so whatever had prevented them from having children prior to my older brother and myself, wasn't a problem anymore. After three boys, however, Mom and Dad were done; thus, no more kids were introduced into the family. As it turned out, three boys were enough.

I will never know why I embellished the way I was brought into the world when I was little; I do know I have always had a wonderfully vivid imagination, and I don't know when I came to believe what I did, but I suppose in the long run, it doesn't really matter. I am here, I exist and I am who I am. I sometimes do wonder who my biological parents were, what they did, where they are now, but those thoughts are always fleeting, and not of real importance. Would knowing any of those facts would have changed my life significantly? Who knows? I may not be where I am today, but I may still have had some of the same problems. What I do know is I would not be who I am right now, doing what I am doing. But I must not get too much ahead of myself...

I don't really have a lot of memories of early childhood. I don't know many people who can remember what they did when they were one or two, but I do have moments when I can see myself standing up in my crib crying with my wet, plastic covered diapers sticking to my butt... holding onto the wooden bars, like a midget prisoner looking out into the world that he is kept from... I have a brief memory (again in the crib, again crying) with a very sore throat—perhaps I had had my tonsils removed or something—the specifics I don't remember. Also, at some point as a baby I apparently was so hungry that I ate some of the wooden curtains that were in the den. Mom said she cried as she pulled slivers out of my tongue (again, fleeting memories)... That sounds more like something I would have done during my drinking years in my mid-forties, but again, I don't want to jump ahead too fast.

I don't remember anything of the first house I lived at in Boise, nor do I have any recollection of the year or two we lived in Yakima, save for me learning to ride a two-wheeler bike, or of the neighbor boy who lived next door who was also named Steve. This was apparently very confusing when one of our mother's would call "Steve!" and we would both answer... I have been told that was quite amusing. I suppose it would have been.

I am not quite sure when, but I was told that what really helped me learn to read was not only the Weekly Reader and school, but since I also really liked TV (that sure hasn't changed) I was frustrated by the fact that I could not read the TV Guide. I really wanted to know what was on television, and the only way I was going to know, was to be able to read. So oddly enough, that was a major influence. That's pretty spectacular, I haven't heard of television actually being a good influence on a child like that in a long time, of course I don't currently watch a lot of children's programming anymore, though once after a night audit shift, I caught an episode of "Sponge Bob and Square Pants" which was pretty funny to an extremely tired mind.

My first two years of elementary school were pretty tame, not much excitement or anything unusual, except for maybe when I almost got my second grade school teacher fired. From what I remember, I was in the lunchroom (I think I was about 7 or eight years old), and a girl threw some food at me, or maybe at someone else, from another table. This was back in 1967 or '68 and our lunchroom doubled as the school gym and all the tables came out of the walls. Anyway, I think I threw food back at her... what else was I supposed to do? The only bad thing is, the lunchroom monitor saw me throwing the food, not the girl, and I was taken to the principal's office. While I was waiting for the principal, my teacher walked by and noticed me sitting there. She came in and asked why I was there, and I told her it was because of food being thrown. I might have neglected to mention that I was the one who was caught throwing said food. Anyway, she told me to go outside and play as she would take care of things. This may have been the beginning of my career of fibbing, lying, or stretching the truth, whatever we want to term it. When one starts out small, one must be careful about where things can lead (but again, I get ahead of myself...). Anyway, the rest of the afternoon consisted of my going back and forth from the classroom to the hall, as the details of the incident were sorted out and my teacher was disciplined for releasing me from the office without knowing the true facts. This seems so simple of a grade school problem when compared to what goes on now, but then again, things were simpler back then. Bottom line, my teacher was not fired, nor was I expelled.

Sometime during the summer of 1969 I believe, we moved into the house my parents had built, where I lived until college. It was a great house, and I do have a lot of great memories and truth be told, lived a good childhood there.

I had a pretty normal elementary school life after that; I recall being a rather popular guy... I remember having a girlfriend for my fourth, fifth and half of sixth grade years, though during the last half year, I must have had a premonition of how things were going, because I remember having two spare girlfriends. But having a "girlfriend" in grade school was really more like having a good pal, who just happens to be a girl. Sara and I did hang out and did things together, and for the most part we were just good pals. I never thought really about anything romantic, because, well hell, I was just a kid! The closest we ever got was a "slow-dance" once at her house, and I found being that close to her was a very strange thing… and also that her breath was horribly bad, not that mine would have been any better, but it did throw me for a loop. But I also remember we caused a little stir when we were probably the youngest kids to ever have a bed scene in a vampire play I wrote in the fifth grade. It just seemed like such an innocent thing at the time. Who knew about sex and all the implications of two 10 year olds sharing a bed back in the late 60's? Even now when I read that play I still laugh out loud! But Sara broke up with me in the middle of sixth grade… I recall sometime after she stated I had hit her too hard with the rubber foursquare ball during a lively round of dodge ball during PE one afternoon. She said I hit her and laughed, like it was the funniest thing I had ever done. Of course I don't remember doing that, I always thought of myself as a gentleman! I probably did, though.

Sometime during my fourth grade year, I talked the local disc jockey of the AM country radio station (he lived behind our house) into getting me airtime for my "Story Hour," where for 5 minutes every Saturday morning, I would read stories live on the air, and encourage listeners to write and send in their stories for me to read on my show. This was truly an amazing thing I think. I mean, how many 10-year olds have their own radio show on a commercial radio station? My show only ran over the allotted time once, and I knew I was in trouble, but I couldn't just stop the story, it only had a few more paragraphs left… but knowing now how valuable air time is now, and surely was at that time as well, it was understandable how pissed off the disc jockey was… I didn't get "fired" though. I only got cancelled once during the year I had my show, only due to President Nixon and some special Saturday speech he gave… I also recall only getting only one story submission from a listener during that year. I did have to heavily correct the spelling and fix major grammatical errors before I could read it. Most of the stories I did read were those that I wrote, and one was from a classmate of mine. I often wonder how many people actually listened to my show… what kid is listening to a country music station at 10am on a Saturday morning? I know that I would normally be out playing or if my parents had their way (which was the case most of the time) I would be mowing the lawn or weeding the gardens....

As a lot of families did back then, my parents took us on many summer vacations to Portland, Oregon to see the grandparents, and then went on over to the Oregon Coast for a week... I remember those as extremely fun times for us as kids. One of those summers I developed a great interest in matches and remember once almost starting a beach grass fire behind an old shed. Thank God for whatever intervention helped and I was able to put out the flames before they got big... beach houses were mostly constructed with wood and **old** wood at that back then.

I always looked forward to those summer trips to Oregon; it was a two-fold treat: seeing the grandparents, and being able to see "Batman" on TV. We didn't get "Batman" (you know the series, the one starring Adam West and Burt Ward as Robin) on any station in Boise. For the longest time I was sure that the show was made in Portland. Why else would I only be able to find it when we were in Portland? I remember trying to talk my parents into taking me to the TV station so that I could meet Robin. I loved his costume, and for several years, the Robin costume was always on my Christmas list. Of course, I was never taken to the TV station, and I never got the Robin costume. I think my parents figured, or hoped, or even wished this obsession was just a passing phase, which it was, though to this day, I still have a fascination for that series.

There was an incident that comes to mind, though I don't remember exactly when it happened, when I was at the grocery store with my mom and little brother. At some point I had noticed a package of those big Sweet Tarts (I had always had a sweet tooth, and currently still do), and since I didn't have any money of my own, I put the package in the front pocket of my shorts. Another customer in the store apparently noticed what I had done, went to my mom and promptly told her what I had done. When confronted by her and the accuser, I became dumbfounded and denied any knowledge of the deed. I did the Cub Scout salute and swore that I wasn't lying and "sincerely" didn't know how the candy had gotten in my pocket. I don't remember the outcome, but I am pretty sure my mom didn't believe a word of my explanation. I probably didn't have the candy when I got home, either, though I am sure I got grounded.

There was the big California Disneyland trip in 1973… that was the year Nixon resigned. I recall that afternoon with clarity. My younger brother and I were on the way to the swimming pool when Mom called to us from the room balcony at the Disneyland Hotel where we were staying. She yelled for us to come back inside "now!" She didn't want us to miss history! I surely didn't understand what could be more important for a 12-year old than swimming when on vacation in Disneyland! But we did go back inside. I remember watching for a minute, then going into the other bedroom and watching an episode of the "Twilight Zone," I even remember the episode where the kids would dive into a swimming pool and swim into a different world, or time or something like that! Funny how I can remember *that* with such clarity and not what Nixon said just a few minutes before. I wonder if that speaks for my current political interests.

As far as kid's lives go my childhood years were generally normal. I had a mouthful of baby teeth that did not want to come out on their own, so I had the pleasure (sarcasm) of having them pulled… and then I had braces for a couple of years. I had a paper route, delivering the "Idaho Statesman" for several years, and I also delivered the "Advertiser," which was a weekly free classified paper similar to "The Little Nickel" a common paper all over the Pacific Northwest. What was noteworthy about that endeavor is I won a ten-speed bike and several other prizes signing up the most subscriptions (which were free) of the "Advertiser" during a special promotion, bringing in the highest new subscribers in the city. I ended up giving that bike to my little brother since I already had one. I mowed lawns during the summers for cash. I did the March of Dimes Walk-a-thon two years in a row. These were activities that were for the most part pretty normal things for a kid to be doing back in the late 60s (this almost sounds like where the announcer then says, "he was a normal kid, living the normal childhood, then, something went wrong…" ha-ha, but nothing as *bad* as all that).

I also did a summer of little league baseball as a kid, though I don't remember exactly what year that was. My position was center field, though I recall the coach had me try pitching one afternoon, to see if maybe I was any good at that. I guess since I played outfield all season, that was the answer to that. It was a pretty good experience as it went, though I don't think I took it as seriously as most of the other kids. I sucked at batting, and the few times I actually made contact with the pitched ball, I rarely got to base. It's funny how later you can really see the meaning of adult terms, like: tunnel vision. After I hit the pitch, all I could see was the path between me and first base, nothing else was there, it's odd that I remember that so vividly now. But it got to where at times I would be so scared of batting that I would lie and say I felt sick and couldn't bat, so they took me off the rotation. Eventually, I would get brave, and want to bat but I was told I could not be put back in once I had been removed. It did serve me right for being a chicken. I remember during one game, I was fielding and it was an unusually long inning, and I had to pee. I had to pee badly. I kept calling, "Mr. Smallwood! Mr. Smallwood! I have to go!!" But he never let me off the field until we finally struck all the batters out. We won only two games as I recall. The funny thing about that was both games were against the same team. Either way, I think our team sucked, but I will never put little league down, it is a good venue for kids to learn to get along with other kids and get good exercise. One piece of advice I would give now is make sure you have an empty bladder before you take the field.

I always knew I had writing talents from an early age, but when I made it into junior high school, I discovered I liked acting. I don't remember why I liked it so much, though. Perhaps it was during the "productions" of my earlier plays I had written in grade school, but I ended up joining the cast of several school productions. It seemed pretty easy to memorize lines and get up in front of audiences at that age. I know that now, I have grown to be very self-conscious and it would be very hard to do the same thing at this time. However back then I remember really enjoying performing. I think my best role was Reader #5 in "Jonathon Livingston Seagull." I know it doesn't sound like an important role, but it *was* Jonathon. We were all so hyped up after that last performance that we begged our drama teacher Mr. Hensen to add on one more night. But it just wasn't meant to be. Mr. Hensen once said that my friend Terry and I were the best actors in the school. I had heard that after the fact, but it still made me feel really good. Being a member of the school drama club gave me the opportunity to stage a few plays that I had written, which was great because I got to choose which characters I wanted to play as I saw fit, and I usually chose to play the lead character in those productions.

It was during the junior high days that I became aware of girls and found I had all the normal attraction to the girls that I had never felt when I was in grade school. I had no idea about sex or anything that went along with that notion, but I was aware of the differences between guy friends and girl "friends"... I know that all sounds so lame and abnormal, especially when compared to how things are today: sex and promiscuity is more rampant (for better or worse) today than it was in the mid-seventies... and I was more or less the clueless kid when it came to that kind of thing anyway.

In the fall of 1975, I think it was September 13, but why I remember the actual date I have no idea, I went to the birthday party of a classmate, Kelly. It was the normal party that teenage kids had back in my day: cake, some presents, the usual birthday party accoutrements. But after all that, we all sat around the living room (there were no parents around, which now seems unusual when I think about it, but having them around would have hindered the activity that occurred), and Kelly, being the birthday girl, was going around to all the guys and giving them full kisses on the mouth, which was great! When Kelly got to me, she sat in my lap and was kissing me (she was a wonderful kisser from what I recall) when she stopped and asked me if I knew what a French was. I had no idea what she meant and all of a sudden her tongue shot into my mouth and attacked *my* tongue, catching me in complete surprise. It was not actually and awesome thing, I will tell you, and I quickly learned how to French-kiss quite easily. But the lesson didn't last long, and before I knew it, she was off to teach another guy how to kiss. I remember sitting in the chair, and I kept trying to get her back for some more lessons. I know this might seem like a preposterous story, but that's my story and I'm sticking to it!

There was another girl, Carole, who was in my class in 8th grade. We had a great relationship agreement – we were boyfriend and girlfriend, but if ever either of us wanted to break up for whatever reason, we could, no questions asked. It was the perfect arrangement, because I felt that I would never want to break up. We went out for a while, and I remember one time, she asked me to come over to her friend's place so that we could hang out. I was supposed to stay home because my aunt was going to be coming to visit the family from Oregon that afternoon. I told Mom that I was going down to the shopping center and play the pinball machine for a while and would be back soon. I rode my bike over and met Carole, and I remember sitting in an easy chair with her, our other friends Jim and Barb were making out on the couch. The curtains in the living room were closed and so the place was dark and cozy. Carole and I were kissing for a while, and then just lay together in the chair, comfortable and cozy. Carole took my hand and put it on her chest, so that my hand was cupping her breast. It was the first time I had belt a boob, even if it was through clothes, and I was on top of the world! But by then, I had been gone for at least a couple of hours and was getting worried that I was going to be in trouble for not getting home at the time I had told my mom. I raced back home and my aunt was there and Mom was furious! She was demanding to know where I had been and why I hadn't been home hours ago! Why hadn't I called? I couldn't tell her I had been in someone's apartment with friends making out and feeling a girl up (even through clothes, as it was); I would be grounded for sure! So I lied and said that I had been playing the pinball machine as I told her I would be, and kept winning and got caught up in the game and lost track of time! I don't think she believed me... and I ended up getting grounded anyway. I couldn't go anywhere after school for two weeks and had to stay at home on the weekends as well. So two weeks for a little necking and a little groping. Would it have gone any different had I told the truth? Who knows? Was it worth it? Who knows? I thought so at the time!

I remember a few months after that, Carole and I and the same friends were down in our basement when my parents were gone one afternoon, and we had the lights out and we were kissing for a little while until we heard noise from upstairs. Mom had come home. We hurried and turned on the lights and turned on the TV just in time before the door to the basement opened and Mom called down to see who was down there and what we were doing. I think in this day and age, kids would ignore the parent and keep making out anyway, but that was a different time. A few weeks later, Carole reminded me of our agreement and said she didn't want to go out with me anymore. I asked her why, and she said there were no questions, did I not remember? And then that was over. But at least I had advanced a bit in the boy/girl sexual department...

11

At some point I had given up my newspaper delivery job. I think it was something about getting up at oh-dark-thirty that was fast becoming old. But the lure of income and the wanting to be able to purchase comic books to add to my collection was still present, so I figured that I needed to get another job, just not one that would interfere with sleep. I had noticed a help-wanted sign hanging in the window of a local record store (yes, of course vinyl was the major form of pre-recorded music at that time—that and reel to reel and 8-track tapes). I was very familiar with that store, as I frequented there with purchases of 45rpms. I filled out an application on the spot and after talking to the owner, he said he would be in touch with me soon. I took soon as meaning in a few days, and after a week of hearing nothing, I called and asked if they had made a decision yet. They told me they had not and told me to call back the next week. As requested, I called a week later and was disappointed to hear the same response. As it had been almost a month with no quality income (mowing lawns just didn't cut it), (excuse the pun, it really was not intended!) I called and told the owner that I was calling because they were supposed to tell me that day whether or not they were going to hire me (this was a lie, but I figured in this case, it was warranted). After a pause, I was asked if I could start the next day. Delighted, I said of course I could, since it would be Saturday. I think I worked there during the weekends and after school for about a year, and it was a good job. I worked well with customers, had no problems with the cash register and even got discounts on purchases.

At some point after getting my driver's license, some friends and I decided to cruise the loop downtown Boise. This was a fun pastime, and it wasn't really a dangerous thing as it can be nowadays. I had heard from other friends that it was a cool way to pick up girls, so we decided to give it a try, see what happens. Ron and I drove the circuit a few times and just as we were about to give up, and go back to our neighborhood, he noticed another car flashing their headlights, seemingly at us. Ron told me to slow down and get a look! There were girls, and they were motioning for us to pull over or slow down or something. I slowed, and we opened our windows. I saw a head pop up out of the sunroof of the other car and this beautiful girl waved and pointed ahead, and I heard the words: "follow us!" I didn't need any more instruction from Ron, as he agreed that we needed to do just what they had asked. So we ended up driving through

Boise, watching the girl's faces keep looking back at us, laughing and pointing, making sure we were still behind them. Of course we were! We weren't stupid... we were just kids with lots of testosterone (didn't have a clue what that word was back then—apparently don't have a clue how to use it now—haha!). We ended up back up in my own neighborhood, in the parking lot of the local country club, just driving around and around, exchanging laughs and smiles. This must have been the way we did things back then, no talking, just waving and smiling... but then they rolled one of their windows down and one of the girls said their friend wanted to meet Me... she wanted to get out and walk with me and talk. That was a new thing for me! To this day, I haven't had that kind of invitation since.

So I got out of the car and told Ron to wait, let's see what happens. Cindi got out of her car and we ended up walking around the parking lot for about a half hour or so, talking about whatever teenagers who have never met before talk about. Whatever we did talk about, we hit it off, exchanged phone numbers and started seeing each other. It was a pretty good couple of months... we spent a lot of time together, though I don't really remember a lot of those times alone with her... for whatever reason or another, I remember whenever we were together, either Ron or Geoff was with me, probably because they had easier access to a car and thus, transportation so that I could get out to see her. Cindi was a beautiful girl, and a great kisser. She and I probably would have been together for a lot longer had I not screwed things up one afternoon. I was a very cocky kid, and thought a lot of the time that I was the shit! The last time we were together, I tried to be cool and joked around and was playing with a big rubber band. I made as if I was going to shoot Cindi with it, and meant to actually release the end of it and hit myself in the face, but things did not go as planned. When the rubber band shot, it went the wrong direction and hit Cindi in the face. She was stunned and furious. I was embarrassed and shocked. I was very sorry and as my pride was sinking to the lower depths of my stomach, I begged her for forgiveness. She was almost crying and yelled at me to get out; she never wanted to see me again. I was almost in tears myself when I left. We spoke on the phone a few times after that, and then she never returned any of my calls. In retrospect, I really don't blame her. I'm sure I would have felt the same way.

But I do remember developing this *huge* crush on one girl, Jenny, who happened to be a cheerleader. I was so stuck on her that I even joined the boys' basketball team so that I could impress her and be near her. I was a horrible player, didn't know the first thing about the game. They tried to teach me how to "screen" an opposing player and I remember thinking I didn't know what the hell they were talking about. I ended up playing on the 5th quarter team, which I thought was pretty cool, not really understanding it was just a pity quarter that didn't count for anything, just making the poor schleps like me feel like they were worth something and made a difference. I didn't really know anything like that at the time, but that is probably for the best.

Poor Jenny, having to put up with me for the entire year... I believe I asked her to *every single* school dance, and I remember she turned me down for all of them. Well, except for the last one. I think she must have gotten tired of saying no, or maybe she just felt so sorry for me that she finally gave in. I don't remember if we had a good time, or what the night was like, so either it was just ok, or it was so bad that I must have erased it from my memory altogether, but either way, I have survived. I do remember that as we were driving to the dance, she sat so close to the door, had it accidently opened up, she would have fallen right out. Yeah, fond memories, right? Not only did she have to put up with my pestering at school, I remember bugging her at the drive-in burger joint she worked at on the weekends. One day I had a gorilla mask on and we drove through and ordered some sodas and I said she probably didn't know who I was, and she said, "you must be Steve..." how could she have known that? Probably because I was the only one crazy enough to do stupid things like that... but I didn't learn that doing stupid things does not impress the girls you like with the actions of my first crush. I made a pattern of doing stupid things with all the girls I had crushes on ever since then... some things more inane than others, and I am sure I will relate those later...

I wasn't always thinking about girls and making out in my early teen years. I was involved with activities at the local YMCA, doing productive things, such as becoming a CIT (counselor in training), which allowed me to go to summer camp and actually have fun without having to pay for it. I met some cool people and had privileges that regular campers did not, like staying up later, and being somewhat of a leader instead of one of the kids. We got to play cool games, have campfires–really have a lot of fun. It was just a great time; life was different back then, more conducive to do those kinds of things... I can't see kids doing that kind of thing now—not with the iPods, cell phones, all the personal gadgets they have nowadays... they don't have time for summer camp... but the point is I was active in doing good things and learning how to interact outside the home... not to mention there were cute female CIT's too. But there are no stories to go into there...

It was sometime during the junior high years that I became fascinated with things like hypnosis, mysticism, things like that... I would see odd books advertised in the classifieds of TV Guide, the Enquirer, rag mags and publications like that, and I began to order some of those books. I got a really neat book on hypnotism that came with a mystical coin that was supposed to help induce hypnosis when you twirled it while attempting to put someone under. I remember trying to hypnotize my younger brother, some friends who I could trust with the knowledge I was weird, so really anyone who would let me try. I don't think I was successful at any of these attempts. There was a nice chapter regarding self-hypnosis, and I tried that on myself as well... I think I always fell asleep before I was able to put myself in a trance... but it was fun to dabble with. There was a funny story involving my acting and hypnosis: for one of the junior high school assemblies, the school had hired a stage hypnotist, and he was putting on a really good, entertaining show. Even though I believed in the theory, I didn't believe that he could actually put any of my friends into a trance, I mean, how could he? I couldn't. It made perfect sense to me. So anyway, I was chosen to get up on stage, and we went through the whole process of getting put under.... "You are very relaxed, you are very sleepy," that sort of thing. Well, I pretended I was put under, and did everything the guy told us to do, even though I knew I was not hypnotized (or was I after all?). I was laughing inside, so very proud of myself for fooling this professional and getting away with it. I don't remember if he had me do anything foolish, like bark like a dog, or strut like a chicken or anything like that... but after it was over and done with, my friend Kirby apparently had been given a post-hypnotic suggestion that when he sat down and was told to stay, he would be unable to stand back up. Well, somehow, this worked on him and he was not able to get up so that he could go to class. He was pissed, but there was nothing we could do. He could not budge from his seat. We had to go find the hypnotist, who ended up saying something into Kirby's ear, and then he was instantly able to stand up. I kind of felt differently about hypnosis after that, though I am still convinced that I cannot be put under...

So I in addition to hypnosis, I dabbled in some astral traveling, and I even attempted having some home séances (JFK never appeared, though I would swear on a stack of bibles that the cupboard door was closed before we turned the light off and turned it back on...), we'll just say if there was a stupid whimsical occultist thing and it seemed like I could use it for fun or profit, then I was all about it, though I would never show my parents any side of this part of me... I wouldn't want them to think I was a strange child.

Mom and Dad were always thinking about our education. Of course they wanted us to study hard, do well in school, and make the grades, like any other dedicated parent. They had done some research about the high schools in the area, and decided that I should get the best college prep education. So thus, they told me that they felt I should attend the Catholic high school in Boise, rather than going to Borah High where I would have gone due to the district we lived in. They were concerned with what they knew about the public school system and the parties, alcohol, drugs, that they didn't want me to be sidetracked by any of that. They figured that at a Catholic high school, with the teachers being Sisters and Fathers and just the whole notion of structure, that I would be much better off going there, and I would obviously get a much better education. I initially fought this idea (though I equated it more as a demandment); I used the lamest excuse I could come up with: all my *friends* were going to Borah, and that is very important to me! I didn't want to part from them and go to a different school, where I wouldn't know anyone, and I certainly didn't want to go to a *Catholic high school!* I mean, come on! A *religious* school? I didn't go to church every Sunday; I didn't even go to church more than a couple times a year by then. When I was little, We went to church most Sundays, though I think the only reason my parents got us to go then was the promise of breakfast at the Pancake House after the service. The bottom line was I was going to attend BK like my parents wanted me to, but I told them I wanted to complete my three years where I already was (BK is a four-year high school) and they agreed to that. I don't want anyone to think that going to a Catholic high school is a bad thing. Quite the contrary. It was actually a wonderful, amazing experience in a lot of ways, although, for as many good things that happened, there was a few embarrassing times as well, as I will relate to you.

When I did begin my sophomore year at BK, it turned out that I was not the only student who ended up there from South. It was only a small consolation, however, I had had only a few classes with Greg, and we barely knew each other, but at least I was not alone. It was fairly easy for me to meet new people and make friends, as I have usually been a fairly outgoing guy. And I was quick to notice the cute girls among my peers. There was one girl in particular, Sal, I did find as quite attractive. But as I was the new guy in the school, among a student body who had more than likely known each other or at least gone to school together since kindergarten years, I found it much harder to approach the girls. Sal was very popular and she also was a cheerleader, I found out, so in retrospect, remembering my experiences with the cheerleader in junior high, I should have left well enough alone. But then I remembered one of the books I had gotten through the mail (remember all the weird books I mentioned previously?), and I just knew it would help me out if I used its methods diligently. The title of this book was something like "How to Secretly Attract Girls to You," or something stupid like that. All I know is I read that I needed to have a picture of Sal and chant some mumbo jumbo while staring at it each night with a lit candle or something like that. The only thing I lacked, was the picture. I didn't have a camera, and even if I did, I couldn't very well just go up to this girl I didn't even know and ask if she minded if I took her picture (remember cell phones with the built-in cameras were available yet... cell phones weren't even invented yet!), so what was I to do? There was a classmate who was on the yearbook staff, taking pictures around the school. He seemed very popular and knew everybody. I saw him taking pictures of the cheerleaders as well, and then of course it dawned on me what to do. I asked Bill if he would take a picture of Sal for me. I don't remember what excuse I used as I am sure he asked me why I was requesting his services. What I can tell you is that this is definitely not a way to make any kind of good impression among people you are trying to get to know and will be hanging around with for the next three years. Bill did take her picture, but I never got one. A few of Sal's friends had asked him why he was taking more than a couple of photos of her, and he told them I had asked him to, and, well, let's just say I would very much discourage anyone from going down that route if they want to get a girl. I mean, really, what the hell was I thinking? How would I react if I found out someone wanted pictures of me for whatever reason and was having someone follow me around taking them? In this day and age, I'm sure I could've been slapped with some kind of lawsuit or another... but oh well, I can't change the past. I'm Sal thought of me as a total creep after and that she has better stay away from. But I did survive.

I never became a hugely popular guy during my high school years. I was never the widely liked jock but I was not a nerdy guy either. I joined the tennis team and made several good friends through that avenue. I also became an active part of the school's newspaper and had a lot of fun with journalism, writing articles and having responsibilities in the advertising aspect of the paper. I remember several times when we would borrow Father Pedro's car to go pick up the *Knight Beat* from the print shop, we would beat the hell (no pun intended) out of his car, speeding through mud-puddle in dirt roads and screeching around corners—things we would never do in our own cars... one day he walked around his car when we had returned and noticed all the caked on mud around the tire wells and asked us jokingly if we had been four-wheeling in his car? Of course we assured him that we had not; we would never treat his car that way! Father Pedro was fun to torment... I don't know why we treated him as bad as we did; I think it must have been because we liked him so much, though I don't think any of us would ever admit. Father Pedro lived at the school in an apartment for visiting priests, and he had given his spare apartment key to us so that we more easily could assist him on projects and tasks involving the newspaper, as he oversaw the entire operations of the school paper. If he only knew all the opportunities that opened up for us (I must admit that I was never the instigator of any of the pranks that were pulled, but what is it they say? Knowing is abetting? Or something like that), but some of the things we did would be considered stupid and immature now, though nothing we did was malicious or life-threatening as what kids do nowadays. A few things that come to mind? Vaseline on the toilet seat, fixing his bed to collapse when he sat on it, having a mannequin fall of the roof when he opened his front door—I am sure there were more, but like I said before, we probably wouldn't have done those things to someone we didn't like.

I still found time to watch TV during my high school years, watching a lot of the shows that all guys liked. "Starsky & Hutch" was one of my favorites. I really wanted to become an undercover cop just like them; it all seemed cool and hip. I wish I could remember why I became interested in the TV show "Family," that premiered in 1976. I know that for whatever reason, I became very infatuated with Kristy McNichol, and even to this day, I still have a hard time admitting this to all but a very few people. I'm still not sure it is a normal thing for a high school guy to have a crush on an actress the way I did. There was no one I knew who did the crazy weird things I did. What can I tell you? There I was, probably at that time a junior in high school, going to the store and buying any magazines that had pictures of Kristy and cutting them out and making my little scrapbooks of her (I am blushing even now as I am going over this again!)… That must have been a sight to see: I would go to 7-11's or Circle K's that were out of area I normally went to so that no one would recognize me; I would carry a picture of her in my wallet; I must have had 3 or four posters of her hanging on my bedroom walls! I used to take my stereo system down into the basement every Tuesday night and set the system up so I could record "Family" onto cassette tapes. I could pick up the audio from the ABC station on our FM dial, making it possible for me to do this. Then I could listen to the episodes whenever I wanted to. Man, what a genius I was (who knew then, that the show would be available on DVD later?). I remember trying to be secretive in carting around my stereo system, so I would not have to explain what I was doing to my parents or brothers. There was one time when my parents had an after school tennis party at our house, and some of the girls on the team made it a point to go up to my room just to see the posters! Somehow it had gotten out in school about "the posters" and me. I even bought Kristy a nice necklace and sent it to her as a birthday gift one year (how crazy was that?). I never got to be a full-blown stalker or anything like that, sending her letters every day, calling her on the phone all the time (though there was a phone call during my freshman year at USC, but we'll get to that), but to anybody who is or knows someone with symptoms like I have just described, please don't let it get to where I was. I sincerely would love to go back and change that part of my life if I could... but then, if I did that, maybe this book would never have been written, hmmm.... That's weird to think about.... But for all of you reading this, please I hope you learn some things that I obviously never did: if you are going to have weird crushes or obsessions and want to indulge in them, please, please, do NOT make this Public knowledge! All that will lead to is embarrassment and unwanted criticism, weird looks and basically getting laughed at and ridiculed at. I wish I had been warned...

Remembering how much fun I had had in junior high school acting in school plays and such, and still full of pride from the raves and compliments from Mr. Henson, I decided to return to the field and auditioned for one of our high school plays. I don't remember the name of the play, what it was about, or anything specific about the play, but what I *do* remember was that I had lost all of the finesse of the craft. During the lunch period one day, we put on a few sample scenes for the lunch crowd; I guess sort of a combination rehearsal and advertisement for the show. I remember that I was full of stage fright, and I know I forgot my lines several times. That is all I can remember about the acting bit in high school, so I must have given up that dream right then. Oh, I still had big dreams of maybe doing something after getting out of school, if I ended up somewhere where I could get into television or movies! I mean, how hard can *that* be? From what I knew, if actors flubbed their lines then, they just would do another take! But at that time anyway, I think I gave up acting and started thinking about other things.

Sometime during my junior year, I had this idea that I could write a movie script about a young guy who lived in a normal town and was an aspiring actor (me) who was fed up with the small town life and did not want to follow in his father's footsteps and end up working for him. The guy would leave his hometown with his best friend and move to Los Angeles and try his hand at acting in the big city. He would just happen to meet and fall in love with an actress (Kristy), get a good job with her and they would live happily ever after. Well, that was the Reader's Digest synopsis of the project and I even got my friend Tom interested in the project, and he helped me co-write the script. The whole deal ultimately went nowhere, but it did go through several re-writes and changes... more detail about this project will be told...

But for all those bad embarrassing times, there were also great times in high school. I had two really good friends during those years. Tom was a normal guy who when I met him had really lost a lot of weight, though I would never have known this at all. He had told be about how he had been made fun of in earlier years. And then everybody who talked about him could not get over how much weight he had lost. I got along with him because he seemed to me to be just a normal guy, and a lot like me, I thought, though maybe a little more reserved. We did share a love for writing and television and we both had great imaginations. Dave and I became friends through the tennis team. Dave was not a jock, but he was quite a popular guy, not only because he grew up with everyone from first grade through high school, but also because he had a personality that enabled him to be everyone's friend. If Dave ever made fun of my Kristy issues, at least he never let on to me personally, however, many of his friends did. That always seemed to bother me deep inside, but I knew there was nothing I could do about that. I just let them have their fun, because what else could I do. Tom never gave me any shit for anything, maybe because he understood more what it was like to have obsessions... I remember he was an avid science fiction fan and read all the time, and in those times, he was probably thought of as a geeky nerd (I am only guessing at this, Tom, I don't know if we ever talked about this).

There were parties and dances and gatherings we would all go to, some of them that were at houses and of course had a fair share of drinking (which I certainly do not condone for anybody under the drinking age, but let's be real, it happens)... I must admit I did not like the taste of beer, wine or hard alcohol at all at that time, so I was not an active participant in the drinking part. It was a lot of fun, though, to watch other people drink and get drunk. I saw one guy dive into a bush brandishing a pocketknife. He finally came back out, saying that it was lucky he was there to stop the bush from attacking us. I remember one party we went to where we were looking for Dave's sister, who was a year younger than us. Dave said we had to get her home before their parent's found out she had gone out drinking. We did not find her in the kitchen, but we did find an empty vodka bottle. What would happen, we wondered, if we filled the bottle full of water and left it on the table, would anyone notice it and then drink it. We did just that and left the room, went outside and watched from the window. Sure enough, someone came in, saw the bottle, and looked to make sure no one was watching and put the bottle under his coat and left the kitchen in a hurry. We never saw his reaction when he realized it was not vodka, but we thought it was pretty hilarious! The things that made us laugh back then, but things were simpler back then, weren't they? We finally found his sister and literally carried her out of the party to Dave's car, she screamed obscenities at us all the way home.

Though I never liked drinking during high school, I was often asked to help provide beer for parties. Why? Well, I guess I looked like I was of age (I can't remember if the legal age was 18 or 19 back then), and though I am sure I was always sweating and nervous looking, I very rarely got carded. Believe it or not, the one place I found it the easiest to buy beer was at the local Kmart. I was never carded there. There was a 7-11 right off the Boise State University campus that I was always successful at well. I know it is sad, but even though I was "used" to buy the alcohol, I felt proud to be a part of the in-crowd, if only for the moment. I am sure that if I was not able to come through with the goods, they would have found other ways to get the beer.

Tennis was a big part of high school for me. I was not the best player on the team, but I kept my own on the court. I played 2nd or 3rd boys singles for a while and did pretty well in the weekly tournaments. Dave and I palled around a lot during tennis, I like to think that he and I played about the same, but truth be told, he was better than me, usually defeating me when we played against each other. We loved playing against teams from schools that were from the smaller towns around Boise. We were considered a smaller school, so we were not in the same brackets as the bigger public high schools though we did play against them as well. But the smaller schools didn't seem to have the best players, (I am not trying to be judgmental, it just seemed that way, but of course, there are always exceptions to that rule), and more often than not we could beat them more easily. I guess you could consider us cruel, and thinking back on it I certainly do, but Dave and I used to get cheap $5 tennis rackets and pretend we were really bad players and trash the hell out of the rackets when we intentionally flubbed shots. The problem with doing that is we would get into trouble from our coaches for our poor sportsmanship behavior. A lot of times we would let ourselves fall behind to make them feel better and then ended up losing the matches anyway. That was always embarrassing for me, and I know I stopped doing that after a while.

Soon after that, I switched to doubles and had a lot of fun with that. One season I was teamed with a Irene, a popular girl and a decent player. We were pretty a pretty good team and also provided good comic relief every once in a while. I remember one time where on a first serve, she hit me square in the back. She had hit the ball so hard, that it bounced clear out of the court over the chain link barrier. I don't know if I fell over more because of pain, or with laughter, but we laughed like it was the funniest thing that had ever happened. I was always pretty leery of her serving after that however.

During my senior year I was partnered with Pat, who was a junior, and we were a great team. Soon we pretty much knew each other's strengths were quite the challenge even though we were classified 2nd boys doubles. Pat and I went to the state championship held in Sun Valley still in the same number two position, though after the first round, when our first team lost, Pat and I progressed all the way to the finals. It seemed we could not miss a shot and we both played like we were on top of our game. It was great! Then there was the final match, played on center court, with bleachers on both sides, which meant we had an audience. I don't know what happened, whether it was because we were the center of attention, or perhaps we were merely playing a better team, but it seemed like I completely forgot how to play tennis. I felt so sorry for Pat, because he was, as usual, playing up to his full capacity. I could not get any good serves in. I could not do anything but hit the ball out of bounds or into the net. Pat might have stood a better chance if I had not been there at all, I felt. Bottom line, we were defeated soundly, and I was devastated. I think I left the court and went off somewhere and wept, I felt so bad. But we did end up in second place, with silver medals. Considering we went farther than our 1st boys' team–that was a pretty good feat. To this day, I still have the silver medal hanging on my bulletin board; though it is a little tarnished (only by age mind you). All in all, tennis was a great part of my high school days. I was even reunited briefly with my old grade school girl friend Sara when we played against her high school, though there was none of the former camaraderie that we once shared. I wonder if she still harbored ill feelings from that dodge ball game so long ago!? I didn't think to ask her at the time. We did end up seeing each other once more after that, but that was way after college. I may elaborate on that later, if I don't forget.

For a few Christmas's during the high school years, I started renting a Santa Claus suit and would deliver Christmas gifts to my parent's friends. That was always a fun time; especially the first year I did that. It was just such an unexpected thing and all of their friends were very surprised but they always guessed that it was Steve, their friend's son inside the Santa Claus suit, but I got a lot of good rave reviews. The third year I did this was during my senior year, and Dave and a couple other friends went with me one night on my rounds. They thought I was crazy, but they got caught up in the fun, we were all laughing and having a good time. It had snowed for the past couple of days and it was snowing that night (it was good to be driving the yellow jeep Wagoneer; otherwise my parents might have had reservations about me driving with the distractions of the Santa suit). Anyway, we ended up in the Highlands of Boise, which was then a more exclusive area of town. The houses were all brightly lit up with Christmas lights and it looked like a lot of them had parties going on, judging from all the cars parked along the streets. As we slowed down one street, looking for addresses, we were all yelling at each other to stop here! Slow down, there it is! Is that the house? I finally pulled over to the side and we were looking at the address my mom had written down. Brian, one of my friends in the car noticed a couple of girls coming down a walk toward us. They had noticed us the first time we had passed and saw that Santa Claus (me) was driving. They asked if I would be Santa at their party and we could all stay for a while. Dave and Brian and Pete all thought that was a great idea! What could be better than crashing a Christmas party! I am so ashamed to write this, but I protested the notion as we didn't know anyone, it was a school night, and I just didn't think it was a good idea. What an idiot I was. My friends argued with me, trying to get me to change my mind, but I was adamant that we could not stay---we had to go. I thought I was being the responsible guy and should just complete the deliveries and get everyone back home safe and sound. If I was trying to impress anyone that night, I failed miserably. Dave, Pete and Brian were pretty pissed (and, rightly so) and it was a cold silent ride back home. The really funny thing about that incident (not really funny when I think back) was when I told my parents about the party and how proud I made the decision to finish the deliveries and get home because it was a school night, Mom said that I should have gone ahead and stayed at the party. After all, they trusted me! I never told my friends that, for obvious reasons, as I never would have heard the end of that one (I am still hanging my head in shame even as I write this)! It is funny when I think about it, the one time I sincerely tried to be a responsible person and do the right thing I would have been just fine had I given in to what I thought I should not do (yeah, really funny now.... Ha-ha).

Like a lot of normal red-blooded high school guys I am sure, I was no stranger to magazines like Playboy and Penthouse and others like that. My friends and I would drool over all the centerfolds and laugh at the Penthouse Forums, because they always seemed to be too far-fetched to really be true. Maybe we thought that because we'd never had experiences to rival the ones we read about (at least I knew I hadn't!) but they were fun to read, and they sure helped get the self-pleasure activities going, if you know what I mean. I thought I would do a test and prove that not all the forums were true. How would I do that? That was simple. I would write one myself and send it in. If you were to check out the November 1980 issue of Penthouse you would see my very first published work. Of course it was pure fiction, but that goes a long way to prove my point that if there is one forum that is made up, odds are that others are just fantasies as well. If one were to scrutinize my story the same way they do now to find mistakes in movies, they would find quite a few inaccuracies in my saga about two guys taking two girls to a drive-in movie and having sex (that happens all the time. The funniest one was the fact they took two six packs of beer (12 total) and they each drank four (16 total)... where did the other four come from? Oh well, I couldn't tell a lot of people about my success, just due to the publication, and since I did not use my initials, I wouldn't be able to prove it. But I know it is mine and I am still damn proud of it!

But to this day I still have yet to have sex in a drive-in on a double date (are there still drive-ins out there?)

There were many other good and bad times during the high school years, but suffice to say, I passed all the finals and graduated. One thing I could recommend to people now is that in the months before graduation, it is important to see your senior counselor regularly for assistance in getting your transcripts prepared properly and make sure you get all your college applications out in time, (though I don't know if they still stress this now), especially for when the college recruiters came around. I don't believe I took much of this too seriously, because I seem to remember getting stern reprimands from one of the Sisters because of my lack of diligence. I must have gotten my transcripts out just in time though, but even my mom was sweating through this process, as you can imagine, she was always concerned where my education was going to take me.

I had always had my heart set on the University of Southern California, I think mainly because it was in Los Angeles, in the heart of television and movie land. Remember, I had that acting bug from junior high and my short-lived comeback in high school, and I had been slowly slaving away on that script that Tom and I had been writing, as I mentioned earlier. I felt that if I went to USC, and we got the script finished, it could be possible that we could send it to producers or movie studios for consideration (thinking back on that period in life, I can't help but think how naïve I was). My parents felt that I should apply to states colleges and consider majoring in something productive, such as business or something where I could learn a good career. But I was really stuck on getting into television or motion pictures, something in that field, and I wanted to go to USC. I never stopped to consider how expensive the school was or explore other schools or options... I had a one-track mind, really. So I did apply there, and a couple of other universities in Southern California, Pepperdine being one of them. One of the side benefits I thought of going down to school in Los Angeles would be all the hot, gorgeous coeds that would be there...after all, I had heard and seen on TV and the movies that California girls were mostly all 10's and I figured that getting laid would be a cinch! Since I had mastered the skills of masturbation, I was eager to jump into the real thing (it is sad, but up to that time, I still had never had sex)! I just knew that I would lose my virginity at USC! I was hoping, anyway!

The summer between junior and senior years, my friend JJ and I drove down to California and actually toured a few campuses, and that was a great trip in itself. I remember he wanted to see Stanford, and it really was a beautiful campus. We toured USC, and I loved it, no matter that the campus was in the middle of Watts, actually being there made up my mind I wanted to go there. JJ had told me he had an uncle who worked at 20th Century Fox Studios, where "Family" was filmed, and I was so excited that we might be able to get in for a tour. I figured I might be able to see, or at least get the opportunity to see Kristy, and I worked myself up into an excited frenzy to go to the studio. JJ was having a hard time getting a hold of his uncle, so we waited outside the front gate of the studio for about two hours, but his uncle never showed up, and didn't answer his phone. We finally left, and I was dejected for a while, great company for JJ, I am sure. So close, and yet… well you know how that goes.

While JJ and I were down in L.A. we decided it would be great fun to go to Disneyland, and take some time away from the stress of touring colleges. I will preface the following interlude by telling you that JJ was the straight-laced guy who never did anything daring or against authority. He was pretty much the epitome of correctness, which by no means is to say anything bad or against him. JJ was a very popular guy in high school, well admired among his peers. But JJ shocked me when we were on the Pirates of the Caribbean ride by jumping out of the boat when it stopped before going around a corner. He wanted to go off and explore, to see how things worked. I whispered loudly for him to get back in, we would surely get in trouble. He smiled and laughed, and then without warning a voice boomed from above, like God talking to the congregation: **GET BACK IN THE BOAT NOW! OR YOU WILL BE REMOVED FROM THE RIDE!** That was enough for him, and it scared the Hell out of me! He quickly got back in the boat (surprisingly, we were the only people in that particular boat). I thought that was the end of his craziness, but I was wrong. When we were inside the Haunted House, he grabbed me by the arm and pulled me through a side door in the dark. "Let's see where this goes!" he said. I told him he was crazy while he slowly opened another door and peered out. It opened into another passageway where visitors were walking and they screamed, but I'm sure they thought it was part of the show. We managed to sneak back into our group without being caught, and JJ behaved pretty much the rest of our time at Disneyland. Let me tell you, it is much more fun and enjoyable going to a theme park when you are older and without your parents. The only major drawback however, we found out, we didn't have our parents paying for everything…

But I digress. I did end up getting accepted to USC, much to Mom and Dad's dismay I am sure. I also got an acceptance letter to another college, which in itself was cool, but the weird part about that was I had never sent them an application. We never did figure that one out.

The summer after graduation was pretty relaxed; I had a job delivering flowers at a local flower shop, which was a a lot of fun. JJ coincidently enough also got a job at a competitors shop that same summer, and when we saw each other on the road, we would often race each other (not a good idea when driving company vans with the company logos brightly painted on the sides). The only problem I had during that job was when I backed up the van and tore off the passenger side view mirror. The owners were ok with it, but they warned me not to do it again; apparently side view mirrors on vans are pretty expensive (I found that out when I worked in service at a car dealership some 20 years later, but we will get there…).

As I had stated earlier I had not yet had alcohol, but it was that summer I decided that it was time I learned to drink. My tennis buddy Dave and I planned things out and went up to the local ski resort where his parents had a condo, to spend the night and get me drunk. We each took with us a six-pack of beer, and after we were there, we found four more beers in one of the cupboards. Now I *had* tried beer and mixed drinks before, had a small sips of wine during family gatherings during the holidays when the grandparents came to visit, but as I relayed previously I had never liked the taste of booze. It was too bitter or just too foul for me. But that night, the beer must have tasted pretty damn good or maybe I didn't care because before we knew it, all the beers were gone. From what I remember, it was a unique experience and we were laughing, talking loud, smoking cigarettes (not inhaling of course) and having a great time.

We made our way to the recreation center and tried to play ping pong, which we both were (usually) pretty good at, but after a short time, we decided that chasing the ball more times than not was not worth it. I remember I couldn't find the bathroom at one point, and couldn't wait, so I thought it would be a great fun to pee into one of the clothes dryers there. It sure seemed like a good idea at the time. Fearing we would get caught and get into trouble, we laughed and raced (more like stumbled) back to the condo and laughed more. We finished off the Oreo cookies that we had found and as the room was beginning to spin pretty well, must have passed out.

Waking up with a hangover was a new and quite unpleasant experience for me. The raging headache was one thing, but the after-drinking farts were the worst I have ever smelled. The aftertaste of the booze was horrible and no matter how much water I drank, the cottonmouth would not go away. It must have taken most of the morning to get the strength to get ourselves together enough to pack up what little supplies we had brought with us and hit the road back home. That was enough drinking for me! I wouldn't be caught dead doing that again for a long time, I thought! At least until next weekend is what a long time turned out to be.

The next weekend was the wedding of one of our cool high school teachers and a good friend of the family. There was a lot of us from our senior class there, who were also friends of our teacher. I don't think we went to the actual wedding, but we did make it to the reception, which was held at the country club near my house, the same country club where I had met Cindi and walked with her in the parking lot that night so long ago. The reception was great, and the champagne flowed freely. The servers never let our glasses get more than half empty before they filled them up again. I don't know how many glasses of champagne we drank, but it was quite a few, when Brian said he was going to go and get some food. We were not feeling one bit affected by the alcohol, and thus we were clearly surprised when after Brian stood up he nearly fell over. We asked what was wrong, and Brian told us to stand up and we would find out. I stood up and that was all it took for the booze to hit me. I went from stone cold sober to feeling no pain after standing up. From that point on, things seemed to happen as if I was in a fog. I don't remember eating anything, and I don't remember where any of my friends went after we left our table on the patio. I do remember dancing a slow dance with Mom (who slow dances with their mother?). Try as I might, I don't really remember too much after that, except I suddenly noticed that I didn't see anyone there that I recognized. None of my friends were around, I couldn't find my parents, and it appeared as if I had been left alone. Was it quite possibly my first drinking blackout? Anyway, I remember running home, and it felt really good to run. I was thinking that I could have run the mile in record time (I would hate to have seen a film of that--- drunk guy running: might have made it on "America's Funniest Home Videos" if that was on then). I did make it home without incident and found my parents sitting on the back porch with some other people, having coffees, or maybe more cocktails and just chatting away. I sat down next to Mom and she did not seem worried about where I had been. I think my head was starting to spin, and I said I think I need to go to bed. Mom said good night, and I told her I think I needed help getting to bed. That's all I remember about that night. But all in all, my first two drunken episodes ever were over, both happening within two weeks of one another. If I had a choice of what to drink, champagne would be my last choice, as the champagne hangovers were always the worst. That was pretty much the extent of my drinking that summer.

As I mentioned previously, I had gotten accepted to USC, and I was going to go there. All the proper paperwork had been filled out and sent as to securing housing on campus, but after a month, we had not heard anything about which dorm I had been assigned to. My mother made a few calls and found out there were no dorms available and I had been placed into a university assigned apartment, which of course was going to be more expensive. That didn't start off a good relationship with USC in Mom's eyes, but I didn't think too much of it at the time. I had applied for a student loan with the local bank, so that plus a college fund my folks had been saving for me would be covering things just fine. As you can probably guess, I didn't start out my college career too seriously, letting my mom put out fires for me, making all the calls… when *I* should have been doing that. I was too "busy" with my job and hanging out with my buddies during the summer instead of really buckling down and preparing for the upcoming year. I remember it was coming down to the wire the last few weeks of summer and Mom was seriously pissed when I came home late one evening from playing cards with my friends, instead of packing up the trunk we had to send down to L.A. But I finally got things together and we did get my things shipped out. I really was looking forward to going to USC, not only because I would be living in the land of my dreams, but also because Tom would be going there too, and we could work on our screenplay and get it sold (I was so deep in my dreaming it was truly a wonder I could even see straight).

Tom and I flew down to Los Angeles a couple of days before orientation (he ended up in the dorm) to get situated and he could not move in yet, so he was going to stay the night in my apartment, which I was sure would not be a problem with any of my new roommates. We found my trunk in the complex office and got the key and went to my new digs. It was totally dark in the apartment when we opened the door and it smelled like they had set off a bug bomb previously. That didn't seem abnormal to me, I figured that was what they did before any new tenants moved in. When we turned on the lights, I was startled by hundreds of little black shapes scurrying up and down the walls and behind couches, anywhere to get out of sight. It scared the shit out of me! What the hell were those things? It was my introduction to roaches. Of course I had heard of them, but I had never seen one before (seriously, I am not lying there). Growing up in Boise, the most common pesky bugs besides mosquitoes were earwigs. I turned around and told Tom that we needed to go the nearest store and buy something, anything to take care of the roaches. I was *not* going to move in to a new place and live with roaches (of course, I learned to tolerate them—I found out one can never truly get rid of roaches)!

We went across the street to the big market that looked like a huge Safeway store and as we passed the beer and wine section, I noticed there was also a large hard alcohol section. Welcome to California where booze was sold in regular stores and not just in state run venues. That would make it easy when I was finally of age to be able to buy it legally! Of course during my sophomore year we found a liquor store named Benji's, which actually delivered and took checks. That would make things easy. Back then we could get a case of Coors's in the bottles for $10. I know this because I had a lot of deliveries my second year at USC, but more on that later.

31

Tom and I found and purchased several different cans of bug sprays, bombs, whatever we could find and went back to the apartment armed for war. I think we used up all the cans before we were done. Then, as it was late afternoon, we realized we still needed to find somewhere to sleep for the night. Luckily, there was a hotel not far from the campus, and we spent the night with the air conditioning at full blast. I know my body was at least a week from being acclimated to a new hotter climate than I was used to. I was sweating just getting out of bed (and I was in substantial better shape back then than I am now).

My life changed when I went to college. I was no longer a kid who lived at home, under my parent's rule. I was my own keeper and although I would live at home during summers and holidays, I think thereafter I felt more of a guest than a resident. Now I was responsible (ha-ha) for my life: what I ate, washing clothes, taking care of all the things that I took for granted while growing up. Now I really had to grow up. But I don't think even getting out on my own made me really grow up, or become more of a mature adult, as it were, as those who read on will come to see.

For the last couple of days, I have been trying hard to remember what classes I took while at USC, any time I spent studying, and anything I did that would actually be considered as academic. And try as I might, I cannot think of many of those things. What I can remember with any clarity is fun things, goofing off, anything *but* academics. No, I take that back. I do recall sitting in the back of a classroom with the instructor's voice somewhere in the background, as I worked on that script. I think by that time, it was in its third draft and Tom and I had done a thousand major revisions since its first inception. Not that it was really any better, but it *was* less silly and inane than the first draft. Now why was I working on the script instead of taking notes and paying attention to the lecture? That goes back to me not taking life more seriously, not buckling down and starting to put some priorities together. Anyway, better that than drawing pictures or sleeping, maybe.

When I was waiting in line at registration, where we chose our classes and schedules, I started talking to the guy in front of me. Scott seemed to be an all right guy, from Southern California, also in his first year at college. He was going to study film, I think, and we talked about our similar interests; I told him about my writing and what I had done, and he told me he really wanted to be a film director. At some point during our conversations, we became friends, and we thought it might be fun to collaborate on a project, my writing something and him filming it with me acting. We did do just that in the next three or four months, and it was actually a lot of fun. It was based on a short story I had written and then re-wrote in script form; we used a girl from the next-door apartment and Chris, one of my roommates also as actors. It was just like a real production. Scott had the bright lights on the stands, he used a meter to make sure the lighting was okay; we had rehearsals and did lots of takes. If it were put on DVD today there would be some great outtake footage with cracking up and flubs and all that good hilarity. But it was just a project and I don't think we ever finished it. Sometimes to this day, I wonder where it is, and where Scott is, if he ever made it in the industry. I wonder if he still has that film of ours. I think I tried to get Tom involved in the project too, but he was busy doing what one should be doing while in school: studying!

That first year at USC was the year I first tried smoking pot. One of my roommates, Gino, was from Jordan and was a fun-loving guy. I don't remember what he was studying, but the two things I do recall about him were that he always seemed to have pot and he had a lot of coins from Jordan that even though they were one cent in his country they were the size of American quarters. Thus, they fit perfectly in the laundry machines, making it cheap to wash our clothes (I think the powers that be caught on to that, because after a while, new machines were installed that would not work with his coins). Tom happened to be over at the apartment one day when Gino asked us if we wanted to get stoned. I admitted that I had never smoked pot before, and Tom said he had not either. Gino couldn't believe it and said we needed to try some of his stuff. What the hell, we were in college now, it was time to try something new! I think I hacked up a lung on the first toke, but I remember it had a kind of sweet taste to it. Tom and I both took two or three hits, holding the smoke in as long as we could each time, and waited, but after about a half hour, neither of us had more than a headache. Tom left to go back to his dorm to do homework and I don't know what I did, but I know it was kind of a letdown that nothing happened. We tried a week later with the same result. Maybe the stuff wasn't potent enough, but judging from how Gino got after *he* smoked the pot, I didn't think that was a good assumption. I remember Tom and I tried it a third time (why it was always with Tom, I don't know, maybe safety in numbers?) and we were thinking that if we weren't affected this time, that would be it. Well, once again, nothing, no euphoric feelings, no floating on air, nothing. That was it. I was getting low on food supplies in the apartment, peanut butter, bread, the usual college kid staples, so we decided to go to the store (the same store where we had purchased our roach war supplies) and do some shopping.

Once we got to the store, Tom and I grabbed a shopping cart and began heading to the bread aisle. This is where things started getting weird. I was starting to feel strange. Not a bad strange, but a strange that I had never felt before. It was a pleasant, warm fuzzy feeling, hard to describe. I looked back at Tom, who was behind me and saw he was looking intently at something on the floor, what it was, I couldn't figure out, because there was nothing except for the floor tile. I started staring at the floor myself, and looked up at Tom. He had a big goofy grin on his face and I started laughing. "Are you?" I remember asking, and he just nodded vigorously up and down and all he said was "Yes!" and we started giggling harder. The pot obviously had worked this time. They say, the third time's the charm (I still don't know who "they" are) and that seemed very true! We were stoned. Everything was funny. We went up and down every aisle and when we got to the checkout stand, we had Oreo cookies, chocolate chip cookies, pop tarts, sugar cereals, potato chips, all sorts of munchies and sweets in our cart. I don't think we ended up with anything that we had intended to get though: any milk or bread. I never did figure out why it took three times to work, and on both us no less? Maybe it was because we were from Idaho... Nah, that wouldn't be it. When Gino moved out that next year, our easy weed source left as well, but we weren't ever getting stoned unless he offered anyway, so it wasn't a worry that we would go into withdrawals. So, that was my first stoned experience. And it would not be my last.

Our apartment had phone jacks, so of course we had a common phone line that all the roommates shared, and we each of course paid for all of our own long distance calls. It was all very organized. After a while we noticed that whenever someone called our phone, the one in the living room and Gino and my room rang, but the phone in Chris and Dave's room was always silent. We thought that to be rather odd, since the ringer volume control was turned all the way up so that couldn't be the problem. So the next time the phone rang, we answered the phone that didn't ring and heard only a dial tone, while the phone was still ringing in the other rooms. The only thing we could figure was that Chris and Dave's extension was a totally different line. But we were only getting one bill for one phone line, so the only explanation was that we had another line, and obviously the phone company did not know about it otherwise they would have turned it off long ago. I don't know who it was that came up with the idea, but I figured out what the phone number was by dialing our number a few digits off in either direction and when the other extension rang, we knew we had the number (why that was a concern, I don't know). Now in retrospect the next idea was the stupidest one, but for a college kid on a budget, it was great! *Free Long Distance!!* We all took advantage of this free phone, totally abusing the privilege, since all of our homes were out of state; Dave and Chris were from Arizona and I was from Idaho, but Gino, being from Jordan, was getting the best benefit from "free long distance." And for about two weeks, Gino was on the phone for hours at a time; arguing and consoling his girlfriend back home. Then, there was the fateful day when the phone book war began. We had several sets of yellow pages and for whatever reason one Saturday we were all very bored and it was hot and muggy out. It doesn't matter who threw the first phone book, but then we were all running around like little kids, dodging books from room to room, and pages were coming out and flying all over. By the time we were done, we couldn't see the carpet anymore for all the scattered and torn yellow pages. There wasn't a full book left either. No one was hurt, and surprisingly there were no holes in any of the walls. If we had left it at that, who's to say, but someone got the idea that we needed to call and order new yellow pages. So I called the phone company and placed an order. I remember my heart sinking when there was a pause and the operator said there might be some problem, as they didn't see any name attached to the phone... well of course not, I was calling from the *free phone!* I froze and I should have hung up the phone right then and there and hoped the operator did not call back; the worst that could happen is the phone would be shut off, but what did I do? I gave them my name and our address like an idiot (it all happened so fast, I didn't know what I was doing until it was over), and then the operator asked how long had we had this line and I must've told her. The bottom line is that one call for yellow pages cost us many hundreds of dollars in long distance charges. Gino, of course was hit the worst, since a call to Jordan is an international call. I think my share of the charges came to about $150, and I had to call Mom and have money transferred from my savings account to my checking to cover my portion of the bill. I don't remember what excuse I told Mom for needing the money, but I am pretty sure I made something up, because I didn't want her to know how I had been cheating the phone company! Needless to say, I was not the most popular person in the apartment for quite a while after that! Understandably!

I mentioned earlier that there was a phone call involving Kristy McNichol (I think we will be done with this subject after this), which I should mention. In all my infatuation with Kristy, you would think my greatest achievement would be actually talking to her, either in person or on the phone at the least. I came up with this hair-brained scheme that was pretty clever in my opinion that just might get me an opportunity to meet her. I talked Tom into calling her up at the studio where they filmed "Family" and arrange an interview with me. He was to tell her I was a reporter for the USC student newspaper and we were doing a story about acting or something like that. Tom really didn't want to do it, but I told him it was the last time I would ask him to do anything like this again. I already had the number for him to call, and he did, certain he would never get through to her. He asked for the "Family" set, and then there was a pause. Then Tom asked to speak with Kristy McNichol, and there was another pause. I was holding my breath, I think I was pacing his dorm room, I was very nervous. Then Tom's eyes widened and he looked at me with an incredulous smile. "Kristy?" I heard him say (I still remember this like it was yesterday), "This is Tom, from the USC Newspaper, and we are doing a story on the Hollywood Experience and I would like to know if you would be interested in talking to one of our reporters." I was staring at Tom, open-mouthed! "Ok, well, thanks for your time anyway. Have a good day." Tom said, and he hung up the phone. I asked him what she said, and he told me she said she was too busy, and that was it. In a way I was pissed because it was *him* that had really talked to her, and not me, but I was the one who told him to talk to her, so I had nothing to be mad about really. I think I asked Tom to repeat what she had said more times than he needed to, but I just couldn't get over how he had actually spoken to her! How odd that we could so easily get through to an actress just like that? My guess is that with all the security these days that we would never be able to duplicate that feat again, and really that is just as well, as there are way too many crazed fans out there now days. So that was the end of my "obsession" with Kristy. Looking back, it really seems like I spent so much crazy energy on things that could have been more productive; but as I have heard so many times, "there is a reason for everything that happens!"

Has anyone ever wondered if they passed up something that might have made a big difference in their lives if they had done it? There have been a few occasions that I think: *If only* I had done *that!* I remember one time I was studying (Really? Studying?) on campus and somebody came up to me and said he was making a student film for a class of his and needed someone to play the lead part. I asked him what it was about. He said it was about a student who was more or less sex-crazed and getting caught in various places masturbating. I have no idea why, but I didn't think I should do something like that, it was too weird a notion and it just sounded embarrassing. So I told the guy no thanks. To this day, I still think back and wonder what would have happened if I had taken up his offer and acted in his film? What if it had led to other acting things? I have no idea who he was, but what if he ended up being some great director who was now making millions today, and maybe he would have carried me with him and … if…. if…. if…. There are always going to be "ifs" in life, so I really should let it go at that.

I think I irked my dad one February Sunday when I was called home and spoke to him on the phone. He asked me how my day was, and I told him I just got back from swimming in the ocean. He told me he had just gotten in from shoveling snow off the sidewalk. He then made a comment that maybe I should have been studying or doing homework or doing something more productive than wasting time at the beach? I don't think I made many more references to any extra-curricular activities after that. But really, a guy's gotta have *some* fun when he's in college! Can't spend all my time in the books! But since I really don't have a lot of memories spending time in the books, it is possible I did spend too much time having fun down in California. I went to all the home football games and I do recall we won the Rose Bowl both years I was at USC. I went to a taping of "The Tonight Show" which was a great experience, except that Johnny Carson had the night off, and so did Ed McMahon. Even Doc Severnson was not there. Richard Dawson was hosting that night and I don't think I recognized any of the guests that were there except maybe Rita Moreno. It got a little crazy when we got into a little shouting match broke out during one of the breaks with a group on the other side of the stage that was from UCLA, and we all almost got kicked out. I also had a chance to go see a taping of the "Newhart" show, the one that where Bob was the innkeeper in Vermont. I didn't go, but I later found out that it was one of the funniest shows to see taped live. The other show I got to see was "The Price is Right." Bob Barker was very entertaining that day, as he kept complaining about this *huge* chocolate chip cookie he had eaten and how it had given him heartburn. My friend Craig who had gotten us the tickets actually had his name called as one the first four contestants, won his way onto the stage, and got to spin the big wheel. He lost, but it was such a great experience! The sound stages are so much smaller than they look on TV I did notice.

My second year at USC I was able to get into the dorms, which I liked better because I was able to meet and interact with more people. It wasn't without some drawbacks, however. I remember making some good friends, but there was a few that no matter how hard I tried to get along with, nothing would work. But that is just a fact of life, I have learned. I ended up with a roommate who really didn't have a lot of common courtesy. There was one night he came back at 2:30 in the morning after being gone for a few days and banged open the door, turned on the lights and made a lot of noise unpacking things, while I was trying to sleep. He didn't shower regularly and had poor hygiene and was generally unruly, but all in all, he did try to be a nice guy. I did feel sorry for him, as he was picked on by a lot of the other guys in the hall. One time when Alex was gone, he had left an unopened bottle of Jack Daniels on his desk shelf. One of the heavier partiers in the hall, Fred, took the bottle and carefully sliced through the seal, emptied out the booze and refilled it with tea and meticulously resealed it so that it looked like it had never been opened. When Alex returned and opened up the bottle, he thought the whiskey had spoiled and took it back to the liquor store. What a surprise when he returned and showed us all the replacement they had given him!

We had some great parties that year (again, I don't recall studying very much, though each year I got at least a 2.5 GPA). I remember a particularly funny Friday night when the desk that Fred was sitting on while drinking came loose from the wall and Fred and the desk crashed to the floor. He was still holding his glass upright without having spilled a drop and was laughing hysterically! Each Friday night, Fred and his roommate Randy would go up and down the hall and take orders for alcohol since they were the only ones old enough to buy the booze. They would come back with two full shopping carts of bottles and distribute them out to everyone who had placed an order. Saturday nights usually garnered only one shopping cart worth of bottles. A lot of the guys were not able to drink quite as much as they did Fridays. I did my share of drinking, but it was *nowhere* near what it was to become later in life (but more details on that later).

I didn't have much in the way of a social life with females during my freshman year, and sophomore year wasn't all that different, though there was a lot more interaction. I became very infatuated with a really nice girl who lived in the dorm next to mine that second year, and we got along really well. The only problem was she basically only liked me as a great friend, which is a situation that has plagued me throughout most of my life. For whatever reason, girls that I fell for only like me as friends, while I always tended to go nuts over them. Tena was no different. I think she was my first real true crush. I adored her, she may have known that and again maybe not, but the bottom line was she never reciprocated the feelings. I did get to kiss her, by way of mistletoe, and it caught her completely off guard. I was so nervous and embarrassed that I am sure I came across as a total nerd. I do remember she had the softest lips I have ever kissed, though. It did not deter the friendship, but I never got to do any more than that. Tena and I stayed in touch for a couple of years after that, though I have no idea where she is now.

One of the shortest, though tougher relationships I had was during that second year at USC. Joan was a cute girl who always hung out with our group in the hall. One week, for no reason that I can recall, she and I started to become a lot closer emotionally. We would eat together, study together, hold hands, I think we made out a couple of times, it was like we were becoming a couple, and I remember being on top of the world! Finally, a girl was liking me the same way I liked her! It was the best feeling in the world! Then there was that enigmatic Friday night. We were going to watch a movie on TV together in my dorm room, and we wanted some popcorn or something like that, so she went across the hall to Joe's room to get what we needed, and I waited and waited for her to come back. I waited for a couple of hours and she never did return. I couldn't figure it out! I finally went and knocked on Joe's door and got no answer. It was the most unique ending to a relationship that I have ever experienced. Joe and Joan went steady for the rest of the year. For the entire next week, I pretty much hibernated in my room, only going out to use the bathroom, maybe to the cafeteria a few times. I was heartbroken, and there was nothing anyone could say or do to make me feel better. I didn't care about anything, didn't go to classes, life was miserable. I would spend the days watching mindless television, and at night I would put on "The Best of Bread," side one and play it over and over. I have never figured it out why, but playing depressing love songs at high volumes always seemed to be the right thing to do. It never occurred to me that doing that just might make my feelings of despair become worse…Then one day I woke up and I guess I was tired of feeling like shit. Maybe I was tired of feeling sorry for myself, I don't know what made me change, but I was ok. I remember going out and acting like everything was fine. It didn't bother me anymore that Joan had left me never to return.

I did stumble upon a way to see some movies for free. I heard someone talking about a senior film class that had Wednesday screenings of films at the Norris Cinema Theatre. I didn't see any blockbusters there, as I was hoping I might, but the one great movie I did see was "The Wild Bunch," which I had never seen before. It was a great movie, and I was glad I got the chance to watch it! As I was getting up to leave after the credits were over, someone got up on stage and introduced the director, Sam Peckinpah, and one of the actors, who I recognized, Warren Oates. I had no idea who the director was; clearly I was no film buff, as anyone who knows film would know he is a great director of many fine classic movies. During a question and answer period, I actually raised my hand and asked Warren Oates an offbeat question about another movie he had been in, that had no bearing on the movie with Mr. Peckinpah. I must have looked like a complete idiot! I am sure everyone there was looking at me with complete shock, probably wondering who I was and why I was there! I did manage to get an autograph, from Mr. Oates, not Mr. Peckinpah, which would have been a great autograph to have, as well. What did I know?

There was one other amusing story of a wine and cheese event. Tom and I managed to crash this function, to have some free cheese and alcoholic refreshments, but we also were there to see William Shatner, Captain Kirk of "Star Trek", who was being honored at the event. We drank more wine than eating cheese, and after an hour or so of waiting for Shatner to arrive, we decided that it would not be good to stay, since we were getting pretty toasted. But Tom was a huge fan and didn't really want to leave, so we left the immediate area and lay down on the other side of this little grassy hill. All I remember is seeing some guy get out of a small economy car, and it looked like he had those trademark slanted "Kirk" sideburns. Tom later told me that he recognized Shatner's car, and stumbled over the hill to try to meet him and shake hands. Tom was so embarrassed, and all he would tell me was that he almost threw up on his idol. But I am sure we both get a chuckle about the event to this day. Tom ended up finishing college in Seattle and has since moved back to Boise. I went to his wedding a few years ago and we still keep in touch, though not as frequently as I would like.

I did manage to get a few more autographs during my time down in Los Angeles. I don't even know if I still have all of them, and most of the people are now dead, but I had John Houseman (of "The Paper Chase'), James Doohan ("Scotty"), David Prowse (he was the physical body of Darth Vader), Warren Oates as I mentioned before and a few others, though I can't remember them all; I just wish I had kept them, they may have been worth something by now, who knows?

One spring break, I ended up driving back to Boise with Don, a teacher's assistant from one of my classes. He had never been to Idaho, and really wanted to go on a road trip for a break in things. It was a pretty uneventful trip, but that week, I ended up with my first traffic ticket. I was showing off and speeding down a street, trying to be cool and ended up being stopped by one of Boise's finest. I don't know how fast he clocked me, but before he drove off, I was left with a $55 ticket. Mom and Dad were not pissed, as I thought they would be, but they told me that I would need to pay the ticket before I returned back to California. The only way I would be able to do that was to sell my comic book collection that I had been working on for years! All of my prized "Spiderman" editions, even the collector's issue where Gwen Stacy died... they all went to the cause of paying the ticket. I still think had I not had to give up that collection, and I had kept them all in the shape they were in back then, I would have had a very nice investment right now. The things we learn as we grow up. Ahh, but the things I still learn to this day!

During the first summer after my freshman year at USC and each summer until I graduated from college, I worked at the CBS television affiliate in Boise. I don't remember a thing about how I got the job, it may have been through an introduction from a friend of my folks, but I started in the film shipping and receiving department. This was a great job, and I enjoyed it immensely. I worked under the tutelage of an older gentleman who had been there for years. He was a crotchety old guy who you didn't want to cross or get in the way of in *his* department, but Jim and I got along great. I would receive movies and episodes of TV shows on film and edit them to fit in the time allowed for each showing, and then pack them back up and make sure they went back to wherever they came from. This was all back in the time when TV stations broadcast things from there on film and video rather than off of network feeds like I know they do now days. During the four summers and holidays I worked at Channel 2, I worked my way into making some commercials for upcoming movies we would broadcast, I did a voice-over for a local TV advertising spot, I ran the studio news cameras, was floor director during the noon news, and ended up as the weekend on-air switcher. One weekend I opened and inadvertently aired two religious programs in each other's time slots, and much to my surprise, we actually got calls complaining about the mix-up. There was also another morning where I could only broadcast in black and white, and after calling and waking up the chief engineer, found I just needed to press a button on the console and suddenly there was color!

I think why I liked that job so much was the fact that I was able to learn new things every day, and the people I worked with really showed an interest in me. Sure, there were those few who were out for themselves, didn't want to let anyone else learn too much about what they did, for fear that they would be replaced or moved out of their comfort zone. But it was one of the few jobs that I have had where advancement was easily obtainable, certainly not discouraged. Too many companies now days don't seem to care as much about their employees, and certainly don't want to offer raises, and if they do offer increases, give only the bare minimum that they are legally allowed to give. But at Channel 2, I was in a very unique environment, one that truly had yet to encounter even up to now, because where I am at today . . . well . . . that will be talked about later.

A perfect example of employee good will: most everyone there had known from the first day I started there that I was only going to be there temporarily during summers and holidays. Yet I was treated as an equal. I think during the second summer I was there, the employees were going to go on strike for wage increases. I was hesitant to join them, because this was my only job and my sole means of income for the summer. I didn't think I could afford to strike and picket with them. I was told to stay on the job, cross picket lines, as it were; they would not take offense and completely understood where I was coming from. There were no hard feelings or grudges. The strike only lasted a day, and they were victorious, all getting the wage increases they asked for. I also got a raise due to their efforts, which really surprised me, though I certainly did not turn it down!

There was a lot of stress on the job; it is not easy operating a live camera during newscasts, trying not to sneeze or cough and jiggle the camera, making sure to cue the correct newscaster at the right time... everything had to be as best as possible to produce a quality news program. But there were also a lot of fun times and I could have submitted several tapes full of bloopers to "America's Funniest Videos" had that been on back then.

I am sure that if I were to go to work at a local affiliate today, I would have no idea whatsoever what I would be doing if I tried to perform the same duties I did back then; technology has changed that much I am sure in the last 25 years!! But like I said, it was a wonderful learning experience. I think honestly of all the things I have done in my life, that job is one of the ones I am most proud of. I had an opportunity to stay in that field a little later, but we will get to that (Spoiler alert!! I did not end up in that as a full time career!!).

After the second year of USC came to an end, it was decided that it would be better to finish my education at University of Idaho, where the tuition would be roughly $7000 a year less. My parents ultimately figured that I could get the same grades and pay less, yet still get a good education. The University of Idaho had a great Telecommunications department, which is what I think I had finally decided as what my major would be. All the proper paperwork, etc. was filled out, transcripts were handled and that fall, I was headed for northern Idaho, where my older brother had just graduated.

Compared to Los Angeles, Moscow was just a puny hick town, but it was full of its own unique flavor and had a great small town atmosphere. I had no desire to join any fraternities there, just like I did not at USC (that is not to say that I never went to any fraternity parties, mind you!), and settled back into the dormitory life. My roommate during my junior year was a decent guy, Rick, who was majoring in Architecture. We got along well, but our schedules were very different, as he would work late into the night at his labs building things and coming back to the dorm long after I had gone to sleep. He would sleep a lot of days into the afternoon, and was a very heavy sleeper so I really didn't have to worry too much about being overly noisy, so that was never a problem.

I actually remember a little more about the academics at the U of I, but I also remember that there was a lot more partying and socializing than there was down at USC. There was one business class I took that I thought would be very interesting , a class which to most people would probably be a piece of cake, but I couldn't get past "amortizing" and "the depreciation values at certain rates and percentages" (I don't even remember the actual terms)... it was all Greek to me! The first test that I took was a multiple choice and after reading the first page of questions, I started laughing to myself, because though I *had* studied and *tried* to learn this stuff, it just had not sunk in. I started marking random answers, not really reading the questions anymore and I think I was one of the first people to turn the test in. I never went back to that class. It was the first and only class that I can remember actually dropping. Maybe I was doing all the other people in the class a favor by having a positive effect on the grading curve with my obvious failing low score! I will never know.

I won't bore you with all of the educational aspects of U of I, except for the fact that I ended up graduating from college in four and a half years instead of the usual four for my B.S. degree. I had to spend an extra semester there because I failed a different business class that last year—I turned in the final paper an hour late. So I had to retake that class. But I had a plan. I would take the same class from the same professor and it figured it would be a breeze since I already had the textbook and all of the old tests. What could be better? What could have been worse is the real question. The professor changed texts for the next semester and had a whole new course direction, which made all of what I had saved worthless. It was like learning the stuff all over again, but at least I passed it the second time around, just not as easily as I had hoped.

There were more fun times in Moscow than not, but that does not mean that I did not learn things from those non-educational experiences. There is just as much that can be learned outside the classrooms, is all the justification that I will tell you at this time. You can form your own opinions, as I am sure you will as you make it through the book.

I met Janie during that first year at Idaho. She was a freshman, two years younger than I was. She was not the typical Playboy bunny centerfold type at all; she was more the girl next door, if you will. But to me, she had a wonderful charm, a beautiful smile and was certainly playful and very much the flirt. Janie was a friend with some guys down the hall, who had become friends of mine, so we all hung around a lot together. The more time that I spent around her and with her, the more attracted I found myself becoming to her. She was felt something towards me, because we began to spend more and more time with each other, and after a while it seemed as if we were a little more than friends, holding hands and kissing when we found ourselves alone. It was after the Halloween party that we ended up in my dorm room alone together. Rick was wherever he usually was, though I surely doubt he was out studying on Halloween night! Janie was wearing this sexy black witch's costume that looked so great on her. I have no recollection of what I was wearing, but we were sitting on my bed together and I think we had a candle lit on the table next to the bed. We were kissing, and we were really getting into things. I know things were racing through my mind, as was blood racing through my body (I don't think I mentioned it yet, but I was still a virgin--- I know, junior in college? I was 22 years old and still a *virgin?* Completely unheard of these days, I know). Even though I can remember this night like it was almost yesterday, it is still hard to describe it. I knew what was/could happen, had seen all the movies, knew what to do, but still it seemed like I had no idea of what I was doing! I felt like the nerd with the gorgeous babe who has to be led by the hand. But Janie said that she was not experienced either, and she was nervous, too. We did manage to take our clothes off or at least the necessary parts and got under the blanket together. Both of us had anticipated that things could go this route, because she and I had made sure there was we had protection.

Funny thing about first times, it was over much too quickly. We had barely started making love, and, well, you know... But it was *so* much better than doing it solo, so different and so much more meaningful! After the initial indoctrination, I began performing oral sex on her, and it was so cool, doing something I had only for so long read about and dreamed about. I remember her asking me what I was doing, as she was shaking all over... she finally told me to stop, I had made her numb over her entire lower body. I was kind of scared, I didn't know if I had done something wrong, but then she put her arms around me and we cuddled together for a while until there was a knock at the door. Our friends had left the party and had come looking for us.

I don't really know how common this is, as I have done no specific research on this particular subject, but I have had a few friends who have experienced the same thing: after Janie and I had made love, I was convinced that we were in love. I remember we made plans for our future together after we graduated; we spent pretty much every waking hour together, we thought we had everything under control. We were so into each other that we began to ignore our friends and classes. I don't remember the circumstances, but as most first loves, first romances, the ones that just are not meant to be, ours went to crap. It must have been Janie's idea (not to be vain or anything, but I still do not really recall being the instigator of any breakups I have been involved in—check that, I was the bad guy in one, horrible breakup, but that will come later), before I knew it, Jamie and I were over.

Now I had been through a bad breakup before, back at USC with Joan, but this one was different, that I was sure of. I had been in "love" and that was definitely different. But ultimately, I am sure it was as devastating as that first time. I have been trying to remember details of this breakup, but they really are not there, though I don't it lasted as long that time. I do know I did not have the "Best of Bread" album to fall back on. After a month or so, Janie and I renewed a friendship and remained in good terms through my graduation. I did bump into her years later during a weekend in McCall, Idaho with another mutual friend, G. If I remember, I will relate that interesting tale later.

I never gave up the idea of playing tennis "competitively" in my college years. At USC, I did not try out for the team because I was too involved in my pipe dream of being in the land of Hollywood and stars and all of that goofy stuff, plus maybe I thought the competition might be too stiff. But once I was at Idaho, more grounded, I thought I would give the tennis team a try. That endeavor did not go very far, though. Again, I don't remember all the details, but I don't think I gave up or chickened out, I just don't think I made the cut. I do remember doing workout drills by myself in the evenings, trying to improve my chances, but I never made it on the team. I don't think I could have been all that disappointed, since I knew that I had given it the ol' "college" try (please excuse the pun—sometimes they just happen).

The rest of the stories I relate that happened during my final college years will bear no resemblance to studying or actual schooling, but they give a little insight of where in my head I was in my 20's. They will highlight some of the things I did that were good in my personal 'education' and some of the things that may have become habits, good or bad in my future. All we can do right now is sit back, relax and read on.

Fun and frivolity, as I remember, seemed to be the main courses I was taking at the U of I. My friend Drew, who lived on my floor of the dorm and I entered into a road rally where all the contestants were to solve a puzzle and find the prize by solving questions. The answer to one question would tell us where to drive and get the next clue, and so on... that was one of the best diversions I had experienced in a long time. We were driving like crazy, trying to get to the next clues, arguing and yelling at each other, having the best time. We got to one checkpoint and were admonished to slow down and obey the speed limit, which of course probably made us even more reckless, because we figured we were doing really well up to then. Ultimately, I think we came in 3rd or something, but it was just a crazy fun-filled day.

Drinking started to make a more prominent appearance during those two years. Much more than when I was down in Los Angeles. I can't think of any particular reason, other than maybe I was around people I was more comfortable with, or maybe it was just easier to get booze or go out and party. In any case, there were a lot of fun places to go out and have fun at. One bar was close to the dorm and boasted the largest dance floor in northern Idaho. You could get just about any kink of drink there, from beer to wine to hard liquor. Their specialty was making a pitcher of your favorite mixed drink, which people would go crazy with especially on their birthdays. There was many a time we would literally carry a hall mate back to his room after a pitcher too many. Personally, beer was my beverage of choice during this time in my life.

Gunnar was my roommate for one semester. He was a cool guy, down to earth, and liked to party hard, but he was also good in school, which unfortunately didn't rub off on me as much as it should have. There was one Thanksgiving I remember when I decided to stay on campus rather than go home for the holiday. Gunnar's home was a few states away, so he was staying there as well. Thanksgiving night we ate Chinese and the following night, we ended up playing caps, the drinking game where the idea is to flip a beer cap into the glass in front of you, and if you make it, the other team drinks. We did this with the two guys who lived across the hall from us, Kevin and Ron, who drank either gin and tonics or Coors's in the bottle. They had one designated drawer in their room which contained nothing but bottle caps, and by the end of the year, it overflowed into at least two other drawers. Anyway, Gunnar and I felt it would be a cinch to beat them because if they got drunk before we did, they would start missing and we would end up winning. The problem was, the drunker they got the better their aim was. Gunnar and I were the opposite and we got plastered. It was a good thing we only lived across the hall because we literally were barely able to crawl back to our room. But I remember it was a lot of fun. When you are in your twenties, recuperation takes so much less time, so by the next afternoon, we were ready for another party!

There was my first time drinking apricot brandy, which I remember was so good tasting going down, and didn't seem to make me overly drunk. But I the drunk did sneak up on me, and I ended up throwing the empty pint down the hall at someone, who luckily ducked into his doorway so the bottle missed him, but it shattered noisily all the way down the hall. The resident adviser was there and I didn't get into huge trouble, but I had to clean up the mess and promise that kind of incident would never happen again. I have never had apricot brandy again to this day.

One morning after a night of drinking, it had to have been a Tuesday because the student newspaper came out every Tuesday; I had quite the intense hangover. I was glancing through the paper, not really able to fully concentrate on anything in particular when I did happen to notice a help wanted ad for "Student Union Film Chairperson." That sounded interesting, so I read more of the ad and found that the candidate would be responsible for overseeing the Student Union Film Program, which showed movies on campus every Friday night throughout the year. The chairperson would choose the films shown and be responsible for the finances of the program; ordering and shipping back the movies... it would be like running your own movie theater. That sounded very cool to me. So I thought "what the Hell!" I cleaned myself up as best I could and went and applied. I was sure I would never get the position, and after I went back to the dorm, I promptly forgot about what I had just done.

As I have found occasionally, some things happen when you least expect them, and to my complete surprise, I ended up getting the position. I don't have any idea how I pulled that off, but I gladly accepted the appointment! And there it was. I was in charge of the student union movies program, which at that time was running in the red, losing money. It wasn't a popular entity, as I guess students had better things to do than go and pay $1.50 for an old outdated movie. It was up to me to turn the program around. With the help of my good friend G, who later became one of my best friends, we decided that we would just order and schedule the movies that we liked and wanted to see. We had a couple of great catalogues to chose titles from and we worked up some theme weekends.

During finals week, we had a "dead" theme, showing George Romero's original black and white "Night of the Living Dead," along with "Dawn of the Dead." Surprisingly, it was a huge success, selling a record number of tickets and making the first sell out showing ever. Another weekend, I had learned that Gene Roddenberry was scheduled to come for a special weekend speech on campus. G and I made it a "Star Trek" weekend and booked the first Star Trek movie that Friday which would tie the two events together. It was another huge success! Being a part of the student union enabled me to be a part of the behind the scenes things and I got to meet Mr. Roddenberry personally. He was supposed to meet us all for drinks after his speech, but he never showed. I did get the opportunity to drive him back to the airport that Sunday so he could fly back to Los Angeles, and I will never forget the last part of our conversation. I had mentioned to him that I was a writer and asked him for any advice he could give me. He told me to keep plugging away at my craft and maybe someday he would be working for me. I told him that I loved everything he had done and hoped that one day I would be working for him. Sadly, neither of us got our wish. An interesting side note: I was at USC when "Star Trek – The Motion Picture" premiered, and was there on opening night to see it (the second showing, at midnight). I stood in line for hours amidst Klingons, Romulans, other assorted aliens and lots of people dressed in Enterprise uniforms, it was all quite festive. Then, after all the waiting and all the hype I promptly fell asleep about a half hour into the movie. But bottom line, when I ended my term as film chairperson, the program was solidly in the black, and I was really proud of what I had accomplished. G and I continued our friendship for many years, though not without life's challenges.

There have been two birthdays I can remember in my life that I partied heavily (only two?) and of course there did a lot of drinking along with the celebrations. The first was during my senior year at Idaho. I had heard previously that for birthdays, some bars or establishments that served alcohol would sometimes give the birthday person a free drink when the proper I.D. was presented. I don't know if that is done in this day and age, but I was pleased to find a few places in Moscow that did honor this particular tradition. I think it was just Drew and a few other guys that went with me, but we went to a few dives and I had a few free beers and paid for a few. We ended up at a favorite local hangout, I can't remember the name of it but I think it no longer exists today. Anyway, when I showed my I.D. and asked if they gave free beers, I was told they did not. However, the bartender said that if I could chug 8 beers really fast he would give me a free pitcher of beer. What my friends later told me was that I was able to chug 2 beers and while downing the last 6, the bartender drank right along with us, and we didn't pay for anything we drank there that night. I vaguely recall we all sang the "Happy Birthday" song over the loudspeaker. My friend G, who was at Idaho State in Pocatello told me that I called him later that night (or early that next morning—it was about 3am) and he had never heard a more inebriated human being in his life! He couldn't make out what I was saying half of the time because I was so plowed, but that I did sound happy and content. I'm quite sure I was far from happy and content that next morning. The other birthday I mentioned happened probably ten years later, I'm sure we'll get to that.

As I have stated before, I had been introduced to pot during my USC years. During my senior year at U of I, I was introduced to a new "party material," or "recreational drug," as people like to call those things: mushrooms. I know I have been throwing out names all over the place and most of them you will never hear again, but bear with me. Joel was another guy in the hall, who was okay, but basically he was the resident stoner – think of Sean Penn's character in the movie "Fast Times at Ridgemont High." He and his girlfriend were going to go see a movie one night and asked if I wanted to go. I didn't have anything better to do I guess, so I said sure. Joel asked if I wanted to take some mushrooms with them. I said I wasn't really sure, as I had never done that before, but Joel assured me it was cool, a lot like smoking pot. I was willing to try it out, and ate what he gave me. About a half hour later, we walked to the movie, and I was fine, feeling nothing different. I wondered if this was going to be like my first time smoking pot. During the Pink Panther cartoon short that I realized that the walls of the theater were starting to change shape, then they appeared to start melting. Then the walls became normal again. Everything became so sharp and acute and suddenly that cartoon was the funniest thing I had ever seen! My guess was the mushrooms had kicked in. I have no idea what the movie we saw was, but after it was over, Joel and his girlfriend left to go to another party, leaving me by myself in front of the theater. That was a totally horrible feeling, all alone, and flying high on shrooms. The high feeling was no longer pleasant, and I just wanted to be somewhere where I was comfortable, with people that I would feel comfortable and safe with. I remember having to piss really badly, and I remember I actually peed in some bushes somewhere, luckily not getting caught. I finally got back to my dorm room and when I tried to sleep, it was like stars were exploding behind my eyelids and there was no way I was going to sleep. What started as a pretty cool experience ended badly, and left a poor taste for mushrooms in my mouth. I think I only tried them once more in my life.

The drive from Boise to Moscow usually takes roughly about 6 hours give or take, depending on traffic and frequency of pit stops. It can be a long drive, or it can be a rowdy, fun drive. Though the latter is the preferred, I would not recommend anyone doing the same things Drew and I did during our last drive together back to school our last year. We were carefree, loving life and not really paying any attention to any of the rules of the road, as I will explain. We had beers with us, not only in the cooler, but open and being consumed along the way (sometimes I think when we're young, we don't think about the sanity of things, and we act like we have a death wish). Somewhere about an hour south of Moscow, we noticed a Blazer, or something similar coming up fast on us from the rear. As it passed, we saw Ron and Kevin waving at us, grinning and laughing! They toasted us with their Coors's bottles they were drinking. We raised our own beers back (it was only polite!). They slowed and rolled down their window when they were right beside us and yelled "do you guys have any more?" I yelled back the affirmative, and then we did the stupidest, most moronic thing I can think of doing while driving up the highway at 65 plus miles per hour. Drew and I passed 2 or 3 beers to Kevin and Ron as they paced right beside us. Thinking back now, I shudder at how dangerous that was, but we weren't scared at all. We were all having the best time! We thought how utterly amazing it was to share our beers with our friends and how convenient was it to be able to do so while driving! Luckily, I am still around today, and have never done anything quite that inane since, at least where driving is concerned. And like I mentioned before, never would I condone nor recommend doing what we did. It was stupid. About the only thing I can say is: Boys will be boys!

I had foot surgery in the middle of my lengthened senior year on my left foot. I was born with an extra bone in each foot, in the ankle joint, which didn't make for disastrous consequences in my life. However that and my extremely flat feet did impede normal foot movements and did cause increased inflammation and pain when I was on the feet for extended periods of time or after excessive walking (March of Dime walk-a-thons, all day tennis tournaments), but it was something I'd long ago accepted, gotten used to. Mom had been doing some research over the years, and had been corresponding with a renowned orthopedic surgeon in northern California, and we decided to have constructive surgery done on one of my two feet, which was removing the extra bone and capping it off. Destructive surgery was considered "no turning back" and would consist of fusing the joint, thereby ending the pain. But doing nothing at all would mean I would most likely develop arthritis in the feet earlier than later in life. So we flew down to Oakland that summer and had the surgery done, and I was in a non-walking cast for the first half of the summer and a walking cast for the remainder. If the surgery was a success, we would plan to have the other foot done as well. What I can tell you in regards to the results is that I did not get the other foot done, and unfortunately it has still been a concern even up to now.

During the last summer of my college years, I remember being at the Idaho State Fair with Dad (I don't remember the circumstances but I can say it was one the time as an adult that I recall being at the fair with either of my parents) and we were walking around some of the agriculture exhibits when some kids ran past us and I got a whiff of a familiar odor. I looked at Dad with a smile on my face and said something like: "those kids must be feeling pretty good!" He looked back at me with a bewildered look and asked what I meant. I told him I thought I smelled pot as they went by. He said, "Oh," and was quiet. It's funny because I remember this conversation as if it happened yesterday. Dad then asked me point blank if I had ever smoked pot. I thought about what I should say and then for whatever reason, I decided to be completely open and honest with him and told him that I had. I thought he would get mad and lecture me on the dangers of drugs, but he simply said, "Oh," once again. Then he paused and this time he surprised me with: "What was it like?" I told him it was sort of like getting drunk, but that you didn't wake up with a hangover, which was the best way I could describe it at the time. He again said, "Oh." And that was all that was said. No sermons, no speeches about anything. Nothing. It was just one of those weird conversations that you never expect. Though very short, it was an awesome moment of honesty with my dad and it felt good.

One thing I should mention is that also during my senior year, I received a letter from a girl I knew in high school. Shelley was two years younger than me and though I hadn't gotten to know her very well, I knew her well enough that she had signed my junior and senior high school yearbooks. I think she may have played on the tennis team one year or something like that. But it was really unexpected, to hear from her since I hadn't kept in touch with her since high school ended. It was a nice letter, just saying hello and asking how I was doing, the usual chit chat stuff. After reading it a couple of times, I thought it would be nice to write back, and we did correspond pretty regularly until I finally did graduate from the U of I. I can't remember if she told me about the baby during those letters or after I got home (it wasn't mine—we had only been friends before). But we'll get to that...

Graduation day came and went. I don't remember the graduation ceremony at all, but I do have my diploma to prove that I did all that was necessary and got all the requirements fulfilled and all the credits needed for my BS in Telecommunications. And then I was ready to go out and face the Real World (not to be confused with MTV's version)! Was I prepared? Had I learned what I needed to begin a successful life? Was I ready? These and other questions are certainly fair game and I know the answer. All I can say is read on, and you can make your own judgments.

THE REAL WORLD – BEGINNING

So now I was finished with college. I had my diploma. I was now ready to get on with life and start doing what any graduate does: Find a career job and be successful! Easy. No problem. Okay, sure, we'll go along with that . . . for now.

A lot of my friends had jobs lined up in their chosen careers for after they graduated. Dave, my high school tennis buddy was going to work in Seattle at a cancer research center. G, my best friend from the U of I was taking two more years of schooling in Pocatello, Idaho and then up to the Seattle area to work at a hospital. Tom was going to work honing his writing in Seattle (funny how they all were ending up in the Puget Sound area). But I was planning to drive back down to Los Angeles and apply at all the TV stations for work, using what I had learned in school and all of my work experience at Channel 2 in Boise. I didn't have anything specific set in stone.

So my thought was to take a couple of weeks to unwind, catch my breath and do some preliminary plans for my job search in Los Angeles. During that time, I caught up with Shelley and we went out a couple of times, better able to become reacquainted in person rather than solely in letters.

Shelley was a very cool young lady, very self-assured, very charming and had turned out to be very strikingly beautiful in my eyes. Her baby girl was adorable, and did not seem to shy away or show any discomfort with me as some babies will do when put into a stranger's arms. Shelley admitted to me that I was the first person her baby had really taken to. I took that as a great compliment that not only was I bonding with Shelley; I had already seemed to with her child. It was easy to talk to her, and Shelley seemed genuinely interested and supportive of what I was going to do and my objectives in life, and that made me feel good. The more time she and I spent together during those few weeks almost made it harder for me to think about leaving, as I also wanted to spend more time with Shelley. I wanted to get to know her more and see where things would lead, but I knew as well that I had to make my journey. We agreed to talk at least a couple of times a week on the phone, promising to keep each other up to speed on how things were going.

I probably should interject here that though I could talk to my parents about pretty much anything, the subject of girls or relationships was never one of those topics. And if you were to ask me why that was, I certainly couldn't have come up with any real answer. Maybe I was embarrassed to talk about those things due to my lack of said subject. Maybe whenever I was in a "relationship" it usually ended up being such a trivial thing or had ended badly that I didn't want to share that experience. Maybe I didn't think they would understand what I was talking about. The bottom line is I have no idea why. Anyway I had not told them any specific details about my thoughts, feelings, or anything else about Shelley other than that we were seeing each other sort of casually and were good friends—although *I* knew that things were developing into something more than just that, and I was sure Shelley was too.

I had already made arrangements to stay with some friends from my old dorm at USC. I think they were seniors at that time, living off campus. Being a member in good standing of AAA, I went and had a 'Trip Tik' put together, mapping my exact route for driving ease down to Southern California. Mom had purchased a luggage rack for the trunk lid of their Toyota Corolla she and Dad had given to me as a graduation gift, and I packed that car full with all of my belongings, including boxes of things I probably did not need to start my "new life," including clothes, stereo system, a small cooler with pop and sandwiches and I was ready to hit the road.

The morning of departure, I had a light breakfast with Mom and Dad, and we hugged and kissed and they wished me well, telling me to call them when I stopped for the night wherever I did so they knew I was ok. I got in the car and drove off to begin my adventure!

I got as far as Shelley's house, where I was given a huge going away breakfast complete with pancakes, bacon and eggs and juice (I was not a coffee drinker until years later). Her parents were very cool and I remember getting along with them very well. I did not have the heart to tell them that I already had had breakfast before I left home, I didn't want them to think I was ungrateful, and besides, the breakfast was delicious. I finally had to get up and leave the table before I would burst or fall asleep, whichever came first. Shelley walked me out to my car after I had given her baby girl a big hug and kiss (for the life of me, I cannot remember the baby's name). Shelley wrapped her arms around me I remember she gave me a very warm and loving kiss—something to remember her by (like I needed help!). She told me to drive carefully, and I promised to call her as well when I stopped for the night. I got in my car and drove off to begin my adventure (for the second time)!

That first day of driving took me out of Idaho, through Oregon and into Northern California. It was getting dark when I made it to the Oakland area, and I was getting tired, having only made a few pit stops to fill up the tank with gas and take pee breaks at various rest stops (funny to remember that gas back then was only 59.9 cents a gallon!). It was a long drive, but I had installed a brand new, state of the art cheapo cassette-stereo player into the car, and when I wasn't able to pick up a good FM station during the drive, I would pop in a cassette tape I had made of two episodes of "Cheers," one episode on each side. You can be sure that by the end of that trip I had all the lines memorized (to this day, if I saw either episode I could recite all dialogue right along with the characters—Gunnar used to drive me crazy when he did that during Mel Gibson's "The Road Warrior!")

So that first night I ended up staying at a Super 8 Motel overnight, and tried to get some sleep after first talking to Mom and Dad, and then Shelley last. I think I fell asleep more from exhaustion than anything else. The next morning I got up and hit the road again.

It felt good to be back down in Los Angeles. Having my own car and no agenda consisting of school and attending classes made being there a whole new ballgame. I finally found where Cheryl and her friends lived near the USC campus and when I got there we hugged and talked about old times and then I was shown where the couch was that I would call my bed for a couple of weeks. I was determined to find a great job and then get a place of my own as soon as I could, so that I would not overstay my welcome.

The first week consisted of one single job application filled out and turned in at one of the local TV stations and the rest of the time goofing off around the campus and partying with my old friends. Surely I was making the best use of my time (hint: sarcasm). The first Friday night I remember I was invited to join the gang on an outing to a hip bar downtown L.A. that was rumored to be a great dance place. They all were pre-partying by drinking cocktails and taking mushrooms and offered me some. I remembered my previous experience of doing that, but I didn't want them to think I was a prude, so I accepted their offer, though I didn't eat as much as they did. I don't recall that it was necessarily a bad experience— actually I don't recall that I was much affected this time at all.

We got to the bar and went in. It wasn't huge, but it was dark with disco lights and loud music and there were people dancing in the middle of the wooden floor. As I began to make my way through the dancers, I noticed two guys dancing together, which I didn't think much of; after all, it *was* the big city. Then the music slowed down and the two guys started slow dancing with each other and proceeded to kiss each other open-mouthed. ***That*** I wasn't prepared for. I then noticed girls dancing with girls and figured out that it must be a gay bar. We may have had establishments like that in Boise, I'm sure you can find one in pretty much every town, but I never had been to one before. But then I just chalked it up to the saying: "to each his own" and left it at that. I didn't want to stare or make a spectacle of myself, so I went into the back by the rear bar area and sat down in a booth, having no idea where all my friends had gone. As I was sitting there, wondering if a waitress was going to come over and take an order, two girls came up to me and asked me if I knew where they could get some coke. I looked at them thinking, why ask me? The bar is right over there. I pointed at the counter and told them they should be able to get a drink there. They looked at me like I was an idiot (which at that point I was), and gave me the finger and walked away laughing and calling me some name. I then figured out they must have meant "cocaine" and not Coca Cola. I must have seemed like such a total dork to them, no wonder they flipped me off! Guess that's what I get for living such a sheltered life….

I did get to meet a TV producer during the time I was looking for jobs. The son of some good friends of my parents knew Ed Friendly, who had produced "Little House on the Prairie" and "Laugh-In." It was arranged for me to meet with him in regards to my interest in the industry and also so I could talk to him about my screenplay I had written. I drove in search of his house one afternoon in a very upscale neighborhood, driving past gated residences and expensive cars that made my Toyota look like something from a very used car lot. I finally found his house and found that I was very nervous about meeting him, but I went to the door and rang the bell, almost hoping he wasn't home. He answered himself and I found him to be very pleasant and non-pretentious, which was refreshing. Mr. Friendly invited me in and offered me a seat in the living room. I remember it was very tastefully decorated and really looked like a normal home, just huge and furnished with everything one could think of. I noticed a few scripts on the coffee table, but I was careful not to appear too nosy. I was trying my best to be as nonchalant as I could and not feel or come across like a fish out of water. I don't really remember in any detail what we talked about, but he did take the copy of the script I had brought and told me he would have his secretary read it and would get back to me in regards to it.

The one thing that really sticks out in my mind about my meeting with Mr. Friendly is that I really had to go to the bathroom, but I remember being very embarrassed to ask him if I could use his bathroom. I was trying to remember where the nearest gas station or fast food restaurant was to his house that I could pee in, but, as does nature make its presence known, it was letting me know that it wasn't going to wait. So I broke through my shyness and asked if I could use his bathroom, which he graciously let me do.

I don't remember how long it was or exactly when I finally received the response letter from Mr. Friendly, but I was pretty much devastated when I read what he had to say. To give you the Reader's Digest version, I was advised not to pursue this line of work, that my script was neither original nor well-written. But if I truly wanted to continue writing, he suggested that I practice writing episodes of my favorite TV shows until I had gotten the hang of things before tackling the big project. He further recommended that I did not show my screenplay to anyone else. I remember feeling as if I had been slapped in the face, after all, it had taken me well over five years to write the damn thing, and the finished product was I think the fourth draft, so a lot of my life had gone into that work. I never wrote Mr. Friendly back and thanked him for taking the time to talk to me, or for his insights, I was so upset (which I now know was wrong, after all, not everyone gets the chance that I did to rub elbows with someone like him). Truth be told, after reading my screenplay recently, I do think he was correct in everything he said about it. It was not that it was childish or immature, but it truly was a novice work, and I would be embarrassed to show it to anyone like Mr. Friendly as it was. But I will never regret what I created. It was a personal project that I saw from start to finish and a great learning experience.

I think I went to roughly around four TV stations and applied, though I don't remember that I had any formal interviews with any of them. I do recall getting a tour of one of the production department at one of the independent stations. What was completely discouraging was when I found out that at that particular time, there was a glut of candidates looking for the same jobs as I was in the television industry and there were not enough openings available to be had. Thinking back, I truly think I used that as an excuse to slack off and not really try anymore to find a job. In addition to that, I am sure I was not as assertive and ambitious as I should have been in trying to start my new life. I was too busy goofing off and having fun, doing nothing productive. I am quite sure my friends saw this, and decided it was time for me to get "off the couch" as it were and finally suggested that I should move out and on. I wasn't too pleased but in retrospect, I am glad they asked me to leave.

There was another friend, Dave, I knew from the old dorm who had taken up residence in Los Angeles, so I called and told him I was in town job searching and he offered to let me stay with him in his apartment for a while. I packed up what little I had taken out of my car and thanked Cheryl for letting me stay as long as she did, and drove to Dave's. Dave's apartment was only a couple of miles from where I was already, so it was not hard to find, and it was right next to the freeway, providing easy access to anywhere I needed to go. His apartment was a small, one bedroom unit, but a decent size and sparsely furnished, and he let me camp out on one side of the living room, which was fine with me. We caught up on how our lives had been since we last saw each other, and got along quite well. I don't remember what he did or where he worked, but I know he had a regular Monday through Friday job, and I think he was earning a pretty decent living, though just getting started in his career. He didn't know anyone who worked at the television or movie studios, and said he was sorry that he could not help me in that area of job searching.

I remember before I left Cheryl's place, I had seen a help-wanted ad in the classifieds for some kind of job at a warehouse in shipping and receiving, so I had gone and applied there, in hopes that I could begin to earn some kind of income while I was down in L.A. I was contacted after I had moved in with Dave and asked to come in for an interview and after talking to some people there I got the job, answering the phones and setting up pickups and deliveries with local companies to ship whatever they needed. I think it was like a version of UPS or FedEx or something like that, though more like a huge currier service company. Anyway, it was a source of money coming in, so I couldn't complain too much.

After working there for a week, I got a call from Mom who told me there might be an opening at the new independent TV station that was opening just on the outskirts of Boise that I might be interested in. She said it was a job doing much like what I had done at Channel 2 in Boise. I got the telephone number from her and called and spoke to the general manager of the station, and was given a phone interview. I told him about all my experience at Channel 2 and how much I would love to be considered for the position and getting back to the industry. He told me to give him a couple of weeks and get back with him to see where he was in the decision process. That was fine. At least I knew I had a shot at what I was already good at, even though it would not be where I had wanted to live. So I worked and waited patiently for the first couple of weeks.

Somehow I found out that Sara, my old girlfriend from grade school who you remember I hit in the face with a foursquare ball, was living in Los Angeles and somehow I had ended up with her phone number. I remember I called her and we talked for a little bit, finally agreeing to meet for lunch and catch up. We met one day in Westwood and when I saw her, I was stunned. She looked absolutely breathtaking! Sara had looked great when we had seen each other back in my high school tennis days, but the years since then had been very kind to her. We had lunch and talked for about an hour or so; Sara told me she had gotten married to a great guy and was very happy. She told me about her job, but I cannot remember what she did, but only that she loved it. I asked her if they had any children, and she admitted that as to this point, they had not yet, but certainly not for lack of trying. It really was nice to have been able to see her and I told Sara that if I ended up staying down in Los Angeles that I would love to be able to have coffee or lunch with her again. We hugged and parted. That was the last time I saw her. I have never forgotten about Sara. I still sometimes wonder how she is doing.

One night during the work week, for whatever reason (who needs a reason?), I was having a few Bacardi and Cokes (my favorite drink at the time), and a few turned into several. The next thing I knew it was morning and I was running late for work, but I got there on time, a little fuzzy headed, but otherwise just fine. Sometime around lunch, I began to feel very queasy and made my way to the bathroom, just off the main warehouse floor. I turned on the bathroom fan, because I felt like I was going to throw up. I couldn't understand why I would be feeling that way, after all, I couldn't have had *that* much to drink! Hoping the fan would cover up any noise, I proceeded to dry heave over the toilet several times and thought I was going to die. That was not in the cards that day, and I managed to straighten up and rinse off my face and go back into the offices. Apparently the fan had not covered up all the noise, as most of my co-workers were looking at me with obvious concern, a few of them asking me if I was coming down with the flu or something. I am sure my face was pasty white mixed with a crimson shade of red due to extreme embarrassment. I said it must have been something I ate the night before that didn't agree with me (like anyone would seriously have believed that). I said I was sure I would be fine the next day. I made it through the afternoon, feeling better and better the closer it got to leaving. I got back to the apartment and Dave asked if I had really had that whole fifth the night before! He then laughed and kidded that I hadn't saved him any... I wish I could say that was the first and last time that I ever drank a whole fifth in one night (oops, spoiler... damn!)

The next week I called the general manager of that Boise TV station and was told he wasn't in that day, could I call back. I did the next day and was told he was in a meeting. I was starting to feel frustrated and was hoping I wasn't getting the run around on this possibility. It was nice enough that the guys at work were letting me call long distance on company time, and I certainly did not want to take advantage of their generosity too much longer. I remember being called into my supervisor's office and asked if I was thinking about staying with the company there, or what my plans were. He said he needed to know if I was serious about this job because if I was only using it as a part time thing, he didn't want to be putting in the time and effort to train me anymore and would start looking for someone who would be more long-term, which made sense. He wasn't rude or making threats, which I appreciated, and I told him what was going on and about my prospect I was looking at back home. He understood but told me that I needed to make a decision by the end of the week if I was going to stay with his company or move on. Understandable but that did add to my need to get a clear answer from the GM in Boise. I wondered if I would have to employ my tactic I used to get my record store job back in junior high. I made what I hoped to be my last call to the TV station in Boise and was told that I needed to come back for an in-depth interview and fill out paperwork, making it sound to me it was a sure deal that I would be hired. The only drawback would be that it would start at barely minimum wage. I don't remember what it was back in the early 1980's in Idaho, but I remember not being too impressed by that. I was hoping that it would be a great starting salary (it was not)… but it was enough of an impetus to get me to come home.

Now I had been in constant contact with Shelley over all that time, and at some point, we had started saying "I love you" to each other. All my time in Los Angeles alone I had realized that I truly missed her and really wanted to be with her. I don't know how deep and profound my feelings were, but I know that we had gotten it into our minds that we were going to get married. She had been telling me that she was thinking positively about my finding a job down there, but I could also tell that she wanted me to come home and we live there with her. She was telling me about things she wanted to start buying like a washer and dryer and maybe kitchen furniture and she was so excited about all that. It sounded really nice, but I remember not taking any of that part of the relationship as seriously as Shelley was… I was just more caught up in the "love" and romance at that time. I do remember buying a ring somewhere in L.A. though I don't think it was really expensive, but I couldn't wait to give it to her and ask her that question in person. That was also a huge push in my mind to get back to Boise along with the job offer.

I told Dave about my plans to move back to Boise and he was happy for me. He had not asked me for any money for letting me stay with him before then, and I told him I felt like I should do something and what he thought would be fair for me to give him. He did not want any money, the only thing he asked for was for me to send him a copy of "Fast Times at Ridgemont High" on VHS (DVDS were not out yet), as that was his favorite movie. That was one of my favorite movies as well. Where else could you see Phoebe Cates come out of the swimming pool looking as good as that? I promised that I would do that as soon as I got back to Boise (at this point, all I can do is say that I'm sorry Dave, that I never fulfilled that promise—I want to add, however that if I ever find Dave now, or hear from him, I would like the opportunity to make good on that promise).

It never took me long to pack up the car back then when I was ready to move, since I had only taken out the things I needed short term at both places I had stayed. I had already given my notice to my supervisor that I would be leaving and been given my last check, so I was ready to go. I was planning to leave early on a Saturday morning, but I was too keyed up to sleep so I said goodbye to Dave and left Los Angeles around 11pm that Friday night. I intended to drive as long and as far as I could and hopefully make it all the way in one drive, maybe a stop or three at a few rest areas. Well, that was the plan anyway.

Around 7 hours into the drive, well into Nevada, I found myself very heavy eyed and all of the sudden snapping alert, in the opposing lane and doing about 80 miles per hour! I pulled over and stretched, jogged around the car a few times, trying to make myself more awake and alert. After getting back into the car and driving again I found it wasn't going to work, as my eyes just did not want to stay open. I again pulled over and looked at the map and was relieved to see a town only about 30 miles away—surely I could get that far, only my tired brain did not realize that still meant at least a half hour's drive. Fortunately I did make it to Fallon and thankfully found a motel that had an available room (it couldn't have been any later than 8:00 am). I wouldn't have cared if they charged me for two nights at that point for checking in so early; I just needed a bed to sleep on. I slept all that day, got up and had a cheap dinner at the local casino using a coupon I got at the motel when I checked in. After the meal, my stomach was full and my eyes were again drooping so I went back to bed until about 6 that next morning. Then it was time to make the last leg to Boise.

You know how sometimes you can remember things from the past as if they happened yesterday, yet other things which you feel should be clear as day often remain in a haze, or like a dream with fuzzy edges, some things clear, other things there but with holes. That is how the rest of my time in Boise was. It is not selective memory; it just is how it is. So if sometimes it sounds like you are reading something resembling "Cliff Notes" I apologize. All I can say is: it is what it is.

So anyway, when I drove up to the homestead, there were no cars in the driveway and nobody was home. I took no offense, as I had not been specific as to when I was going to arrive back in Boise. I unpacked the car and called Shelley to let her know I was back. She said she was going to a party that night and wanted me to go with her. I remember going to her house to pick her up and I think I gave her the ring then. I am sure she liked it, and I probably popped the question when I did, but I honestly don't remember. I know we went to the party and she introduced me to several people as her fiancé, which felt kind of good. I remember we went back to my house, and my parents still had not returned from wherever they were, and I was starting to get worried. Shelley and I made out for a while and then it was getting late and she thought she should get back home; she wanted to make sure her baby was ok. My folks finally returned, and all was fine.

Remember that I did not talk about a lot of personal things with my mom regarding girls and relationships, but I guess I felt that since I wanted to marry Shelley, I thought I should give Mom the respect and tell her something. I got up the nerve and I remember opening up the conversation with Mom by saying "what do you think about Shelley?" Mom said she liked Shelley just fine. Then what she said just affirms that mothers do know everything. She didn't say that she knew that we were engaged or anything like that but just said that as far as marriage goes, she believed that 23 was too young to be married. Mom said she felt a person should not get married until they were at least 27 years old. That way a person was more mature and would have "sown their wild oats" so to speak. And that was all that I remember about our talk. I think what I got out of that was that I was not going to marry Shelley, at least not with Mom's approval. Not that I couldn't, more like I shouldn't. And who knows what my dad would have thought about the whole situation? My mom has always had a strong influence on my life. I have always cared (and still do) about what she thinks, though at times while reading this book, especially regarding certain things I have done or been involved with, you, the reader might not believe that. And if you feel that way, I wouldn't blame you a bit. Not that I have never had any guilt about certain things I have done. I have, but I don't want to get too far ahead.

Anyway, I remember going to some seminar about something and I think I met Shelley there, or maybe I called her on the phone. The gist of that conversation was that I told her what my mother thought about things, and that made Shelley start to cry. I told her things would be ok, I said whatever I could to get her to stop crying and try to make her feel better. We saw each other a few times after that, but I think the damage had been done. The spark or the fairytale romance or whatever it was that we had flickered and went out after that. I know I loved Shelley, or at least I thought I did. Maybe I was just in love with the feeling I had for her, or just caught up with the thought that I could be a husband and father to Shelley's baby. I don't know, I probably never will know. I have thought about all that from time to time, more right now as I am writing this, and wonder what would have happened if she and I had gotten married? Would it have lasted? I know that my life would have been vastly different than it has become, I might have ended up a better person, but then I might not have.

I ended up not taking the job at Channel 12, the independent TV station that I had come back home for. I think I thought the starting pay was just too low, and that I could do better than that. Again, in retrospect, I think I should have taken the job, but that is one part of the story that we'll never read about.

The next few weeks I spent driving between Portland and Seattle, as I had thought it would be nice to stay in the Pacific Northwest. Why there? I don't have any specific justification, though I did like that I would be close to the ocean and not far from mountains and skiing in either state. Good thinking. Think about extra-curricular activities and not specific job possibilities!

In Portland I stayed with one of my cousins and in Seattle (Bellevue actually) I was able to stay with my aunt and uncle, so I had that aspect covered. I don't remember that I had specific interviews set up with any companies or TV stations or any details like that, but I do remember that I spent a lot of time driving and at night wherever I was, whether on the couch in Portland or in the guest bedroom in Bellevue I was never able to fall asleep easily and therefore would have a difficult time getting up bright and early doing the job search.

Eventually I applied for a job at a radio station in sales near Bellevue, which was at least in the field that I had graduated in. I remember taking some kind of a personality test, some test that would tell the employer if I would be a good candidate for working at the job. It took a couple of weeks of waiting and a few more trips between cities before I finally was offered the job on the Eastside. This was great news, and I truly was relieved! Now I could quit my job of looking for a job and get serious about life. I decided it was time to get my first apartment and ended up moving to a place on Seattle's Capitol Hill.

The apartment I moved into was in a three or four story building which was way older than I was. The apartment manager was not the most appealing looking guy; he looked more like the mad scientist's evil helper, complete with a hunchback, facial stubble, greasy hair with white t-shirt and suspenders. He seemed like a nice enough guy, however, and was very attentive and even quite pleasant. I paid the rent and though the floor creaked everywhere I walked the room was clean and had no roaches. And it was my own place.

I must admit that the apartment was not in my first choice of areas, but it did fit my beginning meager budget and was available when I needed it. It also had some benefits, as there was a small food market a block away, and I noted two bars were conveniently located around the corner. I remember going to the first bar (more like tavern, a seedy looking tavern at that) and opening up the door and as I started to go in, I noticed a couple of the patrons sitting at the counter. They had spiked hair and leather jackets with lots of studs and chains... not my normal type of crowd. I backed out and thought maybe the place next door would be a better option. I didn't even get close to the front door of that one, when I saw the guy who came out, who was huge with long greasy hair and laughing like a crazy person, I decided it just wasn't my day to go bar hopping. I ended up going to that food market and bought a six-pack of beer, peanut butter, jelly and a loaf of bread and had my first meal in my new apartment.

So my first post-graduate job was as an advertising consultant at a smaller country western AM station (it is no longer around today, hasn't been for years) that boasted a broadcast range from Kent up to Everett, or something like that. Funny thing, though as I drove around attempting to drum up advertising, there were pockets of Bellevue, less than five miles from the station where I could not even pick up the signal. But it did have its listeners, as I found when I attended my first live broadcast that first weekend. That was kind of fun, being behind the scenes of a live show rather than just a spectator.

I found out quickly radio advertising sales wasn't all fun and games, however. I had always thought that I was a guy who was not afraid to go up to people I didn't know and start conversation, which *is* partly true; however it was a whole different ballgame when it came to making cold sales calls. I discovered early on I was a lot more timid when the manager or owner of a business would come out and talk to me and I fumbled through my sales pitch or tried to explain the different programs we offered. I was more relieved when I was told the person I needed to talk to was not available and I would need to make an appointment or come back later. I did spend a week in training with Don, the top salesperson (the only other salesperson at the station) and was truthfully envious of his charismatic demeanor he possessed. Of course, he had been in the business for a long time, and had tons of experience in the game. He gave me lots of useful pointers and was a good mentor, but what he taught me, either went in one ear and out the other without bothering to sink in.

I did make two sales during my short time at the job. The first was with a Chinese restaurant in Bellevue, where I had eaten many a lunch while avoiding the calls I was supposed to be making. I more or less fell into that sale, as just by luck the manager came by my table and asked how the food was and if she could get me anything. I think I joked and said she could buy some advertising from me or something off the wall like that. We got to talking and I told her about where I worked and what I did and maybe even how I was having such a tough time making my first sale. Perhaps she felt sorry for me, or possibly she just wanted to shut me up, but she ended up signing my first contract for radio advertising. I was so proud and excited, I couldn't wait to get back to the office and show Daryl, my general manager my first sale. He was happy, but not ecstatic like I thought he should be, but in reality, I'm sure he thought it was no big deal. It was what I was being paid to do: make sales. I then found out that not only was that my job, I also had to write the copy and perform the vocal for the ad. This was going to way more involved than I had previously thought.

Soon after that, Daryl hired another salesperson, Monica, because Don was going to retire from the station, most likely to move on to greener pastures. Monica and I got along quite well, and spent some time making some calls together, but after Don left, it was back to the grind. I was having a hard time again, and was I was getting discouraged and really not in to making the necessary calls. I began doing what was totally against the rules of a salesperson in any industry: I started padding my call sheet, writing down places where I had supposedly had gone, writing the 'results' of said meetings and then in the daily afternoon sales meeting, I would tell Daryl I had had another extremely bad day. Tomorrow would be much more successful, I would tell him. The next day I would show up to work and muddle through the morning meeting, show Daryl the call sheet I had made up for the day and then end up going back to the apartment and watch TV for a while. I can't say I didn't feel guilty, but I guess it was easier than going to places unannounced, seeing people who I felt quite obviously didn't give a crap whether I lived or breathed, and attempted to sell a radio station that overstated everything about itself, including its broadcast range. But realistically it was just the procrastination and the laziness coming out, two of the finer things that I was actually good at.

By this time, I had had enough of the commute between Seattle and the Eastside, especially after my little accident one morning on the 520 floating bridge, where I was rear-ended by a guy in a pickup truck with no insurance (I don't think I had insurance either…I ended up collecting about $100 from him over several months). It was strange how everyone at the station knew what had happened before I said anything about it! It didn't make the car unsafe to drive, just had a nasty dent in the rear bumper area.

I had checked out the ads for roommates wanted and found an apartment in Bellevue where they were looking for someone to rent the third room. It was a decent place, even had a washer and dryer in the unit, and a fenced-in back yard with a patio. It used to be the old manager's apartment, and was supposedly nicer than most of the units. I only talked to one of the two guys who lived there, and he told me I could move in. The day I was moving all of my stuff (which I still did not have all that much—only took two trips across the water) I met the second guy, Ben. He was a little miffed that he had not been able to be a part of the decision and I could tell that he and Mark didn't get along all that well anyway. Mark moved out a couple of months after I moved in, and I'm quite sure there was much love lost there.

One of the things I learned about radio advertising was that there were different types of accounts. There were regular accounts where the advertiser paid money for radio spots, which was the most common type. There was also trade advertising, where a business would get radio advertising spots in exchange for services, such as the restaurant that would give us a food for radio time. I had thought about this after my vehicle mishap and then, I came up with what I thought was a brilliant plan. I went to Daryl and proposed to him an idea that I thought would not only benefit me, but the radio station as well. Why not get a body shop on board to repair my car, paint it white and then have it the radio station's logo and call sign painted on the side. I thought that was perfect! Then every time I drove around on sales calls, I would also be giving the station free advertising! And we wouldn't have to lay out any money because we could give the body shop air time for the body repair and paint job. I must have been a good salesman at that point, because I did get the go-ahead to do that. I talked to a few body shops in Bellevue and got one on board who seemed happy to deal with us. Daryl even loaned me his personal vehicle to use while mine was in the shop and when all was said and done, my formally dirty brown Toyota Corolla was now straight and white. I don't remember the reason, but Daryl wanted to wait on detailing the car with the station information, though the body shop advertising went ahead as planned.

I got to know Monica, the other salesperson at work better as time went on. Even to the point of having a beer or two after work on occasion. She was divorced and had two teenage daughters, both beauty pageant gorgeous, but that would be a whole other chapter in itself, so I will leave things at that. Monica was a smart lady, and seemed to have a lot of good ideas about things. I don't remember if she sold a lot of advertising for the station though. One day, we began talking about advertising in general while having lunch at a Mexican restaurant we tended to frequent and she brought up the specific topic of coupon mailers. I told her I was familiar with those, as I knew we got at least one or two a month at the apartment. Monica let on she had been doing some research on the mailers and how much that could be made doing just that. She laid it all out from a business standpoint, and I must admit, it seemed like a very lucrative venture. I said it was too bad we weren't in the coupon mailer business ourselves. She looked at me and asked me what I would think of us creating our own coupon mailer together, going into business as partners. I thought about it and said it would be a great idea (of course at that moment I thought she was just thinking out loud)… but I said there would be no way we could do that! She looked at me and told me that she was *serious!* She knew people who owned a printing shop that could produce the mailers at a reduced cost for her… all we would need to do was to get advertisers, the same way we were already doing, but just for a different medium. She told me it would be so much easier to sell and that direct marketing was a hot market right then. Monica again stress she *was* serious and not to worry, that it really would be easy money. I told her I needed to think about that.

I did think about it, and the more I did, the more profitable the idea sounded. It was such a simple idea! Just drum up about 15 to 20 advertisers, print the coupons and mail them out! What could be easier than that? I called Mom and Dad with the exciting news. To my utter astonishment, they were less than thrilled. They thought that I should stick with my current job rather than quit and go into such a crazy, unwise venture. I thought to myself, were they just crazy and not thinking "out of the box?" Could they really not realize the potential gold-mine such a venture could be? But after listening to all of my ranting about the deal, they finally told me to do what I felt was best. I think they either got tired of listening to my nonsense or just acquiesced because they figured I was going to do this anyway. They asked me if I was going to pursue this in addition to my current job. I told them that Monica and I had both planned on resigning and doing this solo. I think that my folks probably both needed toilet paper after hearing that, if you know what I mean. So after getting my parent's "approval," I called Monica and told her that I was "in!" Monica and I made plans throughout the next week as to what our next step was. We figured that it would look too suspicious if we both quit at the same time, so she gave notice and left a week prior to me. I hadn't even thought about the implication of my car—it still had not been painted with the station logo and all of the body shop's advertising had not even run its course yet. How was that going to look? I found out.

The day I gave notice (I don't even remember if I gave a specific reason for leaving), Daryl asked me if this had anything to do with Monica leaving, as I believe he had suspicions we were going to a competitor and that we might take all of our advertising contacts with us (like I had so many), but I told him that I had no idea why Monica left, where she was going or what she was going to do (another lie). He then told me that I would be liable for paying the station back for the body work and the paint job. Like I mentioned before, I hadn't thought about that aspect. I don't remember all the details, but I did what I needed to do so that I could leave without burning any bridges. I don't recall for sure, but I think Daryl let me leave that day, figuring there was no reason for me to finish up the week if my heart was not going to be in it. So then there I was, unemployed with bills and a new "job" with no guaranteed income. Was I scared? Was I nervous? Probably, but I sincerely don't remember exactly how I felt. Was I stupid? Oh **Hell yeah!** But I just did not know how stupid at that time.

I don't know exactly how long we lasted on our venture, but Monica was handling the business end of the endeavor and I was trying to handle the sales end. I was having about as much luck selling coupons as I did selling radio time, although my effort in and sincerity of in coupon mailers was tremendously higher. I did believe it was a better platform for advertisers than the station I was working for. Now if I had been selling advertising for any of the top radio stations in the Seattle market that might have made a difference. If that had been the situation, I am sure that I might never have left for coupon mailers!

But anyway, I think I brought in two advertisers and that was it. I don't think we got any more on board, and I am also sure that not even one coupon mailer was printed. At some point, we must have admitted defeat, because I remember shortly after I filled out an application for employment at the corner convenience store/deli that was a couple of blocks away from the apartment, just so that I could have some kind of income coming in. The bills needed to be paid, and without an income . . . well, you can do the math.

There was a span of at least a month before I did get that next job, where I had no money coming in, and what money I did have was rapidly dwindling. I did my best to not spend or buy things unless absolutely necessary, and I remember being depressed a lot of the time. I stopped getting the mail out of the mailbox, and when I did get something, it usually was a bill, which I just put aside. After all, why look a bill if I couldn't pay it? I remember getting a letter from my folks, which I either read and did not respond to or just plain ignored it. I didn't call them or return any calls, probably because I was too embarrassed that I had failed miserably in my "great venture of coupon mailers," and I didn't need Mom and Dad in any way reminding me they had told me that would happen. I did open one letter from Mom one afternoon because I think my name and address was typed on the envelope, which Mom never did, unless she was pissed. She would always address the envelope with her unmistakable handwriting. My heart sank as I read what she had written. The letter was also typewritten, again, something she rarely did when corresponding to me. The gist of the letter was that if I continued to ignore them, they were going to disown me. That was it. In retrospect, I think Mom was trying to open my eyes and get me to see reality. Would she have followed through and disowned me? I wasn't about to take the chance and find out.

They say Moms know everything, that they often have a sixth sense and can feel it when things go wrong for their children. I truly believe that. Over the years, my mom has been so intuitive about so many things in my life, that it is scary. I'd bet she knows things about me that I could swear I have never told her. But I digress. Anyway, that letter did wake me up, and I think I called her that night and we talked about how things were, what was happening and what wasn't happening. She told me that whatever I was going through, they supported me and no matter what, would always love me. Of course those words made me feel better about me and my life. She may have told me that if I needed some extra money to help me through until my next paycheck, she would be glad to give me a loan, which I am sure I took her up on.

I was now starting my second "real" job, working at that local deli/convenience store. I was behind the counter, making hoagie

73

sandwiches of all kinds, being the cashier, making coffee, sweeping, cleaning, you know, all sorts of fun stuff. But it was a job. Because it was minimum wage, it did make me miss the salary I was making at the radio station. But it wasn't really all that hard and the people I worked with were friendly enough. What made it more of a challenge for me was the fact that I was on my feet for most of the time I was there. My feet were so sore after I got off shift that I would literally be limping as I walked home. I had no other choice but to tough it out, as I had no other job options available to me at the moment. I remember sometimes during my work week when I got up to go pee in the middle of the night, my feet were so cramped, I would crawl to the bathroom, I seriously could not walk. Thinking back, I do not know how I lasted at that job as long as I did.

I had some fun times working there, and like I said, I met some cool people. My supervisor was a girl named Gloria, and though she was very matter of fact and stern, she was also quite pleasant. I was probably around 24 and she couldn't have been too much older than me. Gloria and I went out a few times for drinks and we would each try to see who would leave the bar with someone first. I remember one night in particular that both of us indeed did not leave alone. That night was my one and only "one night stand" that I can remember. As most one night stands commonly go, names usually are not exchanged, and if they are, they are not remembered. The truly peculiar thing about that night and after we had done the deed and were putting out clothes back on, she said to me "the next time you will see me will be in my casket." I thought that was the most morbid thing I had ever heard, and I asked her what she meant. "I have leukemia," she told me and then she left. That was just too weird, and I am sure there was no significance but as I watched her drive off, it started snowing for the first time that season. I never saw her again (like anyone ever really sees their one night stands again anyway).

About 4 months into my time working at the deli, I was promoted to shift supervisor and undoubtedly got a little raise. That was pretty cool, but it did come with more responsibility, mostly having to insure that everything got done prior to the next shift starting. That was not always easy to do, especially when the prior shift didn't complete all that they were responsible for. That was my first taste of graveyard hours, which in itself was not bad, because there another person to work with and usually not a lot of customers to bother us. What I really liked was there were no managers hovering over our shoulders. However, not having supervision can often lead to hi-jinx and bad habits which I indeed did succumb to. There were a few times in the cooler when we were stocking the shelves with beer and wine I remember helping myself to citrus coolers and munching on the pre-sliced deli meats we stored there. I can also remember a time or two when I would drive to work and park in the back and when I would leave in the morning, I would have a case of beer in my trunk. I want you to know that if I come across as bragging or boasting, I am not. I am certainly not proud of those actions, and truth be told, I *am* embarrassed. I would like to tell you that those were the worst things I have done in my life, but unfortunately that is not the case.

Working graveyard hours at a place like that does have other more positive advantages, one of which is you get to know a lot of the policemen that patrol the area. And yes, they do come in for doughnuts… I just thought I would throw that one in, ha-ha. It was most always interesting talking to them; they always had curious stories to tell. There was one time Don and I were back in the cooler, and we had just finished smoking a joint when I saw through the glass cooler doors two cops come into the store. I immediately got paranoid and told Don that there was no way in Hell I was going out into the store to help them. I just knew that they would know that I had been smoking; I figured my red eyes would give me away. I don't think I ever smoked pot at work again after that. I remember Don just laughed at me; he didn't care if they noticed, he said as long as they didn't smell anything, they would just figure we were tired since we were working all night. I stayed in the cooler until the cops left.

Since the apartment I lived in had a backyard (small though it was) that was fenced in, I figured it would be cool to get a dog. I had grown up with Springer spaniels, so when I saw some kids giving away dogs outside of a Safeway store one afternoon that looked just like Springer pups (they were actually half Springer/half Australian shepherd), I just had to take one home. The fact that they were free was a huge bonus! I got the puppy home and then asked my roommates if they minded if I had a puppy. He was so cute and friendly, I don't think they could have said no even if they wanted to. That's the wonderful thing about puppies. I named my dog Luke, I think after the Luke character from the afternoon soap "General

Hospital" (yes, I watched that show for years, more during the Luke and Laura years) and Luke easily caught on to his name.

Luke became my friend and companion, and I would play with him all the time, take him for walks every day after work, and basically take him everywhere I went that I could. The only problem I had with Luke was that he would constantly escape by digging under the fence and running away if I left him unattended for long periods of time. That was fun chasing him around the neighborhood. As he got a little older, he stopped getting out and was much easier to handle. It got to the point where when we went on walks, I didn't need to keep him on a leash, he would always stay near my side. I remember one time when I threw a ball and told him to go fetch, I hid behind a tree. He ran back past the tree and stopped and looked around, then ran back the other way, stopped again and didn't see me... he just sat down and started whining. I felt bad so I poked my head from behind the tree and when he saw me, Luke ran and jumped full into me. He knocked me down onto the ground hopped on my chest and then growled in my faceThen he proceeded to give my face a bath with his tongue, happy that he had found me. I think he growled as a way of telling me never to hide from him again. It really was a touching experience and I think any lover of animals would probably know exactly what I am talking about.

After almost a year with Luke, it became apparent that he was getting too big for apartment life, even though we had the backyard. There was no grass back there, just a small patio and beyond that, mostly shrubbery and weeds, and more often than not, Luke just wanted to dig his way out. I loved my dog fiercely, but I knew that with my night time schedule and how big he was getting, there was just no way I was going to be able to keep him if I was going to continue living at that apartment, and at that time, I had no other options as to where I could go and still afford to live at that time. Though I did not want to give up Luke, I had to try to find him a better home for him than what I was providing. I had hoped that one of my friends would be able to adopt him, which would be a perfect solution, allowing me to see him as often as I could. I tried for roughly two weeks, but unfortunately I found no one who could adopt him into their homes, for whatever reasons. That sucked.

I had thought of a contingency plan in case I could not find him a home myself. The only other humane choice I could come up with, because I was not going to drive around and just drop him off in another neighborhood to fend for himself, was the Humane Society, of course. What better place to take Luke, I figured. They would certainly be able to find him a good, loving, quality home. The only problem was I knew it was going to be very hard on on Luke (which is really weird to say, after all, Luke was just a dog, how could he *miss* me?). Some great family with children that wanted a dog would be delighted to have such a devoted and intelligent dog, I kept telling myself, to justify what I needed to do. I put Luke in the car and took off his collar so I could say that I found him wandering the streets and wanted to find him a home. I would tell the Humane Society that I was unable to take him in myself and take care of him properly (which wasn't totally a lie), and could they help me.

Walking Luke into the building was probably one of the most difficult things I had to do, giving up my best friend, leaving him with strangers and not knowing where he would be going. Luke did not want to leave my side and he whined and if I didn't know better, I would almost say by the look in his face he *knew* I was abandoning him. I hugged Luke, and he licked my face, which created a huge lump in my throat. I had to get out of there or I was going to start crying and probably take him back out. He started barking at me as I was leaving the building, and as the girl was taking him into the back, he struggled and tried to get away from her. I could still hear Luke barking as the door to the Humane Society closed behind me. I got to my car, got in, sat down and closed the door and started crying like a little baby. I didn't care if anyone saw me, I was just overcome with grief and regret and shame at what I had done. I don't know how long I sat there before I finally drove home.

A week later, I still didn't feel much better about things, but I was missing Luke like crazy. I knew it wouldn't really make a difference, but I had to find out if he had been placed in a good home, so I called the Humane Society and asked the receptionist about the dog I had brought in the week before. She said she would check and find out what she could. I was put on hold for about five minutes before a new voice came back on the line. I was asked if it was regarding the spaniel/shepherd mix that was brought in the previous Friday or something like that. I said yes. Then I was told something like this: "I'm sorry sir. After you dropped off the dog, he barked for two days straight, would not eat or sleep and he made himself sick, so he had to be put to sleep." I killed my dog. I hung up the phone and I am sure I started crying again, probably got drunk, too. I couldn't believe it. I tried to do the right thing, but all I did was kill my dog. I don't think to this day that I have forgiven myself for that. I have vowed that never again will I own a dog until I have a house with a fenced yard and can take care of it the way it deserves to be taken care of. Even now, over two decades later as I write this, it still hurts.

Even though I haven't mentioned anything about girls in a while, that doesn't mean there hadn't been any progress on that front. There were two girls I had gotten to know while living at that apartment in Bellevue: Trudy and Darla, the red-haired co-worker from the deli.

Trudy was the younger sister of a lady who was a neighbor in the complex. Trudy and her sister were from England, her sister lived in the complex with her boyfriend and Trudy lived with her parents in Redmond. She was pretty and seemed like a friendly person, and was my age. Trudy and I never really dated, though we spent enough time getting to know each other and enough time for me to start to really like her. I am not sure if my attraction was due to Trudy as a person, or because of her truly sexy accent. I have always been fascinated by women who speak with the English accent, I don't know why, but I am. I'd always thought if I had the choice between a woman with an American accent and an English accent, and everything else was the same, I would probably strive to end up with the latter. Anyway, what made me want to pursue Trudy even more was her refusal to see me as anything more than just a friend.

I remember we talked about pretty much everything under the sun, things we liked, things we were indifferent about, movies, sports, food, where we had been, the whole nine yards. I loved just listening to her and was fascinated with her, as she had been more places in her life than I probably would be in my lifetime. I don't remember if she had a boyfriend, but if she did, I don't think it was a serious relationship, or maybe he was back in England, but I know that I asked her out more than once, and she would always decline, but not in a direct way; it was more like we'll see, or not this week, or that she wasn't ready to go out with me yet, lots of different excuses, but never that she specifically did not want to go out with me. And that made me want her more, which drove me crazy. I think sometimes she would antagonize me on purpose, tease me and pretend that I had done or said something to make her mad. There was one time that she would not answer her phone or return any of my calls or messages for a week. Then when she finally started talking to me again, she said I had pissed her off by making a derogatory remark about her having a teddy bear, or something like that. I think in the long run, Trudy really enjoyed the attention I was giving her. She wanted to be the center of attention, but did not want things to go beyond that. Some guys could live with that, but it drove me crazy.

Trudy was taking classes at the now defunct business college in downtown Bellevue, and I remember one time I bought a red rose beautifully wrapped up with baby's breath and placed it on the windshield of her Nissan pickup, which was parked in the college's parking garage next to the building where her classes were. I parked across the street where I could watch without being seen for what seemed like hours, just so I could see what her expression would be when she got back to her car and saw my gift. Would she know it was from me? How could she not? It actually was hours, and I had no idea what her schedule was, but I don't remember her ever going to her car while I waited, and finally I left. I called her later that evening to say hello, but mainly to see if she would say anything to me about the rose. She did not. I finally had to ask her if she had found anything on her windshield that afternoon. She hemmed and hawed and finally said she found the rose and then asked me if I had put it there. I said I did. Very matter of fact she asked me why I would do that. I was shocked. Did she not know what it meant when a guy gave a girl a rose? Of course she did. She was just playing with me again. But she was serious when she asked why I did it, because she then tried again to tell me that she was not interested in me in any way more than good friends. It was then that I think it finally hit home and I finally understood where I stood with her. Admitting defeat to myself, I didn't give her any more flowers or special treatment, and I think she ended up going back to England because I don't remember seeing her very much if at all after that. Maybe she knew she was leaving and wanted to let me down the easy way. Maybe I should just keep thinking that.

Darla worked with me at the deli and we had never become really good friends, though the flirting between us was very evident. She would always say things about how I looked with sexual undertones and she was definitely hot herself, very pleasing to the eye in pretty much every aspect. I have never been really attracted to redheads for whatever reason, but Darla was a true exception to that. I was very turned on by her. The flirting and sexual innuendos went on for weeks until one of us decided we needed to do something about our obvious attraction to each other. I don't remember if it was Darla or me who initiated the encounter but it probably was her, as I was pretty much always the one who let others make the first move.

One morning after the graveyard shift, Darla had agreed to come back home with me, so at 7am, we both left, though not exactly at the same time so as we wouldn't draw unwarranted attention to what we were doing. She followed me back to the apartment, and we quietly went to my room and closed and locked the door. Once we were inside, it was pretty much a no-brainer; the clothes came off and we were naked and groping each other's bodies like two people who had been deprived of any physical contact with the opposite sex in years. It was great! I didn't consider this like a one night stand, mainly because we knew each other, and also because I was pretty sure that if we liked how things turned out, we would probably do this again, or at least not rule the possibility out, of course. Our bodies were soon covered in sweat and the sex was great. It was at that point that I finally knew how to tell a redhead was truly a redhead.

After we were done with the first workout, we laid together for a few minutes, catching our breath, and as I was still a young guy, I was ready to go again pretty quick. Darla told me that she really needed to be going however, because she needed to be sure she was home before her husband got home. Now this was news I was not expecting to hear! She had not told me about a husband, and I was pretty sure I had not seen a wedding ring on her finger. She saw me looking there, and smiled and told me she didn't wear it to work because she didn't want to get it dirty or risk losing it. I asked her how long she had been married and I don't remember exactly what she told me, but it had been for a few years at least, and I don't recall her saying they were having any problems. Darla sensed my apprehension but said not to worry, she was safe, and this was the first time she had done this sort of thing. I think I probably believed it at the time, I was still pretty naïve in those things. She got dressed, kissed me and thanked me for a wonderful time, and then left. I remember lying there, wondering what the hell I had done. I didn't think I would ever be involved in an affair with a married woman! That was just wrong! I would hate to have that done to me, so why would I ever do that to another person! I vowed I would never do that again! Well, except for the one other time with Darla on my birthday a few months later. She wanted me to have a special birthday present, and who was I to deprive her of that exceptional gift. Did I keep my vow after that? I wish I could say I did, but that would be lying, and I do try to keep that trait in check these days, but that story comes much later.

Up to this time, though I drank booze, smoked pot, and done mushrooms, I was still a virgin to smoking cigarettes. I had been pretty proud of that, as most of my friends smoked. I just had never felt the urge or need to smoke. I didn't see what the big deal of smoking was. But one day I decided to see what the whole deal was. I thought I would try smoking and actually inhale like real smokers do (remember back in high school, my buddy Dave and I "smoked" the night of my first drunk but did not inhale). I remember buying my first pack of cigs: Camel Lights. I took my break and went outside and thought how neat it was, I was going to be like everyone else and take a "smoke break." How cool! I lit the cigarette and took a drag, inhaling the smoke and instantly began coughing until tears were running down my cheeks. What a silly hilarious sight that must have been (I am laughing right now thinking back at that moment). I took another drag on the cigarette, thinking that maybe after two or three puffs I might get the hang of it. After the fourth drag, I was able to hold the smoke in without choking to death before exhaling and then as I finally did blow out, my head felt very different, I can't describe it better than I felt extremely light headed, and I thought for a moment I was going to pass out. Then that feeling subsided and I just felt and heard a major buzzing going through my brain. So *that* was what it was all about! Not bad, I remember thinking. I finished the smoke and flicked the butt onto the parking lot as I had seen all my friends do. I felt cool now. I had a smoke! And it was okay, after all, I knew that one cigarette would not get me hooked. I could smoke and not get addicted. I would *never* become addicted to cigarettes, any more than I could become addicted to drinking booze!

So now that I had learned how to smoke and be cool, it was fun to drive around town and smoke in the car. I have no idea why I thought that was so cool, but I remember thinking just that. I would drive around with no particular place to go, just smoking and enjoying myself, throwing the butts out the window, just like everyone else did no worries. I also felt like part of the in crowd when I would go out with my friends to the bars and drink (remember back when it was legal to smoke in the bars?) I was never without my pack of smokes and my lighter. At some point I switched to Marlboro reds, though not after trying pretty much all the brands, just to see which one I would like better.

I remember one of my roommates thought I smoked too much and he was really on me about quitting. I told him that I could quit anytime and not to worry about it. I think he dared me to quit, so I did, just to shut him up. That didn't last long though. I began thinking about why I had just quit. Why should I quit just because I was dared? That wasn't a good reason. But if I started smoking again, he would think I was weak, that I didn't have the stamina and he would rag on me for starting up again. So I figured that I just would not smoke in front of him. He would never know. Why I went that route is beyond me, why I didn't just say I am going to smoke and deal with it like a normal person I couldn't tell you. I took the easy route and hid my smoking. I would smoke in my bathroom with the fan on and use air deodorant, I would smoke in my car away from the apartment, and anywhere he wasn't. Then one day I was in my car in the car port with a lit cigarette and my roommate came up, got in the car and started talking to me, not even noticing I was smoking. I was trying to hide what I was doing, and all of the sudden his eyes opened wide, and he got this pathetic hurt look on his face and walked away. I felt like shit that I had deceived him. But in a way, I was glad it was out in the open and I could smoke again without hiding it. You would think I would learn how stupid it is to try and hide smoking! But I didn't. And apparently it seemed I could not quit any time I wanted, could I?

At some point during my time at that apartment, I met a girl named Sheri. To this day, I don't know exactly how or where I met her, it was probably at a bar, but we ended up sleeping with each other a few nights after that. She was a nice girl, about 4 years older than me, but pleasant enough and though we started out in just a casual sexual relationship, we ended up being pretty good friends after that. She told me a few months later that she had gotten pregnant after our first night together, but that she had taken care of things. I think I may have asked her why she didn't tell me when she first found out and she said she thought I might never talk to her again, or something of that nature. I think she said her parents knew, but she never told her dad who the father was, because she was certain he would have come after me with a shotgun. Even after all that, our friendship remained intact. We slept with each other many times after that, but always made sure to use the proper protection at all times of course, for obvious reasons.

Sheri had a female friend, Lynda, who lived in Seattle who I had been introduced to, another fiery red-haired lady, who was beautiful, a talented singer and an aspiring actress. Lynda lived with her boyfriend Andrew, and I remember Sheri and I went to their place one night to party, drink and just have fun. We started drinking early, but casually, as we didn't want to get so messed up that we would pass out and not have any fun... at least not real early. I remember after it started getting dark, we thought it would be great fun to have Sheri call my room-mates, and ask them if they knew where I was. She made the call and they said they hadn't seen me. Sheri said she hadn't seen me either, and that I was supposed to be over to see her two hours ago. They said they would watch out for me and have me call her as soon as they saw me. It didn't seem like any big deal at the time, but later they told me they had been worried sick about me and that they even thought about calling the police and reporting me as a missing person. I am glad they did not do that.

Anyway, as the night went on, we, or should I say I got drunk, or maybe you could call it wasted. I remember becoming aware of things and was sitting on the couch. I could not open my eyes, but I could hear everything that was happening plain as day. Sheri, Lynda and Andrew were all hovering over me; they lifted my arm and watched it fall limply back to my side. They were laughing and commenting about what a lightweight I was, they didn't think I had had *that* much to drink, but obviously I had. Then one of them got this bright idea that it would be tremendous fun to put a dress on me, lipstick and a wig! And then someone said then they could take pictures! There was no way I wanted *that* to happen! But try as I might, I could not move, I could not talk, I could not open my eyes. There was nothing I could do to prevent anything from happening. I remember being dragged off the couch, my head bouncing off the cushions and onto the floor. They undressed me down to my underwear and someone shaved a patch of hair off one of my legs and a little patch off my chest (I was pissed when I found that out—it took a couple of months for that to grow back!). Then the dress was put on, the lipstick applied and the wig put on. I think somehow they got me back up on the couch and I remember seeing the flash of a camera go off through my closed eyelids and that is the last thing I remember about that night.

The next morning was Hell on earth, as is most mornings after a night of heavy drinking. The head was pounding and the mouth was full of cotton. The only thing I could even fathom was a few spoons of cottage cheese (why I have no idea) and a small glass of cold water. Anything more than that and I was sure it would come right back up real quick. I had no recollection at that point of what they had done until I had the wherewithal to notice that I was wearing a dress. Then something sparked in my brain, and I managed to find a mirror and saw the rouge and lipstick and then it all came back. I was too sick to show my anger, and I just lay on the couch for the afternoon until I had gathered up enough strength to go home. I often wonder if pictures of that night are still in existence. I sure hope not!

I had not heard from Shelley for quite a while. She and I had more or less fallen out of touch since I had moved up to the Seattle area, and the last I had heard from her, she had met another guy and had gotten married. At first I had thought that was sort of odd, and rather quick, as she and I had been in "love" and were planning on getting married ourselves. Then to hear that just a short time after it had become obvious that she and I were not going to be going down that aisle, she meets and finds another guy and marries him? To be honest, I was not jealous, or put off with that; possibly I was never really in love with her, and it was more just infatuation, or deep affection at best and a real desire to be a father to that super sweet little baby of hers. Who wouldn't have fallen in love with a baby as cute as hers anyway! I don't remember where I had gotten a number to reach her, but I did. She and her husband had moved to eastern Washington and were living the good life there, I found out. I called her one night, for no other reason than to tell her that I had no hard feelings, that I wished her the best and that I hoped we could remain friends. She was very quiet and didn't say much, I don't know if she was embarrassed to talk to me or what the deal was, but she said she still was my friend. We said it would be great to keep in touch and I wished her the best. I hung up the phone and felt weird, like a part of me was sad, but then again, a part of me was glad to have closed that chapter. Shelley and I have never spoken to each other since then. I have no idea where she is or how she is doing. Years and years later, through Facebook, I have since become her 'friend' again!

During my time working at the deli, I went through about five room-mates, and out of the last two, Stan (the roommate who had wanted me to stop smoking) and Karl (he was an asshole mainly when he and Stan hung together). For whatever reason, Stan and Karl liked to pick on me, probably because they were bored and had nothing better to do (maybe to get back at me for worrying them so much when they had thought I was a missing person)…but maybe also because they knew I wasn't one to really fight back. I wasn't a pansy or anything like that; I just had better things to do than to tolerate their bullshit.

This is an example of how childish they could be and how they would not let up or seem to get tired of their pranks. I had gotten home from a graveyard shift probably around 7am and I was extremely tired, and just wanted to get to bed. I went into my room and closed the door, and got into bed. Stan and Karl would open the door and stand in the hallway and laugh with obvious glee, until I got back out of bed and closed the door again. They would open the door and laugh even more, and this went on probably three or four more times. They were enjoying the hell out of tormenting me, and all I wanted to do was get to sleep. I don't remember how that scene ended, but I think at that point I had had enough. I went through the paper and finally found another place to move to, a little studio apartment in a small five unit complex downtown Bellevue. One Saturday morning I moved out with the help of some other friends of mine. I didn't have a whole lot to move and I think it only took one trip, but that was fine. I remember Stan was gone, and Karl had been awakened in the process; he was upset because he said he was sick and was trying to sleep, but I didn't give a shit about him at that point. I didn't care that I had not given either of them any real notice that I was moving so they could try and find a new roommate. Too bad that they probably had a hard time splitting the rent between the two of them for that month, I didn't give a shit. I know I went about the whole deal in the wrong way, but I did what I had to do, and to this day I don't have any regrets about it.

I ran into them a few times in the deli after that, and they really didn't say anything to me, which was fine by me. I didn't go out of my way to avoid them, but I didn't run up and give them hugs and kisses either. Then one night before I was supposed to go to work, Stan called me and asked me if I could meet them so we could talk about what I still owed on the phone bill. He sounded sincere and didn't give me any shit over the phone, so I agreed to meet them before I got to work. They met me in the parking lot of the deli and asked me to get into their car so we could talk over things in private. Though that sounded weird, I got in against my better judgement and they immediately accelerated out of the parking lot and said they were going to beat the shit out of me for having them in the lurch. I remember my heart sank to the bottom of my stomach and probably started to shake with fear.

I had never before been beaten up, and what truly frightened me was they were furious and serious. They drove to the parking lot of the high school near the apartment complex I had just moved out of and pulled me out of the car, calling me names, and pushing me around. They said I was a pathetic piece of shit and wasn't worth the ground they walked on. I remember standing there and taking it (I have never been a fighter, never hit anyone in anger, this was all too new to me), not really knowing what to do. They poured a can of pop over my head and called me more names, and then I just started walking away from them. I don't know that they expected that, as it took them a moment to realize that I was going to get away. I remember running out to the main road and then Stan caught up to me and actually threw a punch and caught me in the jaw. I still did not hit back and just turned around and ran to the deli parking lot. I stopped and noticed they had not followed me there. I stood there for a few minutes, shaking and not knowing what to do. I don't remember crying, but I knew I better get inside before they decided to come back and try something else on me. My friend and coworker Mark saw how distressed I looked and asked me if I was okay, and I think I just told him to leave me alone until I could rinse my hair or something. The rest of that night is a blur, but I do remember talking to one of the Bellevue cops who came in regularly and told him what happened. He told me I could file assault charges if I wanted to, but I never pursued that avenue. Maybe that was the pacifist part of me, the part of me that did not like confrontation (I am still pretty much like that today), I don't know. I don't think I saw either of those guys again after that.

My new apartment was just downtown Bellevue off of Main Street, in an older residential area. It was the kind of place where one would have to have explicit directions to get there otherwise one might never find it at all. I remember when I was first looking for it to check out, I had to call and get directions from the manager twice before I finally found it. It wasn't the best place I had ever seen before in my life, but it had all that I needed, which suited me fine.

I thought that if I had such a hard time finding the place, it probably would be equally difficult for a pizza delivery place to find as well. Back then, Domino's Pizza had their delivery deal of 30 minutes or free, so I put that to the test. I called and ordered, gave them my address and they verified I was in their delivery area and told me it would be there in 30 minutes or less. I hung up the phone and noted the time and started the countdown. Thirty minutes went by, then forty minutes, no pizza. Finally I got a call from the driver and he had no idea where I was, so I gave him the directions and I think finally after almost an hour he arrived. Bingo, free pizza. It didn't matter that it wasn't piping hot, I didn't care—I cared more that it was free! I think I tried my scheme one more time and got one more free pizza, and after that, they must have had my particular address circled on their map, because the third time I ordered, it must have been to my door in less than 20 minutes. I swear I have never had a pizza delivered so fast!

My friend Don and I put together a Halloween party at my little apartment that year. We injected a fifth of vodka and a fifth of rum inside a watermelon and let it sit for at least 24 hours before the party. Only a few people showed up initially, but eventually we had probably about 15 in total. We did manage to keep it relatively toned down, at least we didn't get any noise complaints that I recall. What I do remember was that watermelon was one of the worst tasting things I had ever tasted in quite some time, but it was potent, mind you. I don't remember how many slices

I had, but we finished it off before any of the other bottles that people had brought with them. When most everyone had left, there was a cute blonde still in the apartment who was playing with the tuner on my stereo. I'm not sure quite what she was trying to do, but I did note that she was pretty wasted, which I thought I could use to my advantage. I led her over to the bed and think I tried to make out with her. She kissed back for a few minutes and then pushed me away, claiming she had a very bad headache. My head wasn't all that clear either, but I remember telling her that I knew the best way to get rid of a headache. She asked what that was, and I told her that the best cure that I knew of was having sex. She wasn't buying my idea, but she did stay long enough for me to at least do a little snuggling with her before we both passed out. I woke up with a head-banging hangover in the morning and also alone in the bed. She had gotten up in the middle of the night and left me without so much as a note or a good bye. Pity me.

One day, and I remember this day specifically, as it was exactly a week before my one year mark at the deli, I was called into the office to talk to Pam, the store manager. She sat me down and told me that they were letting me go. I asked her why, and she told me that I was never able to complete the tasks of my shift and so the morning shift was always starting behind schedule. I told her that it wasn't my fault, because the shift prior to mine was the same way, so our shift was constantly trying to catch up. It was a never ending cycle, so why was I being canned? But it turned out it wasn't just me, all of the shift supervisors were let go in the ensuing weeks. I figured that with me they couldn't have timed it better for their sake. After all, if they had let me stay just one more week, I would have been eligible for a week's paid vacation. Again, pity me. So there ended my deli career.

I went through the next week feeling depressed and gloomy, basically feeling sorry for myself. I had purchased a baggie of some good pot from my friend from the deli the week before, and found myself smoking a lot during that week, probably trying to escape from the dreary reality that my life was at that time. But even no job and no income would keep me from any opportunity to experience that wonderful thing known as sex.

Sex was something I liked but didn't seem to get enough of (I'm sure that most guys in their 20's would agree), and it didn't matter if there was a relationship involved or even if you knew the girl or not. I was given the phone number of a girl who I was told loved having sex, without all the fuss of getting to know each other, which was fine by me. We talked on the phone for a few days and finally made a "date" for a get together. We may even have had phone sex once during our talks. It was a very long couple of days waiting for the big night. Being jobless and having nothing to do during the day didn't help with the time—I couldn't believe how slow it passed by! But then finally Friday arrived! I remember taking a shower and got all clean and nice for her and waited for her appearance. There was a knock at the door and I opened it to find a pretty nice, attractive girl at the door, no Playboy model, but, as they say, do-able (I was bad like that back then).

Showing her (I don't remember her name at all) around my little apartment didn't take but a few minutes and then I was ready to get down to business, but she wanted to go out and get something to eat. We drove to Wendy's and got some burgers, and again I found the time to be going by at a snail's pace, I (sad to say now) had a pretty much one track mind then. We finally finished eating and ended back at my place and then I think I lit some candles and we made a little more small talk. Finally our clothes came off. I remember she had a really tight great looking body and beautiful breasts. We had sex and then I became what I now call cold and an asshole. I didn't ask her to leave or show outright rudeness to her, but I didn't want to cuddle or lay in bed with her, I know she wanted that, but I put on my shorts and got out whatever I was writing and started working on that. She watched TV for about an hour and a few times I remember her asking me to come back and join her in bed, but I said that it was times like this where I wrote better, that the ideas were flowing out of me and I needed to write while the ideas were fresh. So I continued to ignore her and finally she just left without saying too much. I think back and wonder how I could have been such a cold-hearted bastard, but I guess I got what I wanted and that was that. What an idiot I was!

So money became tight and I thought I had better start spending as little I could and cut out on purchases that were not really necessary. What would be a better time to quit smoking cigarettes than right now, I thought. I remember I was back to smoking Camel lights and for some reason I was out driving in the car later at night because it was dark when I made the decision. I didn't even want to wait until I finished the pack, so I rolled down the window and tossed the pack out and kept driving. I felt good that I was finally done with smoking. I drove back home and watched TV for about an hour, more or less twiddling my thumbs and wondering what to do. I didn't have money to go drinking, I was out of pot and I didn't have any smokes because I had just thrown out my smokes. Then I thought what the Hell and got in the car and drove to where I thought the smokes might still be. Thank God it had not rained and that no one had found them before I did. It seemed like pure heaven to me as I lit up that smoke. I guess I wasn't ready to quit yet. I would just have to figure cigarettes into my measly budget.

It was time to begin looking for another job, either full time career wise or temporary; it didn't really matter at that point. I needed money and I had already put my apartment manager off once before, so I didn't want to have to ask for another extension. I figured maybe I should call a temporary agency to help me find some work. I had heard of Kelly Services before, and so I made the call and they had me go to the local office and fill out some paperwork, take some aptitude and typing tests and then said they would give me a call as soon as they found something that fit my qualifications. I hoped that call would be soon.

The first job they sent me on was at the division office of a major grocery store chain, in the pricing department, inputting data. I had never really used the Lotus 1-2-3 program before, but I found it pretty easy to learn. Each week I was given all the information as to what items were to be included in the store's newspaper ads then I input them into the spreadsheet with the regular retail prices along with sale prices for all stores in Western and Eastern Washington. I would produce this advertising booklet that would be distributed to all the departments that needed the information. The information was checked and after any final changes were made, I produced the pamphlet that ended up in the advertising department where the ad was produced that would be distributed to stores and newspapers. It was a great job, and I picked up on all the requirements and learned the processes with ease. The people in my department were fun to work with and I was having fun as well as earning some money. They were impressed with the speed and accuracy of my work and I was getting better and faster each week. As the end of the four week period that I had been contracted for was coming to an end, I found I was actually sad that I would be leaving. I got the feeling that those I worked with were not entirely happy to see me leave as well.

That Friday that was to be my last day there, the pricing manager asked to see me in his office. Curious, and also with a little anxiety, I went in and as he motioned for me sit, I did. I tried to think if I had done or said anything that might have gotten me into some kind of trouble; it would be a shame to be leaving a good job, temporary or otherwise in a bad light. He began by telling me what a great job I had been doing for the company, and how much they had enjoyed my work. He asked me if I felt I had done a good job, asked how I liked working there. I told him I enjoyed things very much and it was a job I could see doing all the time. He seemed pleased with my answer, and told me that they would like me to stay on working there full time. I told him that as far as I knew, that was up to Kelly Services, since technically I was an employee of theirs. He then told me that what they wanted to do was to hire me away from Kelly, if that was something that I wanted. I couldn't believe what I was hearing, and I was almost beside myself. Of course that was okay with me, I told him. So about a week later, I left Kelly Services and became a full time employee of the Company (as I stated much earlier, I chose not to use the actual name of the business, due to what happened later, so I will just call it the Company).

Sheri was coming over a lot lately, and though we were not ever a couple or dating we did spend a lot of time together. She was a lot of fun to be around, and the sex was always good. I had called her after I got home the day I got the news that I had been hired full time and she told me she would come over that night and cook me a special dinner. Sheri was a great cook, and she loved cooking pasta. She had her own exceptional goulash she had improvised from a couple of recipes she had used before, and it was out of this world. We ate dinner and drank wine and beer and had a grand time. Sheri then told me that she had to move from where she was living and asked if she might be able to stay with me for a while. I was feeling really good right then and so I told her it was okay, but I reminded her that we were just friends, and that I didn't want her to get any other ideas, we had a great friendship going and I didn't want to change any of it. She said she understood and agreed. Then we had great sex and went to sleep.

Sheri and I lived in that small studio apartment for another couple of months, and it was pretty cramped as I remember it. We were not saving as much money as I thought we should be, what with both of us sharing all the expenses (I don't remember her having a job for whatever reason), but she did her best to keep things clean and helped out with the cooking and such. People at work sometimes asked if I had a girlfriend, and I would say no and I didn't tell anyone about Sheri not because I was necessarily embarrassed about her, but I didn't anyone to have any reason to think I wasn't available. And there was one girl who I had found pretty striking, but more on that in a bit.

It became time to make a move to a bigger place and Sheri and I found an apartment much closer to where I worked. It was a nice one bedroom apartment in a modest sized complex just a few blocks from work which would save me gas, as I could then walk and not have to drive all the time. Gas was still pretty cheap back then, but every little penny one could save was helpful. And Sheri was still not working steadily if she had a job at all, I still have no memory of any job she had back then.

I don't know when it started, but Sheri and I started arguing more and more, not about hugely important things, but about anything that she did or that she didn't, and though things were never thrown, our voices were raised often at each other. I think Sheri wanted our relationship to be more than what I wanted, and her thinking was that since we were living together, it should be more serious. That was so much farther from the reality that I wanted to be living in. I remember one bad, horrible fight after we had been drinking where she ended up storming out and I slammed the door after her. I don't remember if she just decided to go or whether I kicked her out, I didn't care at that point. She didn't call or come back for two days, and I found myself starting to worry about her. She did call finally, and we talked more calmly and I asked her to come back so we could talk about things in person. She did, and we decided that it would probably be in both of our best interests if she moved out and we lived apart. We both respected each other enough to realize that our friendship was more important than losing it over something stupid. So that afternoon, she packed up what she had and left, I think she moved in with another friend in Seattle.

I felt so relieved to have my own place again, and was able to start enjoy living like a bachelor again. Work was going very well and I was feeling very comfortable in my job and getting to know more people at the workplace. But living alone also had its drawbacks and I missed not having someone around to talk to and pal around with. I missed being able to have sex on a regular basis too, funny that!

Every once in a while I picked up the Eastside Weekly and would scan the classifieds for fun and read all of the sex and chat lines ads that weren't long distance as far as I could see, they were I think 876 prefixes (before the 900 numbers). So I tried a few and found I could record a greeting and then fish through all the greetings of the females then I could pick and choose who I wanted to respond to live. It was pretty cheesy but it became kind of fun when you drank a lot of beer and spent a lot of time pushing the number 3. I did this for hours on a Friday night and finally fell asleep after 2 a.m. and then after sleeping most of the day Saturday, I went down the little convenience store down the street and picked up another 12-pack of beer and got ready for another fun night of 876 numbers. I remember talking live to this one girl and though it was a pretty bad connection, we agreed for her to come over and we could mess around and she could spend the night with me. I know that sounds like a pretty risky venture, but I was young and stupid and horny, and what could possibly go wrong with doing that?

About one in the morning, there was a knock at the door and I opened it and there was a young girl, I think she said her name was Star, waiting outside. She wasn't bad looking, but you have to remember I had been drinking a lot, so in my eyes, she was female and looked fantastic to my beer eyes right then. I invited her in, and she and I undressed down to our underwear and relaxed on the hide-a-bed in the living room in front of the TV. We didn't fool around too much because it was so late and we both were tired and shortly fell asleep. I remember waking up when it first got light, and started caressing all over her body. She woke up and started kissing me back. We got naked under the covers and I remember teasing her by just about entering her and then stopping. I would do that several times and I think it was driving her crazy because she grabbed my butt and pulled me inside of her. It was very sexy and I loved it. But it ended up being very quick and then we fell asleep. I woke up a little later and she was gone, which was not necessarily a bad thing, but the first thing I thought of was that I should check around to make sure nothing was taken. After all, I didn't know the girl and she could have robbed me blind when I was asleep, not that I was rich with cash or anything. I looked around and did not find anything out of place or missing, so I was relieved. I cleaned up the living room, put the couch back together and showered, but for some reason, I felt a little dirty.

The next few days went by as normal, and I was looking forward to seeing my parents who had planned on coming to Bellevue to see my Uncle (Mom's brother) and his wife as well as see me. I really wanted to take them around and show off my apartment they had not seen yet and take them by work and introduce them to everyone I worked with.

It was during the second day that I started to think something was not quite as it should be. Every time I took a piss, when I was done it started to hurt. And then I started noticing a brownish discharge in my underwear. All I could think was this was *not normal*. What the Hell was happening? I began to wonder if this might be connected to the sex I had had the other night. I had not used any protection and I started to get worried. Had I picked up one of those sexually transmitted diseases that I had heard about? That pissed me off. How could I have been so stupid? That bitch! I called her every name in the book I could think of, and was so mad that she would do that—she must have known she was infected! And she had sex with me anyways! I wanted to call her up and chew her one side and down the other! I went to the library and looked up about sexual diseases and figured I must have gonorrhea. I read that these little crab-like things that were infesting me down there didn't like the cold, so for the next couple of nights I slept completely naked and with the windows wide open. Obviously that had zero effect on my conditions, and I did the next thing that I could. I called my friend G from college—after all, he was studying medicine and would know what to do.

I called him the next day and after the usual little pleasantries, he asked me what was wrong. He knew me too well and could tell that something was bothering me. I skirted around the subject for a few minutes and then just blurted out the symptoms I was experiencing. He told me that I needed to get to a clinic immediately! He told me to quit wasting time and quit being stupid and get it taken care of right then or things would get worse. I promised him I would, and I meant it. I think I went to Overlake Hospital at lunch that next day and after filling out some paperwork, I was taken into the back and a nurse came in and asked me some questions.

The whole process was quite embarrassing, I had to pull down my pants and she looked at my poor member while asking me to describe exactly what was happening. As I was telling her, she took a Q-tip and stuck the tip inside my penis to get whatever she needed to get. I had no idea that was possible and the intense pain was like nothing I had ever felt before! I thought I was going to pass out. She then asked me who I had slept with recently and I told her I honestly did not know her name. She looked at me with such disapproval that I almost started crying. The nurse told me I did have gonorrhea and that she was going to give me a shot for the treatment. I was relieved that that was all I was going to get, after all, it couldn't be any worse than the Q-tip procedure! She left for a moment and came back in with the biggest shot tester I had ever seen and said that it would hurt a little bit more than a regular shot. That I believed. I bared my rear and she stuck the needle in and I swear she left it in way longer than she needed to, but she told me it was a concentrated antibiotic that she was injecting me with and it was necessary for it to go in slow, so I just grit my teeth and bear through it. I did and then she was done. She gave me a prescription for some pills and said it should be okay in a few days. I thanked her and left, wondering if my pride would ever come back. Before leaving the hospital I went to pick up my prescription and then went back to work and waited for my parents to call, as they were to arrive that afternoon.

I had not heard from them before I left work and after I had been home for couple of hours I finally heard from my uncle they had arrived and had been trying to call me all afternoon, which I found strange, since I had received no calls. I went to their hotel and when I got to their room, Mom was all but yelling at me that I was irresponsible and just trying to avoid them again, like I had done the prior year. I protested and told them I had been waiting for their call all afternoon. As it turned out, Mom had written down my phone number incorrectly and had been calling that number, not reaching me of course. The whole thing got sorted out and she calmed down, but it couldn't have been a worse end to one of the worst weeks I had had in a long time. There was no way I could never tell my parents that I had an STD because I knew the lecture I would get and knew how disappointed Mom and Dad would be in me and I just could not take that. But other than all that, the visit went well, and the gonorrhea went away and things went back to normal. I will say that I do not recommend anyone having unprotected sex, and I also do not recommend to anyone getting infected with an STD. I don't know how they treat that now, but the memory of that Q-tip will certainly last me a lifetime!

I think part of living on your own and having a job is a good test of how one keeps his finances. I was not a good student in that class, because it seemed that I was always living from paycheck to paycheck. I don't know if I was eating too much fast food, spending too much on booze, buying too many unnecessary personal items, too many magazine subscriptions, but I was bad. But in fact, this was not a new thing; I had been bad with finances ever since I had been on my own. I don't know that I had ever truly learned the value of money. If I had, I think life might have been a little different back then. But as it was, I was slowly falling further and further behind the financial ball, not seriously bad at first, but it got to the point where I was putting off one bill for another bill, borrowing from Peter to pay Paul. If something didn't happen, I was going to be in trouble, and I was too full of pride to call my folks and ask for help—after all, I now had a good job and was making a decent wage, I didn't want them to know I wasn't able to properly manage my money or handle life on a budget.

G called me one afternoon and told me that he was finished with his schooling (he had graduated with a degree in radiology I believe) and was planning on moving up to the Seattle area and had a job lined up in the Everett area. I asked him if he had already decided where he wanted to live and he told me he had not. I told him he should consider moving to Bellevue and we could share an apartment, which would save us both on all the normal monthly expenses (I think I was thinking more about me at that particular instance). He thought that was a pretty good idea, and I thought it was a *great idea!* By combining finances, not only would I have a good friend as a roommate and someone to party with, I also would not be as bored or prone to go out as much just to relieve the monotony of being alone. So I checked with my apartment manager and he said it would be fine to have a roommate move in, but that we would need to move to a two bedroom apartment, which would be fine, since the rent would still be less than me paying for a one-bedroom unit all by myself. It would only be a month until a two bedroom apartment became available, which was fine.

G arrived and we ended up getting our two bedroom unit and got settled in. At some point, as we were discussing finances and how we would be splitting up bills, and as I had not signed up for cable in the previous unit, who's name would be put on the cable bill. We then began to talk about my bleak financial situation. G was concerned, I think more for himself, as he probably didn't want to start his new life with someone else's financial problems. He asked me to itemize out all that I owed, all the bills I was behind on and he would see what he could do to help me. I did that, and what he then did was truly amazing, and showed me what a good and true friend he was. He wrote me a check for what I owed bringing me current on everything. He did admonish me to try to be a lot more prudent in my spending, to budget more carefully and take control of my money, don't let the money take control of me. I promised that I would. I can't tell you what a relief it was to finally be out of debt and in the clear. It was like having a full bladder and not being able to release it for a long time, and then all at once, you are empty and can bask in the feeling of relief! That is a good way to describe how that felt. I don't remember if we ever drew up any kind of contract, but I am sure I told him that I would pay him back.

G has pretty much always had my back, even back in the U of I days back when Janie and I broke up. He helped me get my head back on straight through my heartbreak, and he was there to keep my head on straight that summer after I graduated when we went camping near McCall, Idaho. Janie had grown up in McCall, but it was still a surprise when we ran into her in town when G and I had been buying our beer for the weekend. I invited her to come back to our campsite and she accepted, much to G's dismay. While she and I drank beers together, G busied himself making the campfire and setting up the tent, something I'm sure I should have been helping with, but I was becoming dewy eyed with Janie and she was being very affectionate, something she hadn't been in a long time, giving me playful attention. I think G pulled me aside at one point and warned me to be careful, advice which of course went in one ear and out the other. She and I went off into the woods and drank our beers and ended up making out again (I had forgotten how great of a kisser she was) and I don't know how long we had been gone, because all of the sudden we noticed the sun was almost at the horizon and G was calling our names, wondering where we were. Janie looked at her watch and abruptly said she had better be getting back home. I remember asking her to stay and eat dinner with us and she said her dad would be pissed if she didn't get back really soon. She promised to come back out and see us the next day and left. I told G that I thought that things were going in a great direction again for Janie and me, and I was so excited. He wasn't at all convinced and told me that tomorrow would tell. Well, of course when she never showed up the next day, I was almost heartbroken again, but G was there to drive home some good sense and didn't let me get too down on things. He is the best kind of best friend anyone could ever have!

G got the job in radiology that he was up for at the hospital in Everett, so he was very happy. Life seemed great for both of us.

I remember becoming a member of the local Jaycee organization and became involved in a lot of the activities they put on. During late June and into July, our chapter ran a fireworks stand in a local supermarket parking lot. I volunteered to stay overnight one weekend in the camper we had on site, to make sure no one stole any of the fireworks. That was a lot of fun. I made sure to bring my cooler with beer and I even brought along my small black and white TV so that I had some entertainment after the stand closed for the night. The only problem with that was there was virtually no signal that I could receive in the camper, so I ended up just getting buzzed both nights instead. I think Sheri, who was also a member came out and kept me company for a little while the first night, but she got bored and went back to her place.

There was another weekend where there was a statewide Jaycee convention held near Tacoma and our chapter had about four rooms rented at a Best Western where the event was. Sheri and I drove down in one car, so that she could leave early if she wanted to, as she was not one who was really comfortable in huge crowds. That was a great weekend with lots of people and lots of drinking. I remember sitting in one conference room listening to whatever was the topic being discussed there, and I was paying more attention to a girl who was sitting a few seats away from me. Neither of us was paying much attention to the speaker but we *were* enjoying looking at each other more than anything else. At one point, I moved so that I was sitting right next to her and we started whispering to each other about how boring the speaker was. She asked me if I would like to go someplace that was quieter and get to know each other better. I wasn't stupid, and I said of course I would like that. We made our way to the rear doors and left. I had no idea where Sheri was and really didn't care at that moment. I was not going to try and find her to tell her I was going to another girl's room because I didn't want to cause any scenes. I knew that Sheri still harbored a secret affection for me, and I didn't want to make her overly jealous especially at that particular moment.

Julie and I ended up back in her room and when she started taking off her pants and shirt, I knew where this was going. I couldn't believe my luck. I had never before picked up a girl with such ease, and I really think she was the one who had picked me up. Anyway, we both ended up in her bed naked as jaybirds and having great sex. She was amazing and enjoyed our lovemaking as much as I did. We finished with her on top and we laid there together for a while, just resting, catching our breaths and caressing each other. She had a fantastic body and as we lay together, me still inside of her, I soon found myself recharged and we started moving together in rhythm until we were spent once more. Then it was too hot and we had to move apart to allow some air to cool our sweaty bodies. That was the first time I had ever done it twice in that short of a period of time, and it felt great. Usually it was just a one time, thank you very much and it was all done. But with Julie it was different. And it was okay that when we were done, we were able to leave the room and have no further expectations of any commitments. She and I talked about that while we were getting undressed that this was just sex and nothing else and I was fine with that. I think that if two people have that understanding beforehand, there is less chance of misperceptions as to what happens next, and that is a more mature way to handle things. That made the next time—a couple of weeks later, just as good as the first time. Though she really confused me when I thought she called me "love" when she was leaving. That scared me and I didn't call her for about a month after that. We spoke some months later at a chance meeting and she asked me why I had never called her and I told her why. She seemed confused, as she didn't remember saying such a thing and said even if she did, I must have misunderstood or took whatever it the wrong way, but it was alright because she had met another guy by then and I think was engaged.

There was a girl at work who caught my eye named Gloria who had the most killer body I had ever seen. There was just something about her that really turned me on and more than that really attracted me to her. I fell more in lust with her than anything, but like all the girls that I really liked, she just viewed me as a friend. She was very sweet with me, though, and she seemed to enjoy and really feed off the attention I was giving her, not in a way that could be construed as using me, but really relishing my doting all she could. Despite knowing how she felt towards me, I still fell more and more infatuated with her, and ignored her cues that she was not interested in me in the same way. Maybe I felt somehow that if I just showered her with affection, cards, flowers, that eventually she would fall hard for me too. I don't know how much I time or money I spent, but I finally decided to write her a note telling her exactly how I felt and put it in a card in her car. I had shown G what I had written and he shook his head sadly. He was properly embarrassed to know what a sick love stricken puppy I had once again become, but as always, he put up with me, knowing that whatever he said, I was still going to give her the note and make a fool of myself. One afternoon I when I noticed she had left her car driver's window open, I put the envelope with the card in it on her dash and left. I didn't hear anything about it for the rest of that day and was on pins and needles that whole night.

The next day, Gloria came up to me at work and told me that we needed to talk and wanted me to meet her by her car after work. I could feel a thousand or more butterflies fluttering around in my stomach for the major part of the day, almost dreading the time when I had to meet with her. Part of me was hoping it would be a good talk, but I had a sinking feeling I knew exactly what she was going to say, and sadly, I was correct. She told me that she was flattered and truly touched, but that she was just not the right girl for me. She said she was the type of girl who was the trouble maker and always got into trouble, and I deserved better than her. I couldn't believe what she was saying about herself. I figure now that she was just trying to say anything to put me off of my feelings any way that she could. She ended up giving me a hug and told me it was all for the best, and then said those words that every guy hates to hear: "I hope that we can still be friends." And she got into her car and drove off. I walked dejectedly home and as I went in the door to the apartment I slammed the door shut behind me and sat on the couch and sulked. I may have cried, I don't recall, but I do remember that I felt like shit.   When G came home from work and saw me on the couch, he didn't even have to ask how things had gone. He just said that when he was done with changing his clothes, we were going to go down to our local watering hole that was just down the street and tie one on. I had no objections to that. At that point I was ready to tie a lot more than one on! I don't remember how many pitchers of beer we had, but I think I had four too many, and for about the last hour that we were there, G told me I was basically a zombie with my head on the table for much of that time. We were not causing any trouble and since we were regulars, the waitresses knew us pretty well which probably was the only reason that we were not asked to leave. I think for the next few days I was in my funk and not very communicative at home, just hanging out in my bedroom; some fun I must have been for G, but he was used to my moods by that time. Of course I got over my despair, and soon was myself again.

I think it was after I had been with the company for about a year that I received a promotion to Pricing Analyst, which was a great surprise for me. I don't remember if I had applied or petitioned for the position, but however it occurred, I graciously accepted the promotion. It was a big deal to me, as it meant a nice raise as well as business cards, and my picture even made it into the local paper as a result. It was one of those times that I felt respected by those who I worked for. In that position, I was responsible for comparing the retail prices of competitor stores in different areas with ours and adjusting our prices accordingly. Of course, we didn't want to be too far over or under everyone else's prices but we still needed to retain a certain percentage of profit. It was a great job, and I was able to see myself staying with the Company for many years to come (at least that was my intention, anyway).

When G had moved in with me, I was still smoking cigarettes, and he knew that. Over time, he would kid me about the long term dangers of nicotine and lung cancer and all the bad things that are always associated with smoking. I did seriously listen to all that he said, but I did not want to stop right then. I enjoyed smoking and told him not to worry, when the time was right, I would quit. But after a while, maybe I did get tired of spending all of my hard earned money on packs (I don't remember, but back then it couldn't have been more than $3.00 per pack—and why I didn't buy them by the carton, I have no idea), and I may have been tired of seeing the look on G's face every time I went outside to light a cig up (even back then, I never smoked inside the house), I decided to quit smoking. I told G about my decision and he said that he would support me in my endeavor in any way he could. He was so proud of me!

I think I lasted a couple of weeks before I broke down and bought a pack. Of course, now pride was involved and I couldn't tell G that I had fallen off the wagon! He had been so proud that I had quit! So once again I did the only thing that I could think of: I hid my smoking. I had not told anyone at work that I had quit, so smoking there was not an issue. Back then, smoking was still allowed inside buildings, and I even had an ashtray at my desk. Hard to imagine that now! It wasn't all that hard to conceal my smoking from G, at least so I thought. I would smoke on the porch when I got home from work where I had a view of the road so I could see him coming back home, and I burned incense in my room to cover the smoke when I dared to smoke in my room at night. I kept the charade going up to the day when we no longer lived together, though now I have to think he knew. How he could not know? I think he just kept mum to keep anything from becoming an issue.

Pot was still a part of my life during this time. G knew I smoked it, and he didn't have a problem with my occasional toking. I remember one time that I had run out of my stash and I was craving a hit like crazy. I was short of available funds and I wouldn't be able get any more until I got my next paycheck. I was sulking. G came over to me and said that I should go into his room and look inside the middle cupboard of his waterbed headboard and see what was there. I asked him what he was talking about, and he repeated that I should go look, I would find a surprise. I did as he said, and found a little baggie with a couple of chunks of pot. I was happily astonished. G would never buy any pot himself! I came back out with the baggie and a shocked smile on my face and asked him where the

Hell it came from. He smirked and told me he had taken some from my stash a few weeks ago in case I ever ran out. It worked for me! Have I mentioned before what a great friend G was?

I was still driving my little white (remember it used to be brown) Toyota Corolla, and up until then it had been quite the reliable vehicle. I hadn't had to put too much money into the upkeep other than oil changes (when I remembered to do them). But then I started to hear noise when I applied the brakes, a low squeaking noise, that most of the time went away after I had been driving for a bit, I just figured that maybe something had gotten caught in the brake pads or maybe that was normal for brakes as they wore down (I was not that car savvy, obviously). Shortly after that, they started making a grinding, metallic sound and that was when I started to get worried. I took the car somewhere, I cannot remember where now, but I had the brakes checked and was told that the pads and rotors needed to be replaced. I was horrified! How could that happen? I didn't think that was possible because I was never hard on the brakes, never slammed them or was a crazy driver, and how the Hell was I going to afford that? They quoted me a couple hundred bucks to make the repair. Now one would think that with my good salary, surely I had money saved up for emergencies—uh uh. Nope. Believe it or not, I was still living paycheck to paycheck, though if you asked I couldn't tell you what I was spending my money on. But I knew I had to get something done, and I couldn't ask G, he had already bailed me out once before! Luckily, one of my co-workers heard me talking about my brake problem, and she told me she would help me out with a loan, and I graciously accepted her offer. It took a while to pay her back, but I did do that.

I don't remember exactly how, but G and I became involved with the Boy's and Girl's Club of Bellevue, and became the coaches of a young girls' basketball team. The reason this is odd is because I know nothing about basketball rules, plays, etc., but it was more believable that G was with me because he *loved* basketball and could tell you anything you wanted to know about it. He and I had gone to a few Seattle Sonics (that was when they were the "SuperSonics") basketball games and I was always asking him about what was going on. Anyway, our team was comprised of 15 or so early teenage girls, most of who didn't care about the game and I had no idea why they were even there. Practices were crazy and we had a hard time keeping the girl's attention on what they were supposed to do, and it showed in the outcomes of the games we played. I know that the girls didn't win an single game, and even though they never seemed to care about anything during practices, they were really bummed at the outcome each time the final buzzer went off. I remember one game telling the girls in a huddle that if we won, we would buy them all pizza; however it was finally changed to if they even scored over 10 points they would get pizza. We got them pizza anyway.

One day the Pricing Manager called me into his office and asked me if I could do him a personal favor. I said of course, because you didn't want to say no to Len. He was a great guy and never had a bad thing to say about any of his employees. He told me that a personal friend of his was transferring to our division from Eastern Washington and would like me to pick him up at the airport, take him to his new apartment, show him around, and basically be his new friend here. I felt pretty honored that Len had asked *me* to do this for him, because he could have asked anyone. But the fact that he wanted me meant a lot. It showed trust and faith. I couldn't have been more proud, really. I *was* a little nervous; I had no idea what he looked like, who he was or anything at all about him except that he was a personal friend of Len's. I think when I was at the airport waiting for him, I might even have had a sign with his name on it held up for all the incoming passengers to see. When I met Marty, he shook my hand and introduced himself to me, and I found him to be outgoing, yet soft-spoken. He was very pleasant and had no superior airs about him. During the ride to his new apartment in Kirkland, I learned he was probably 10 years older, but we seemed to have much in common, many shared interests. It is hard to describe, but I could just tell that we would be more than just work associates; we would also be good friends. During the next couple of weekends I had introduced Marty to G, and the three of us went bowling and had beers, and I am sure I introduced him to our hangout. I was doing all I could to show him everything I could to make him feel comfortable in his new surroundings.

Now you remember I had had the brakes replaced on my car not long ago? Well, it seemed like too short a period of time after that, at least in my opinion, they started making the same noise again, that metal on metal sound. I don't know that I took it back to where I had the brake job done before, but I think it must have been too long after that repair to qualify as any kind of warranty work, or claim that the work had been faulty, so I figured that I would be looking at another expensive repair (obviously I had not gone to Midas, but maybe they didn't do brakes for life back then, who knows). I didn't want to rely on my friend who had paid for the brakes before to help me again pay for them again. Who knows, maybe I was too hard on the brakes? But they had lasted for years and years previously. Anyway, so what was the next cheapest thing to do besides pay for new brakes? How about trading the car in for another one?   Yeah, that sounded like a good idea to me, so I drove the Toyota on its last drive down the local Ford dealership on auto row in Bellevue, just down the street from my apartment, pulled into the parking lot and somehow barely got the car stopped in a stall. I think everyone in the dealership could hear me braking that time, the grinding was so loud! There were at least three or four salesmen that were making their way over to me; they could smell my need of a car a mile away. I was shown around the used car section and I looked around for at least an hour; I had no clue as to what kind of car I wanted.

Then I saw it. A red Ford EXP with turbo. It was almost as if it was calling my name! I looked at it inside and out, and finally decided it was fate that I should have it. The salesman and I went in and spent lots of time with paperwork, and after all was said and done, I drove off in my new (used) Ford EXP. My credit wasn't as bad as it is now, and I qualified for an auto loan with the Company's credit union and I was all set. It was only later that I found that the turbo did not work, and since there was no clause in the used car limited warranty that extended to turbo repairs, I had to live with my turbo car actually being a non-turbo. But it was not really a deal breaker in my book. It was a cool looking car, and it drove nicely. And the brakes didn't make any noise, so that was already a bonus!

The basement of the Company housed the offices of the security department as well as the print shop. The print shop was where bulletins that went to all the stores were printed, as well as inter-office memos, bulletins, and all of the advertising inserts for newspapers were printed. I got to know the people who worked there pretty well over time. Barry was a cool guy who usually worked in the afternoons and evenings. He was my age and seemed pretty easy going and friendly. There was a girl who I noticed who worked during the days and I would say hello to her when I was delivering things there. There was something about her that caught my eye, maybe it was her infectious smile, her eyes, or just the way she talked and walked. Occasionally I would run into her in the lunch room and finally I went up to her and introduced myself to her. She told me her name was Martha, which I think by that time I had already known. I felt so awkward and probably embarrassed, but I was glad I did it. For a while, I used every excuse I could to go down to the print shop, just so I could see Martha. I think we might have eaten lunch at the same table or maybe had coffee together in the morning with smokes (she smoked as well) before work in the cafeteria. I remember a few times when we actually had time and had longer and more than just casual conversations, we found that we had a lot of things in common, not just liking to party and smoke cigs. She was into football—loved the Seahawks (she and a friend had season tickets) and I when she let on that she smoked weed, I was pleasantly surprised. I was really started liking this girl. And she sure wasn't giving me the brush off either, so that was a good sign.

After a couple of months of passing in the halls, and casual chit-chat with Martha when I went down to the print shop to deliver something, I finally got up the guts up to ask her out. I was so sure she would find some way to let me down easy and say no, and tell me I was nice and everything, but she just wanted to be friends. But Martha shocked the shit out of me when her face lit up with a broad smile and she said she would love to go out with me. I just about fell over in surprise. I hadn't been prepared for that response so when she asked me when I wanted to take her out I had no idea. She gave me her phone number, and told me to call her when I knew. I gave her mine and I thanked her (I'm sure my face was redder than a fire engine by then) and went back upstairs to my desk. I probably called G to let him know what I had done I was so excited.

There was a place near the apartment where I liked to go to play pool, pinball, video games and darts. It had virtually any game you would expect a bar in the 80's to have and was a popular hangout for people over 21, since they served alcohol. I used to go there a lot on the weekends when I wasn't down the street at my regular hangout. My favorite game was Galaxian and I could spend hours playing and drinking and lose track of time. I figured that would be the perfect place to take Martha on our first date, it was low key, not a dive (at least in my opinion it wasn't—but I also used to consider Denny's a quality restaurant), and just a casual place where we could have beers and talk and get to know each other. I remember putting on some nice shorts, a Hawaiian shirt, white socks and sandals—I wanted to look cool and suave for our date. We met at the place and she did look at me kind of strange and then smiled and we went inside. Funny how that is all I remember about that night, but I do recall that Martha said later that she almost never went out with me again after that because not because of me specifically, but because she thought I had no sense of style in the way I dressed. She had been mortified especially by my sandals and white socks! I'm sure life would have taken a completely different turn had she done just that and never dated me again… but then again I probably wouldn't be writing this book!

So you are probably figuring that we did go out again, and you would be correct. We went out many times as a matter of fact, but I'll be damned if I can remember many of them. I remember one time we were in my car in front of my apartment after coming back from somewhere, and after making out for a while, I suggested that maybe we could go inside to my bedroom where we could be more comfortable, not meaning sex necessarily, mind you. I was too embarrassed to bring that up with her, especially that soon because I was really into her, and I have found that when I get really stuck on someone, in the beginnings, I have no backbone, and I sometimes let any risk-taking attributes fly out the window. In any event, I am sure she took that the wrong way because the make out session ended abruptly and she said she was tired and really needed to get home. We did of course eventually have sex, but I do not remember when our first time together was, or anything about it. I have usually had a pretty good recollection when it comes to my sexual episodes it has seemed, but for some reason I do not remember the first time with Martha. It certainly couldn't have been that bad, otherwise, I don't think that we would have continued on our path.

The one other time that really sticks out in my mind and shows my fortitude of sticking to my conquest, was when I called Martha on a Sunday, early afternoon, and her roommate told me she was not available, and maybe I could call back later. I think in total I called at least 5 times, and even G told me that maybe I should just give it up, maybe she didn't want to talk to me, or maybe it was her way of telling me things were over. But sometimes, I do become stalwart, and keep trying. Maybe she was tired of hearing the phone ring, or whatever the reason, but Martha finally did get to the phone to talk to me. It turned out she had been partying pretty hard the night before and was massively hung-over, and just couldn't get herself out of bed until then. In a way I felt relieved that it hadn't been anything that I had done to make her want to avoid me. And maybe that showed Martha that I was the kind of person that would not give up easily in his pursuits, and that I possessed good qualities.

I don't think there was an official "will you be my girlfriend?" or "I think we should only see each other" statements between us, or at least I don't remember either of us saying those exact words, but after a while it was pretty evident that she and I were a couple. She was probably the only thing I talked about, and I would hope I was the same to her, but that is what all guys would hope of the one that they are "monogamous" with. I remember Martha staying overnight at my apartment many times over a month or so. At one point I felt bad that she was always the one coming over, so I suggested that maybe I could go and spend the night at her apartment. I remember that she was really surprised to have me offer that, and I recall having a hard time finding her place in Lynwood, but that after I got there, we watched *Knots Landing* with her roommate and then we went to her bedroom to do our thing and go to sleep, as we both had to get up earlier at her place than mine to get to work.

I thought it might be fun to go on a little weekend road trip, just Martha and me, and spend some time quality alone time together, so we drove up to Vancouver Canada. I had not made any reservations, and as it was not on any special holiday weekend that I knew of, I thought that getting a hotel or motel would be no problem. I could not have been more incorrect. You know the saying: never assume? Well when we got there, it just happened it was during some special Canadian celebration and pretty much all the lodging in Vancouver was booked. That was not a good start in my attempt to impress my girlfriend. We finally found a motel on the outskirts of Vancouver, and it seemed like things were going to be okay. When we got out of the car to enter the lobby, we could hear loud music emanating from the club right next door. This was a much better sign. We checked in and I used my credit union Visa card to guarantee the room. We got to our room and took our stuff in. The accommodations were not high end quality, but they were ok, the room was clean and didn't smell dank or unpleasant. The phone rang and it was the front desk informing me that they had run my card twice, but it had declined both times, and they needed another card or cash. I did not have another card, or the extra amount of cash, so Martha had to use her card. I was so embarrassed and apologized to her, but she said that things happen, she was not upset in the least, and we were going to have a great time!

After taking care of the finances with Martha's card, we changed our clothes and decided it was time to check out the club next door and see what it was like, and have some drinks. I figured that was a great idea, as we could both use some booze to unwind now. We walked across the parking lot to the entrance and Martha opened the door and started to go inside. The music was much louder when the door opened and all of the sudden Martha did an about face, grabbed my arm and said that we were going back to the room. I had no idea what was going on, had no clue what made her do that. I didn't see anything but people moving around inside. She was actually starting to laugh as we walked back to the room and it took a minute for her to finally tell me what was going on. It turned out that the night club was actually a stripper bar, not a classy lounge as we had thought, or hoped. Was this strange night going to get normal? I think not. Anyway, after we got back to the room, I made us some cocktails with the alcohol we had brought from home and we turned on the TV and started to channel surf, hoping to find a movie channel so we could relax to a flick, kick back and enjoy each other. We found a movie that I had seen and I explained a bit about that parts we had missed. I remember going to the window and looking outside for a minute and then I heard Martha say something like, "what the Hell?" I turned back and saw her pointing to the TV. Now suddenly there was a different program playing on the screen: hard-core porn! I asked her if she had changed the station and she said she had not. Apparently the movie channel changed to the porn channel at midnight, because that's what time it was. At that point I had lost track of all the strikes against me, though I don't think Martha was looking at things quite like that. I have always had a sensitive side, and I'm sure that I was taking things a lot more seriously than I should have, but all

I can say is that I couldn't have planned any of these bizarre little occurrences if I had tried. I don't remember anything else about our little trip, but obviously it didn't turn her off of me. She still liked me.

Martha invited me to Thanksgiving dinner at her parent's house, so that I could meet them and at that point, I figured that she must be pretty serious about me, as I was of her. After all, I didn't think a person would go to those lengths and make a big deal about bringing the parents into the picture if things weren't getting serious. The week before Thanksgiving, I was starting to get nervous. It wasn't that I was afraid of meeting them, but I didn't know anything about them, other than what Martha had told me, except that they were nice, easy going, and they were looking forward to meeting me. With Shelley's parents, it had been a little different. I had known them before Shelley and I got serious, so I already knew what to expect, but here I was heading into unknown territory. I didn't want to go in and say stupid things and embarrass Martha or myself, act like an idiot, or seem like someone with no goals or ambitions. I wanted to put on my best show face and "wow" the hell out of them.

So I remember we got to her folk's house that afternoon, and I went to the door with Martha, and she knocked on the door and then we went in without waiting for an answer. I think she knocked just to let them know we were there. We went into the family room where her parents were, sitting in their easy chairs and watching TV, and the odors of a great meal were overwhelming. I shook her father's hand and her mom's and they were very nice and receptive towards me, I don't remember being given any highly stressful third degree questioning or anything like that. That's pretty much all what I recall of that meeting. But apparently the dinner went well and I was accepted as their daughter's boyfriend.

Things were okay as far as my mental state and being in a more serious boyfriend/girlfriend relationship. I felt like I was in good control of things, that Martha and I were both equal partners in things. I didn't feel like she was any kind of a control freak any more than I was, and things seemed to move along pleasantly. Work was progressing well; I think after a year after I was promoted I was given a raise, which was appreciated. As far as anyone looking in from the outside, one could say life was good for me. I don't think many would say they were insanely jealous, but they could give me a solid thumb up. I only say that because as you know, life has a tendency to change, sometimes for the better, sometimes for the worse.

After the Thanksgiving meeting with Martha's parents, I felt pretty confident about things, because I remember G and I going to find a ring. I had told him I thought things were going really well between Martha and me, and what he thought of my asking her to marry me. He told me that if I was sure of my feelings and hers, then I should do it. I don't think G really wanted to go ring shopping with me, but he was a devoted friend, and wanted to support me.

My budget was not of the caliber that I could go to *The Shane Company* or *Zale's* or any of the higher end expensive jewelry stores, so we ended up going to *Best Buy* to look through their collection of 'fine' diamond rings. That retailer hasn't been around for a long time, but if some of you don't know what kind of place that was, it would be like going to the Fred Meyer jewelry section and getting something, not that what they offer is bad, just more affordable; but anyway, we picked out a nice (at least I thought so—you could see the diamond if you squinted) ring with a small teeny stone, whatever $125 could afford. I was really excited and couldn't wait to plan some way to give it to Martha as a surprise. It's funny, though when I stop to think about it, I must have asked her at some point what her ring size was. Now if someone asked me what my ring size was, I think I might be a little suspicious of why I was asked, and might be expecting something then... I can't believe she would be thinking any different...

G and I had had a party at the apartment's cabana once before. It was pretty handy, all we had to do was put down a deposit and we had use of the kitchen and recreation area, and it was ours for the night. As long as we cleaned everything up just the way it was before, we would get our deposit back. Things had worked out very well the first time, so we thought we would throw a little Christmas party there, and invite work friends from each of our jobs and then I could take Martha aside and give my present to her, which would be the ring. I would put the ring in a little box, then that box in a little bigger box, then that little bigger box in a little bigger box... well, you get the idea. I know how stupid that whole thing sounds, but you have to remember, I was a hell of a lot younger and "in love" what did I know? And I was timing things just right as per what my mom had said about the age to get married. Remember she had said that any age under 27 years old was too young. And right then I had just turned 26, so what could be wrong with anything (providing Martha said yes when I asked her)? By the time we said our vows, I would be 27. So we reserved the cabana for the party and sent out our invitations and things were all set.

I don't remember what all I had told my parents about Martha prior to that point, but I am sure I would have at least told them that I was dating, maybe that things had progressed to where I was seeing only one girl, but those details I do not recall now.

The night of the party came and we had decorated the cabana pretty well, we had provided mixers, chips, all the things good hosts should provide. I think it was probably a bring your own beverage deal, as far as alcohol went, but I remember G and I had purchased our favorite brands of beer and had our own vodka and whiskey that we liked. When I took Martha aside and told her I had a present for her, I recall the excited look she got on her face. I went into the kitchen area and then came out with the huge box, decorated with a large bow and ribbon. I think Martha had figured out my trick with the boxes after she found the second box inside the first, but she played along with me, as she was having a great time as well. When she got down to the last little box, Martha found it to be a little more nicely wrapped, but she ripped it open anyway, and pulled out the ring box. Her eyes opened wide and I think she may have gotten a little teary eyed. Knowing or having a suspicion of what you are going to get and actually getting it are two completely different things, I believe, yet I was very touched by Martha's reaction to her gift. She opened the case and looked at the ring as I got down on one knee to do the proposal as a gentleman should. I took it out of the case and I remember getting the lump in the throat as I asked her if she would marry me. She said yes and I put the ring on her finger, then we hugged and kissed and I have to believe that was truly one of the happiest moments of my life up to that point. I felt elated and joyous, just so caught up in the whole proposal and acceptance deal that I wished I could have frozen things right there forever. I couldn't tell you if Martha felt exactly the same way, but she seemed pretty damned happy herself.

So life was starting to go in a great direction, and Martha and I were ready to start making decisions on the important things, such as when we should get married, where the ceremony should be, colors, flowers, all the things that I hadn't the foggiest clue about. I had been on such a one-track mind, which was asking her to marry me that I hadn't even fathomed the thought of everything that comes after the affirmative answer. I think as soon as she started bringing up all of those issues, I may have gone into an internal shock, though I did not come right out and show that. After all, that would be so unlike a prospective groom, wouldn't it? I should have been prepared for all the consequences of what happens after Martha accepting. Problem was I most certainly was not. I figured I would feel a lot better after I called my parents and told them what I had done. I remember when I canned Mom and she answered the phone. I think I pretty much blurted out the news, something like: "Mom, you remember I told you I have been seeing this really cool girl Martha? Well, I asked her to marry me and she said yes!" There was a pause on the other end, and then Mom said she was so proud of me. I know I got a huge lump in my throat and probably got teary eyes, I could hear a hitch in her voice as well. That really was really touching and it was such a great feeling. I was bursting with pride and I knew I was doing the right thing.

That next week at work, things felt so different. Some of my friends there knew that I had been planning to pop the question, some did not, but by the end of that first Monday, everyone knew that I was no longer a single guy, and I got many congratulations as I am sure Martha did too. There was only one person who told me if I ever hurt Martha, I would have a lot of explaining to do, and that was from her boss, which in retrospect, I thought was pretty cool as it showed Martha's supervisor had a lot of love and respect for her. But truthfully, it scared the shit out of me, as I think she really could have kicked my ass!

It is strange and I know I had heard of this phenomenon before, but never really believed it, but it seemed like the moment I got engaged, girls came out of the woodwork, coming on to me, asking me out, or flirting with me. There were girls who I had never met before, or had only had seen casually and did not know about my engagement. It seemed like they were all coming on to me and wanting to go out with me, hitting on me. Sadly, there was nothing I could do about it. Martha had given me any kind of engagement ring, so I didn't think these girls were outright trying to seduce me just because I was taken, but maybe I was just exuding some king of "taken" magnetism. I don't know, but in a way, it felt kind of good to be getting all of the attention that I had not gotten before from so many different women! And I didn't want to be so rude as to completely blow them off! There were two instances where I remember I could have gotten into trouble.

The first was with a girl from the bowling alley I had met while I was bowling on the Company league every Wednesday. She worked at the lanes and I had gotten to know her before Martha and I had ever become an item. I don't even remember her name now, but I had been attracted to her for the longest time, but she had shown no interest other than being a flirty friend. As soon as I became engaged, it seemed like they were no longer just flirts and were more to the point of actions. At one out of town tournament I attended, she really came on to me and somehow we ended up kissing and I could tell it would lead to more if I didn't stop things. That was the hard part, because a part of me didn't want to stop! I had waited a long time for that, but I was engaged now. The one thing that worried the hell out of me as I was driving back home is I knew I was meeting Martha for dinner or something and here I was with another woman's perfume clearly noticeable on me. I'm sure you would have howled in laughter or sadly shaken your head at my pathetic attempts to cover my "indiscretions"---I had the driver's window down (it was raining cats and dogs) and I was frantically reaching for the rain on the windshield to try and wash off the odor from my face so Martha would not smell it on me when I saw her. Part of me reasoned with myself that I had not cheated on her in any true sense, it was only kissing, but I seriously did not want or need Martha to find out. Fortunately, I lucked out in that incident.

The other time involved a gorgeous blond that I had met somewhere, that I had had lunch with a few times during the work week. The liaisons were harmless, though if this girl had made any serious moves on me, I seriously do not know what I would have done (though I have a pretty good idea). Like I said, I was having so much attention paid to me that I had not had for a long time, and before all this newfound attention, it had only been Martha. I know I sound like a cad, and I really cannot defend my actions but I am honestly glad nothing came of those meetings other than lunches. If my recollection is correct, she had broken up with a boyfriend or was going through bad relationship problems, so she was using me as a shoulder to cry on, and that is why I probably had no qualms about those meetings with another girl. Should I have told Martha about what I was doing so she would have had no worries should it ever come out? Yes, probably. Did it matter in the long run? No.

Martha had a great idea for a honeymoon—any one of the Hawaiian Islands. I loved the idea as well, so I got brochures of all the hot spots and resorts on all the Islands and started having great fantasies as I looked and read all about the locales and beaches and everything. Then I started studying the prices for the vacations and nearly shit my pants. I had no clue how expensive a honeymoon in a nice place would be! I knew that I would never be able to afford that, but I had to figure out a nice way to tell her that we should think a little more conservatively about where we should go. She was quite adamant about Hawaii, and I wanted so much to please her that it was easier just to go along with her ideas, at least as long as I could. That was the beginning of my mistakes—always trying to please.

Martha and I took a long weekend to drive to Boise so that she could meet my parents. It was a fun drive and Mom had a nice dinner planned for us, as well as having some close family friends over that evening. Everyone loved Martha, and she seemed to fit in very well, especially with our neighbors. I remember they had so many nice things to say about her. Mom was old-fashioned and adamant that since we were not married, we would not be sleeping in the same room, which we respected (not really): but I realized when staying under the parent's roof, one must abide by the parent's rules, of course. It seemed like such a harmless request and it didn't seem like a big deal until we all retired for sleep that first night. I kind of expected/hoped Martha would sneak in and snuggle with me for a while (or at least have sex) after Mom and Dad had gone to bed, but all she did was pop in for a quick kiss and then off she went to her room like it was no big deal. I remember being really offended and feeling pissed off, extreme childish behavior I know, but I wasn't going to 'get any,' and being the spoiled guy I was, though I covered it up relatively well, I think I sulked and let that affect me that entire weekend there. We showed Martha all over Boise and I remember I was embarrassed because when I tried to drive her to my old high school. I could not for the life of me remember where it was. I thought maybe it had been torn down or moved, thus being unable to find it. But after we got back home, Mom told me it was still in the same place, and she too, was surprised I was unable to locate it. That wasn't the last time I had problems with driving and directions and finding things when I was with Martha, but we will explore some of those later.

A month or so later, Mom and Dad came up to Bellevue to meet Martha's parents and we all had dinner at a nice seafood restaurant in Kirkland. I remember Martha being a little on edge, because she wanted everything to go perfect and whenever she was stressed, I stressed, but our folks all seemed to get along well with each other, which made the evening go a lot smoother. Even so, I couldn't wait until the dinner was over and we had all said goodnight to each other so that I could get to the car and have a smoke. No, I had not told my parents that I had picked up that nasty habit, which Martha could not understand in the least. All I could tell her was that my dad used to smoke and I was the reason he quit, and I figured it would really disappoint them to find out that I smoked. Martha repeatedly told me that it should be no big deal, I should just tell them and they should just accept it, after all, it was my life! But, as I have pointed out before I am not a big one on confrontation, so it was just easier to hide it from them. That should have been a big red flag for anyone starting a relationship like we were embarking on, if I was hiding simple things like that, what could I possibly hide in the future? What and from whom? Those questions will be answered, I promise.

Anyway, the wedding date of the middle of the following August was decided upon, I think I more agreed with what Martha had come up with (remember it was easier to agree with her—that will be a commonality in our life together), and that was fine, because when we first announced that date, it was over 8 months away, so very far in the future. But as the days progressed, and preparations were starting to gel, things inside me were probably not all that normal. I was starting to become a different person, more on edge and less my old "Steve" that everyone knew and loved. I began to feel the pressure of the impending financial responsibilities of the wedding as the figures for each part came in; flowers, photographers, cake, tuxes, ring, you name it, everything was becoming an overwhelming hodgepodge in my brain. I remember my close friends were started to get worried about me, they could see that I was showing signs of nerves, shaking, not eating properly. Marty, my close buddy at work also had recently gotten engaged to a wonderful woman he met at the gym he worked out at told me that I did not at all look like a happy person. I think I shared my concerns about money and everything Martha had planned and that she wanted us to do most of the wedding things so that we would have more control, and that she was driving me crazy, but also I didn't want to cause waves. He told me I had to stand up to her now, early in the relationship or I would be running into problems later. I remember always saying I understood and I would talk to her that night. Of course each day Marty and my other friends I would talk to would have the same conversation with the same results. I was too chicken-shit to say anything to her. My thought was "a happy Martha was a Martha easy to get along with."

I had a conversation with my Mom when she mentioned that I didn't seem like myself when she and Dad had last seen me. She noticed that I was more nervous than she had ever seen and told me that if I had *any* doubts, this was the time to vocalize them, before we got too far into things. I remember telling Mom that everything was okay, it was just wedding jitters, I was sure of it. I assured her that when everything was over and done with, things would be back to normal. I *was* sure of that, but what I didn't tell Mom was that Martha was so into what we were doing and she was proud and happy with the way things were going, how could I even say anything about my inner butterflies or my thoughts about toning things down because that would surely piss her off and being around her when she was pissed off was never my ideal way to spend an evening.

About three months before the wedding, Martha and I moved in together, and that was a hard thing to do because I was leaving G and my comfort zone and heading into new territory which one would think should have felt like a good thing. But what I was ultimately doing was settling for what she wanted to do. My gut said we just stay in the apartment where G and I had lived, because it was affordable and close to work, but she had her mind set on moving somewhere different and nicer and newer. I so much wanted to somehow convince her it was unrealistic and we would be seriously over our heads financially. I didn't because I also knew she would have had serious fits and just call me cheap and a tightwad. I didn't think I was being cheap by not wanting to move the way she did, I seriously thought it would just be better for us to conserve our money, but I caved and we got a townhouse in Kirkland (it *was* nice) but it was over double what she and I were paying together separately for our old places. I joked that just up the street from the new place there was a drug and alcohol rehabilitation center as well as a mental hospital so I would be safe if she either drove me crazy or drove me to drink (funny how things work—shhhh….).

One more obvious piece of evidence that I was a person who could not stand up to my convictions and especially stand up to my future wife was when my mom made some suggestions regarding colors for our wedding. Whether they were for the flowers or dresses but it was something to do with color coordination and Martha did not approve of those suggestions and sternly told me to tell my mother that. She intimated that she wanted my mom to butt out with her ideas and even though I took offense to that, I did not stand up either for my mom or myself and that internally made me feel like shit, really just adding to the pressures I was already feeling about what was going on.

I ended up getting a part-time after work job in order to make some extra money to help with wedding expenses. The work was pretty easy; I worked as a phone solicitor, calling up customers who at the local K-mart and sell them extended warranties on what they had purchased there. The thing that I didn't like about the job was that I was calling people during the dinner hour and the majority of those that answered the phone were either pissed that I was interrupted the family meal, or just purchased the extended warranty to get me off the phone. The thing I did like about the job was that it was located in a little strip of stores that contained a liquor store, which was where I think the majority of what little extra income I made went to. We would buy our pints during the breaks and imbibe and then chew gum before going back inside. I also would use the extra money to buy take out for me and Martha a lot of nights on the way home from the phone job. So in reality, the extra money I made didn't really amount to much toward the wedding.

A funny thing happened on the day Martha and I went to get the wedding license. The plan was for us to drive to Seattle and she and I would get the license, then she would meet up with her parents and go with them, while I went on to enjoy my bachelor party. Basically things went as planned, though not without some unplanned occurrences. We had parked my Ford in what I thought was a 30-minute parking zone, giving us ample time to get done what Martha and I needed to do. We went in to the building, got the license and when we came back out to the street, I couldn't find the car. Martha thought this was pretty normal, because she assumed that I had just forgotten where I had parked. I was pretty sure that we were where the car was supposed to be, but it was not. It turned out that my car had been towed less than five minutes previously, and I was pissed. I was sure we hadn't been inside more than 20 minutes. But as we looked at the sign, I had not read it correctly, and it turned out I had in fact parked improperly, thus it had been towed. Now I was furious at myself and also extremely embarrassed, because here was something else I had screwed up when I should be the man, impressing my intended. She was impatient and said she needed to leave to meet her parents. Martha said something like "I'm sure you'll get things taken care of," and then absently kissed me and left. I made a call and found where my car had been towed and roughly $75 later I was driving to my party, relishing the fact that I would be downing some much needed drinks there!

I picked up my friend Mike and we drove to the house where the bachelor party was being held. It was planned that I would spend the night there, knowing I would clearly be in no condition to drive, which as it turned out, was true. I had invited, or given names to whoever was doing the inviting, all my close friends from the Company, and my supervisor from my new part-time job and we had a great time, playing poker and listening to music. Oh, and drinking of course. As would be expected at any bachelor party, the doorbell rang a couple of hours into the festivities, and when someone answered the door, they found a female cop waiting on the doorstep. Quite a beautiful young 'cop' she was. She came inside and said she heard there was some sort of a disturbance and she had been called to investigate. Of course, she then brought in a boom box with her, and I was repositioned to a chair in the middle of the living room. I didn't put up much of a stink on having to leave the poker game, as long as I could bring my bourbon and coke with me. The 'cop' tuned on the music and then did her stripping routine amidst all the hoots and cat calls of the rest of guys at the party. She disrobed down to her bra and panties, doing what strippers do best for the intended groom. I was getting pretty toasted by this time, but of course immensely enjoyed all the attention. Several of the guys were trying to give her more money to take me into the bedroom and send me off with the final fling, but she refused, telling them that she was a stripper, not a hooker. I was told later that she was offered a nice sum of money, but that she adamantly refused. She had morals, you know. She did allow me to take a shower with her, though I seem to remember that she did not take her panties off (I may have also been wearing my own shorts I don't recall), not that in my current state at that moment that I would have been able to do anything other than just stare at the wonders of what was covered by the panties; I doubt even a dose of Viagra would have made any difference with the amount of alcohol I had consumed by that time. I was standing behind her, soaping up her back—cut to black.

I opened my eyes and squinted at the obtrusive light, momentarily blinded. I was lying under covers in a bed, and as I looked around the room, I saw some pictures on the walls that I did not recognize. What the Hell? For a few minutes, I had no idea where I was, what day it was, I was as clueless as one with a bout of amnesia. Then it slowly came back to me. Yes, this must be the morning after my party, and I was slowly noticing the booming headache starting to occupy my head. I tried to swallow, and had very little liquid in my mouth, it felt that I had eaten a bowl of cotton and it had absorbed all of the available spit. I was sick, miserable and now I had to go home and try to survive until I became myself again. Then I remembered the stripper and briefly panicked. Had I had sex with her? Would Martha find out? I couldn't remember for certain, but I'm sure that Martha and I had talked about the bachelor party and I probably made the promise that I would be a "good boy" and there would be no hanky-panky. I made my way into the kitchen and found Dale sitting at the table having a cup of coffee. He looked at me and started laughing, the sound of his laughter making me wince with pain. I asked him if I had slept with the stripper because I couldn't remember, and he said no. Thank God I would not have to face the wrath of Martha. But as it turned out, Martha knew about everything that happened at the party without me saying a word; it was like she had spies that saw everything or she had been a fly on the wall. She did admit that my party sounded a lot more fun than the one her friends had thrown for her, after all, who could have fun with your mother there.

At some point, I did manage to convince Martha that going to Hawaii was just too ambitious of a honeymoon idea, and that it would be much more fun to take a long week and drive down to Big Sur California where we could spend some quality time on the beautiful California coast. I don't know how I managed that, but she agreed and put me in charge of the honeymoon plans. I felt a little better after that but as it turned out, my research on that final destination left a little bit to be desired.

As I had stated before, Marty was also counting down the days to his own wedding and he and I began a daily ritual which was quite amusing. Each morning, we would calculate the days, hours, minutes and seconds to each of our ceremonies and would tape the results to our computer monitors at our desks. It probably was the worst thing I could do, because it just reminded me every day of how close the day was coming.

I think the only really smart thing I had done in preparation for the wedding and honeymoon was going to the Company credit union and getting a loan for the honeymoon festivities. I think it amounted to about $2000, which I felt gave us a nice buffer zone to play with. Martha's money and my money combined would ensure we would have a great trip. At least that's what I had thought, but we'll deal more on that later.

Since Martha was Catholic (I am Episcopalian), we were required to take a marriage class sponsored by the church. Now I don't know any guy who is really turned on by something like this (perhaps there are some, but I am speaking generally here), but we go because we don't want to piss off our prospective mates by saying opposing this notion. It wasn't too bad, though the hours we spent at this class seemed to be the longest hours I had spent, but we did learn some good things and I did think I came out of the classes with good advice and techniques on how to successfully communicate with our mates, and how to anticipate problems that can arise in any normal marriage. Ultimately I do not think anything I learned could have made any difference in this particular case.

Martha and I had decided it would be a good idea to live apart for the last month so that we would appreciate each other more after we became married. We still saw each other at work, and she would come to the apartment to see me after we both got off, but she would always leave when it was time for her to go to bed. I knew that she really would have loved to stay with me, anything would have been better than living back at home with the parents, but it was best to stay celibate until the wedding night. It was strange not sleeping with her every night but I figured it would be worth it in the long run.

The week before the wedding came and my younger brother came into town, as he was to be my best man. He was helping me take care of the things I had to do for the wedding. Martha was doing most of the things that a wedding planner would be doing, and she seemed to be very good at it. She did not ask me for too much help, which was fine, I certainly didn't want to get in her way and mess anything up—I know she didn't think she thought I had any real sense of style anyway. She didn't like the way I wore my hair, because she had me grow it out longer in the back and change my hairstyle, not that I didn't like it. I don't think I ever asked her to change anything about herself.

The night before the wedding was the rehearsal and dinner which went fine. The dinner was held at a yacht club in Bellevue, and I remember drinking more than I should have, but not to excess, since I had to be coherent and reliable at my wedding and make sure I didn't do anything stupid. I remember when Martha and I wanted to smoke a cigarette, I wanted to make sure we did it where my parents could not see us, and she told me it was time to just let them know that I smoked. No more hiding things! I knew she would not let up unless I told them, so we went over to them to say hello, and I did tell them that I was a smoker. Martha was right, they did not go ballistic, and I think they appreciated my telling them rather than them just finding out. I did see disappointment in their eyes however, but there was nothing I could do about that, except maybe quit right there on the spot. But that was not going to happen.

So the day of the wedding came and a lot of little problems started to occur, which didn't necessarily ruin anything, but really tested Martha's patience and tolerance. You may have had similar experiences so these things might make you laugh. One of my groomsmen pulled a no-show, so the husband of one of Martha's bridesmaids volunteered to stand in. His body size and structure was totally different so we had to be unusually creative to get the tux to fit him. The pants were too tight and he could not button them, so we fitted the cummerbund over the button to hide the obviousness. Martha broke the heel off her shoe in a grate behind the church. I don't remember if she ended up with a new pair of shoes or the broken heel was temporarily repaired. My parent's arrived late, as they had to go back to where they were staying to retrieve their wedding gift and I think they got lost as well, so pictures had to be taken separately (that pissed off Martha to no end—I didn't hear the end of that for a long time!), and then there were two ladybugs found in Martha's wedding veil (I heard that if you find one it is considered good luck—but two?). But even with all those things happening, the wedding turned out to be a success, and I heard from more than one person that they really enjoyed the ceremony. I know I had my tunnel vision eyes on, because I don't remember much other than what was happening right in front of me. I remember talking to my friend G later and asking him why he had not come to the wedding, had he not gotten his invitation—and he said that was crazy! He had shaken my hand after the ceremony during the receiving line, did I not remember? Guess not... that was kind of funny. There was a video of the wedding that I ended up with that I kept for the longest time, but there was nothing spectacular about it, nothing to send to America's Funniest Wedding videos or anything like that.

Now Martha had wanted the entire wedding party to turn around and face the audience with dark glasses on and shout out some kind of "hurrah!" when the priest announced us as husband and wife, but I just felt that it was a wedding "ceremony" and not a stage show with theatrics and I suppose I seemed to Martha to be like an old fuddy-duddy with that notion. We never had a knock out discussion over that, but that idea thankfully never came to be. We did turn to our audience and kissed each other as a newly married couple. I think we gave people high fives as we walked arm in arm down the aisle to the back of the church, but I think that was about as showy as we got.

Someone had gotten us a stretch limo to take us to the reception hall where the festivities would continue, and I remember we told the driver to take us there via the 'long' route, which ended up making us a half hour late, but even I did not care at that point. We had champagne waiting for us in the limo and as we were riding and beginning to celebrate, I think Martha popped her head out of the open sunroof and did a few whoops and cheers, I probably did the same. As we were going to open up the champagne, we noticed to our surprise that there were no glasses in the limo to drink from. We didn't want to drink from the bottle, so we had the driver pull in to the nearest convenience store so that I could get some glasses. It was kind of funny because I remember going in and couldn't find any single glasses, plastic or otherwise, but the manager was understanding and ended up giving me two Styrofoam cups to use. I think I tried to give him some money and he just said congratulations, as he could guess from my tux and goofy grin, not to mention the limousine in the parking lot that I had just gotten married. So we had our first toast in Styrofoam cups, I think they were used because they didn't look to me all that clean, but what the Hell, we didn't care at that point.

We finally got to the reception and found everyone waiting for us, our parents had been a little frantic, but were relieved that we had finally shown up. We did the reception line thing, and then the dreaded first dance. I don't remember the song that we danced to, but I do recall that it was very long and very hot and it was just a lot of going around and around in circles and I could not wait for it to end. I know I should have that dance in my memory as the most special dance Martha and I would ever have, but I think the most special thing about it was when it was over (no offense Martha, but I can't dance and it was brutal!)! We cut the wedding cake and Martha had pre-warned me that if I mashed the cake in her face in any way that she would never let me forget, so I tried to give her the bite as daintily as I could, not smearing a bit. This was our wedding day and I certainly wanted the wedding night to go as planned, if you know what I mean. I think she tried to slop a little on me, but that is just the woman's prerogative I guess. I don't know what all we had to offer the guests as far as food or drink, but I remember only having one glass of champagne and I don't think I even ate one whole piece of cake, I think I was still so nervous and numb after the whole deal. I don't know that I had yet begun to grasp the change that I was now married, that my life was never going to ever be the same as it was before.

I had been given the assignment of choosing the hotel where we would be spending our first night as a married couple. I remember laboring over that task, as any choice I made that ended up being less than perfect could affect the mood and outcome of what should be the perfect night. This was back in 1987 and home computers with access to the internet were not as prevalent as they are today, so my research consisted of the yellow pages under the heading 'hotels' which I know in retrospect was not the best way to explore my options. I began with the first entry which at that time was the *Alexis Hotel*. I called and told them what I was looking for and what they described to me seemed pretty adequate, and the rate was reasonable, so I figured having exhausted all my resources (which really means picking the first one), I made the reservation. We got to the hotel, and it really wasn't too bad. Not that we needed a washer and dryer, but there was one in the room. There was a plush bathrobe along with the towels (I wouldn't have been surprised if didn't find its way into the suitcase before we left) and I think they even had slippers that we could use if we chose to. We were pretty worn out from the long day, but we did consummate our marriage as most newlyweds do. I do remember thinking that making love for the first time as man and wife should be the most special feeling, the most moving union that two people could experience, but strangely, I recall that to me, there were no fireworks; it was not a mind-altering, breathtaking or earth shattering occurrence, it seemed to be just another moment in the sack, too quick to the conclusion (probably due to our abstinence) and then it was over. I remember afterwards, Martha went into the living room area and reclined on the couch with the TV and I stood by the window gazing out at the night sky for a while, fingering my wedding ring, wondering why I didn't feel more special, why I felt so damn strange and so out of sorts. I think I just chalked it up to nerves and that things would be better once I got some good sleep.

While we were at our reception, we had been offered the use of my uncle's station wagon to take on our trip, thus saving the cost of a rental car (Martha did not trust my Ford EXP to take on the trip, and frankly, I didn't either), but though I was okay with that idea, Martha was totally against it. She wanted us to start our life together doing things on our own, with no hand-outs from others, even family. So I (regrettably) turned my uncle down, though being sure to politely thank him for his generous offer. First thing that Sunday morning, being the dutiful husband I left my beautiful bride to go and procure the rental car (why the Hell I had to get one from somewhere all the way down near the airport to this day I have no clue). One of my buddies from Boise went with me to follow me back home with my car, and we had a most difficult time finding where the rental office was, taking us over an hour, which shouldn't have taken even half that time.

When I went inside and filled out the paperwork, I was pulling out my VISA card for them to use as payment, but they said that they did not use credit cards for out of state rentals, and I would have to pay for the rental with cash, and would get a refund if one was due when we returned the car. This was something that I had not planned on in the least! I told them I was not informed of this when I called them on the phone to reserve the car, but the agent couldn't care less about my protests. He said cash or he could not rent the car to me. I thought about calling Martha and telling her we should take my uncle up on his offer, but then again, I thought about what her reaction would be to that. I was fucked. I reluctantly pulled out the majority of my travelers' checks so I could get the car, and this was the beginning of the end. I wasn't counting on using the cash I had on hand for the rental, as that was to pay for everything else on our trip. I didn't have any huge line of credit on the card since I had used that go get the travelers' checks. Martha would be furious if she knew that from the get go we might have money problems on our honeymoon and there was no way I was going to start out our trip by filling her in on my first fiasco! So my friend and I left with the rental and took my Ford back to the apartment and then the butterflies were working overtime in my stomach as when we headed to the apartment, and I realized I had forgotten the key to get inside. Another faux pas! Was anything going to go right? We left the key to the Ford in my golf bag on the back patio and then I took my friend back to his car, thanked him and raced back to the hotel, sure I was going to get a lecture on my poor use of time. Luckily Martha was absorbed in a movie and hadn't really noticed how long I had been gone, and she was actually excited with some news to tell me.

I learned two things about Martha that day that I had not known about. The first was when she showed me what one of our mutual friends had given us for our wedding gift. She pulled out a little baggie from her purse and showed me the white powder. It was an eight ball of cocaine, of all things! Smoking pot was okay, as she and I had done that together many times, and that was fine. But I had no idea that Martha did coke too. Not that I was aghast and that I was now going to leave her. I hadn't snorted the stuff before, but I had done other drugs, and at least it wasn't LSD or something bad like black tar heroin or something like that. So I told her that was very cool of them. She seemed to be in a great mood and happy, so I wanted to keep her that way and did not mention anything about using most of my cash for the rental. We got our stuff in the car and were ready to take off on our new adventure. Oh, the other thing I learned about Martha was that she loved sunglasses, and not just any sunglasses, but really *expensive* sunglasses. We hadn't even left town before she discovered that she had either lost her pair, or had left them at her parent's house. And there was ***no way*** she was leaving on the honeymoon without having a new pair to take with us. That was not problem with me, as I loved my dark glasses as well. In fact, I had just picked up a nice pair of dark glasses at the local *Bartell Drugs* for about $12.95—might have been less, because I think they had been on sale.

So our first stop before leaving town was at to get her a new pair of sunglasses, I don't remember if it was a specialty store or maybe it was a sporting goods store, but Martha picked out a really nice pair, but one of the most expensive pair on display! I inwardly cringed as she pulled an envelope out of her purse that contained some of the cash she and I had gotten as wedding gifts, and handed over to the clerk about $125 I think including tax. I just couldn't fathom spending that much for dark glasses! But I just couldn't fathom actually telling her that either, and risk dashing her good mood this early in the trip. It wasn't just the cost of the glasses that bothered me; it was also the fact that she used 'our' money for 'her' purchase, not to mention that was cash that could be better used for our trip expenditures! If only I had had the balls to tell her about our financial situation before we left! If only, if only! Seems like my life has always consisted of 'if only, but in retrospect, I don't think that would have mattered all that much. I think things would have run their course as it was. More on that will continue.

The first leg of our honeymoon journey brought us to Seaside, Oregon, and we stayed at the Shiloh Inn, which was a nice hotel right on the beach. We walked down the promenade along the beach and enjoyed the afternoon sun and the fresh salt air. It really was invigorating. We then went back to our room and before going out and finding somewhere to eat dinner, enjoyed a few cocktails together. It seemed we walked quite a ways before we found a place to eat. I remember saying something like "this looks like the restaurant was advertised in the hotel brochure." Martha looked at me with a sarcastic smile, and said it *was* that restaurant! I don't know if I was just affected by the alcohol and didn't have a clue we had walked into the restaurant from the back side of the hotel, but I sure felt like the stupidest idiot when I realized she was right. I don't know if she was trying to intimidate me on purpose. I think I was doing the perfect job of that all on my own. After we ate, Martha wanted to set some fireworks off on the beach to celebrate, and I remember getting all paranoid that we would get ourselves into trouble somehow if we did that, but her persistence won out and we lit off the fireworks and then ran back to our room, unscathed and no law enforcement waiting for us.

Soon, we had made it down to Big Sur, and I remember wondering where all the beaches were. All that I could see were mountains on one side of the freeway and cliffs overlooking the ocean on the other. Now, I think if I had studied all the brochures on Big Sur, I might have realized that there were only motels on the cliffs above the beach and not *on* the beach like they were in Seaside. Martha was looking at me like I had no idea what I was doing, and she really was correct in that assumption. She asked me if I had made any reservations somewhere, or if I knew where we were going to stay now that we were in Big Sur. I had to admit that I had not made any reservations but that I was sure we would find a nice place to stay. Most of the nicer looking places of lodging we passed all had "no vacancy" signs lit. Finally, I saw a green sign with "Vacancy Here!" all lit up and so we turned right down that road. We ended up at a cozy looking, older motel situated near the edge of one of the cliffs. It actually did have a great view, but if one was looking for a four-star hotel, this were not going to find that place here, no matter how hard they looked or how much they paid the desk clerk. Martha was tired, and starting to get cranky from the long drive, so I went in and got us a room. As I left the motel office, the clerk said something about no refunds, but I did not pay much attention to that at that time. We got to our room—all the rooms were actually little one room cabins, and when we opened the door, I saw it had not yet been made up, the beds were not changed and it looked as if someone had used it and just checked out. I told Martha to stay in the car and that I would take care of it. I went back to the office and they checked and gave me the key to the cabin next door. The short of the story was the room did not have a TV or a telephone, just an old clock/radio that looked like it had seen better days. Martha turned around after she had entered and said there was no way she was going to spend the night there. It would have been fine with me, truth be told, but I had no choice but to agree with her; and then I remembered the no refund policy. She looked at me and told me she didn't give a shit about that rule and to get our money back and we were going back to Monterey. I remember going back to the office and telling the clerk we could not stay there, as we had to be back north for an emergency. He mentioned the policy and told me there was nothing he could do, and I told him that I wasn't trying to be rude, but that he really needed to refund the money, or my wife would be coming in, and I don't think he would want to deal with her. I think he saw something in my eyes that made him change his mind, and he did give me the money back. I went back to the car, got in and told Martha, there was no problem, of course!

So we drove back up north to Monterey and spent the night at someplace like the Hyatt or the Sheraton, and spent a fortune and then I knew we were officially in trouble. I sometimes wonder if had I actually asked Martha for any help with the cash, she might have chipped in out of her stash, but I was too proud, trying to be the ever providing husband and do everything myself. I remember the next morning, Martha went to the beach to lay in the sun and I told her I would be out to join her soon, as I had to do something, I forget what I told her. I was out of cash and I called the credit union from the room and actually got a hold of the lady who had been helping me personally. I explained what was happening, the problems with having to pay cash on the rental, and that had run out of cash and was not sure what I was going to do—I was hoping desperately for an extension to my personal loan I had gotten before we left. She put me on hold for about 10 minutes and came back on the line, and I don't remember exactly what she told me, but I think she may have added another $100 do my checking account, but nothing else she could do to get any more money added to my loan, that I was extended as far as I could get at that time. I thanked her and hung up. I went down to the marina beach and found Martha, wondering what I was going to tell her.

Of course, Martha was completely oblivious to our financial situation, because I was too busy doing everything I could to ensure that Martha was having the best time—after all, that's what a honeymoon is supposed to be! The best time ever! I think one of the things that was helping me was that the pro football pre-season had started on our wedding night, and there that every night there were evening games that we watched during our trip—that and the booze! And we also made took full advantage of the coke that had been given as a wedding gift.

I think Martha could see something in my face and after she asked me what I had been doing and what had taken me so long, I think I told her I was just tired, and was kicking back in the room, resting up for a great dinner. We had planned to go eat at the restaurant in Carmel that Clint Eastwood owned, that it would be fun to say we were there. We had heard that sometimes Clint dined there himself and there would be the chance we might run into him. I remember it was pretty good food, but when we got back to the hotel, I realized I had left my wallet back at the restaurant. I made up some excuse (there was no way I was going to let on I was so careless to lose my wallet) to go out and get something special for us, and took off like a bat out of Hell, probably breaking all speed limits, but did get my wallet back and I think came back with some ice cream. Martha was into the night's football game, and hadn't noticed that I had been gone longer than I should have. I keep thinking in retrospect how much easier things might have been if I had just been more vocal about things, let her in on just how human I was, but it seemed better to let her stay in the good mood she had been in and not get her pissed off at my stupidity.

My one other time of speeding off and not telling Martha where I was going or where I had been was when we stayed in San Francisco on the way back home. I secretly drove to where my Uncle lived in the Bay area and hit him up for a loan. He questioned my motives for keeping this a secret from my wife, and I told him exactly the extent of how deep in shit I was. He was a tough sell, but he did loan me $375, he said he wished he could loan me more, but that was all he could give me. He also stressed that I needed to be serious about paying him back, and I agreed on I think $75 per month starting that following October, which gave me a month's grace period. I remember racing back to the hotel with another excuse about where I was. I certainly was not proud of lying to Martha, but I was feeling a bit better about having cash again in my wallet. I never did tell her about that loan.

We drove to some big park in San Francisco and Martha and I walked around for a little while, looking at everything, the trees, flowers, other people walking dogs, couples old and young strolling casually some hand in hand, some not, I don't know what Martha was thinking about, but then she led me over to a bench and we sat down. She asked me what was going on, she could tell something was wrong. That gave me the opening, the perfect opportunity to tell her everything, the money problems, the visit to my uncle, the loan. I looked at her and could see the worry in her eyes and I decided that I couldn't tell her anything, that it would just ruin our vacation, and destroy any faith or trust in me and my ability to be a good husband (like my lying and deception wouldn't anyway?), so I just told her that my cash flow was starting to dwindle faster than I had anticipated. That *wasn't* the complete truth, but that was about as honest as I could get. Martha thought about that for a few minutes and then said that maybe we should cut the honeymoon short and just go home. I didn't know what to say, she didn't sound really happy about doing that, but I knew that was probably the smartest thing we could do, and it would slow the outflow of the small amount of cash I had. I knew already that I had a huge debt that I was going to have to start paying back when we got back to the real world, and I would have to buckle down and be responsible. So I put on my best sad face and told Martha that she was probably right, it would be a good idea to start heading back home. I told her things would be ok, I would make sure of that. I kissed her and we headed back to the car and began the drive home.

Our last night on the road ended in Vancouver, Washington, and we settled down in a motor inn of some kind, at that point, I think even Martha didn't mind too much that it wasn't the classiest of places, she knew that money was a concern now. The room wasn't that bad and we turned the TV on and found another pre-season football game. I told Martha that I would go find us some vodka and bourbon so we could at least celebrate our last night and left to find a liquor store. As I was looking for the store, I walked by a guy on one corner and he asked me if I was looking for anything. I said just the liquor store. He told me that if I wanted anything else (this seemed pretty bold in my opinion), like blow or weed, to look for him. I said sure, whatever and then walked down the sidewalk. I got around the corner and thought it might be cool to surprise

Martha with some coke, as we had run out days before, and it might cheer her up, so I turned around and went to find who I had talked to. He was not around, but I found another guy and casually asked him if he knew where I could get any rocks—sometimes you just know if a person is ok to talk to. He said he had a nice rock, and pulled out a baggie and showed it to me. I thought it looked pretty decent, so I said sure. I don't know how much I gave the guy, but I got the baggie and went back to the liquor store and bought some booze and finally got back to the motel. Martha was waiting for me and said it was about time I got back. I told her I got her a surprise and pulled out my special purchase, telling her how I thought it was a pretty good deal on a nice size rock. She had a big grin on her face, gave me a really nice kiss and took the rock out of the baggie and put it on the table. When she tried to cut it down, she looked at me and grinned, but it was a sad smile. "You got a rock all right," she said. "A real rock." I couldn't believe it. I had been taken pretty good. It *was a real rock* and not cocaine as I had been led to believe. That really pissed me off. I put on my coat and told Martha that I was going to find the guy and get my money back or get some real stuff. She tried to talk me out of it, telling me it was a sweet gesture, that the alcohol I had gotten was fine. I told her it was principle now. I was not going to create any problems, I just wanted to find the guy and tell him what I thought. I think she knew how serious I was and said ok. I thought maybe this might show Martha I had some balls after all.

I left the motel room and went back out in search of the guy I bought the 'rock' from, holding onto the baggie in my pocket as the evidence of the foul play. I walked to the street where I had seen him and it found it deserted. As I turned the corner, I ran into the first guy who had offered me his services. He seemed like a guy who might care, so I told him my story and he let out a compassionate little laugh, saying that sounded like what he had heard about that other guy. He said he was sorry, but there was nothing he could do about my original purchase, but he said what he *could* do was sell me the correct stuff at a reduced price for my hardship, he would give me the original amount I had wanted for only $50. I thought that was pretty nice of this guy, after all, because by giving me the bargain, he would be losing the profit off of this sale, (boy, I was stupid in those days!). So I traded him the 'rock' and $50 for a new baggie with real coke and thanked him. I turned around to go back to the motel, and kind of got turned around and disoriented, so it took me a little longer to get back to the room than I had expected, but I did make it.

When I opened the door to our room, I saw the most unexpected sight I had ever thought I would ever see. Martha was crying and she came almost at a run and embraced me tightly, giving me sweet kisses and telling me she was so relieved to see me. I asked her what was going on, why was she crying. She told me after I had left, she had gotten scared and really angry with herself for letting me go back out. She was certain that I would go out and probably get myself hurt or even killed by messing with drug dealers. She was afraid I would piss them off and they would shoot me and she would never see me again. And the fact that I had been gone for almost an hour, really made her think the worst things. What would she have done if I had gotten murdered? How would she be able to live with that? What would she tell people? It was really touching, seeing all of these emotions come out of Martha, not that I had never seen any emotion previously, but never this kind, and showing true love and devotion towards me! Really, thinking back from that moment until now, I don't think I have ever had any other girl show me that much concern since then, except for one and now two, but they come along over 15 years later. I did get Martha calmed down, and that night, even with the alcohol and drug enhancements, I felt the most happiest I had felt with Martha, second to the night I had asked her to be my wife. That was probably the last time I was to ever feel that whole and complete with here again.

Now you are probably thinking that this marriage isn't going in a really solid direction, there are too many obvious things happening that are going to be *huge* problems as time passes, and you would be correct in thinking that. So rather than tell you what happens each day, I will just highlight certain events that will solidify *not* the fact that this marriage was a horrible one, *not* that Martha was a bad wife, *not* pointing fingers at anyone specifically (expect for maybe me), but just to show you readers what happens when you do brainless things, take actions without thinking about the consequences, or conversely taking actions while fully knowing that what you are doing will snowball back on you worse than you can possibly imagine. Because I do believe now more than ever that everything one does, if it is bad, will come back and bite one twice as hard! So anyway, bear with my ineptitudes and know that in my heart (at the time) that my intentions were good, at least that is what I will continue to tell myself.

As I have previously mentioned, I was making a decent wage at my position of Pricing Analyst, but with Martha's and my lifestyle, it just wasn't enough. We didn't go out to expensive restaurants every night, we didn't cook enormous meals at home that required us to buy tons of food (I think we had only two home cooked meals, each time when Martha's parents came over for dinner), we didn't snort cocaine every night, we didn't host wild parties paying out huge wads of cash to supply everything. So what was the deal, you ask? It was partly because I was so far behind in everything I owed before the wedding and having to pay all the current monthly bills along with what we had decided would be my portion of the still current wedding bills. I recall I had to pay the photographer and the florist. With all that, I was not able to see *anything* at the end of that lengthy tunnel. Martha did contribute to our bills, I am sure, but I know that we had never sat down and drawn out a budget plan to where each of our paychecks would go to pay our bills. I know later on, we did try to implement a schedule like that, but I think it was too late at that point. Too much had happened, but we aren't quite there yet.

There were several times that Martha had overheard me saying that we had plans to do something even though we didn't so that I could get out of seeing my older brother, or tell a story to get out of a phone conversation, and she was getting tired of me not just telling people how it was. If I didn't want to do something, why couldn't I just tell them the truth? That came to a roaring boil one night when my brother showed up at our door unannounced. After I told him that Martha wasn't feeling well, and we were going to go to bed early, he left, and then she came into the room, her face was red with anger and she was furious! I think she was ticked off more because I had used her as an excuse not to see him more than anything, but she started yelling at me and told me that was the last straw! No more lying! She was so tired of that and she didn't want to see me right now, that she just wanted me to leave, to get out, and she pushed me to the front door. I almost went out, but then I turned around and told her I wasn't going to leave, this was my place too. I told her that I only did what

I did so that we could have a nice quiet night to ourselves. She wasn't buying that line at all. I think that night I slept on the couch.

I was starting to drink beers more often, just to wind down before coming home from work. My drive home was what I called a two-beer trip (usually 12 ounce cans), and if I took the longer route, I could make it with 2 - 16 ounce cans. Then when I got home, I would hit the fridge and help myself to another beer or two. Martha would never know that I had already had beers. My nerves were getting so rattled with the finances and the effort to conceal all of my problems and emotions from Martha that I would wait until she went up to bed and then go out to my car. I would then bring in more beer that she didn't know about so I could drink and get calmed down before going up to bed myself. Usually I would throw out the empty cans or bottles before going to bed so she would not know about my extra-curricular consumptions, but often I would be tired and lazy and would stash the empties behind the couch in the living room, intending to throw them out the next day or whenever I could without Martha knowing.

One day I came home from work and heard the vacuum cleaner in the living room and thought it was unusual that Martha was cleaning house on a weekday. Then I saw all my empties that I had hidden behind the couch sitting *ON* the couch. Martha saw me and turned off the vacuum cleaner and looked at me with accusing eyes, I had not seen her look like that before. She asked me (not real nicely if I remember correctly) what I knew about all the empty beer cans and bottles. She told me she was deep cleaning and when she moved the couch to vacuum, she was shocked at what she had found. So here was the perfect opportunity to fess up to something, to tell it like it was, to be completely and utterly honest and tell her the truth. I looked at her and told her that I had no idea how those empties had gotten there. I know, I know, that has to have been one of the stupidest things I have ever said. And the fact that I even had a notion that she would believe it should put me in the front of the line of the nearest insane asylum. I can't even believe it now, all these years later that I tried to pull that lie off. But that was my line, and I stuck to it. I don't think I ever admitted to putting the empties there, and I think Martha got tired of being mad at me for my obvious lie, though I'm sure she never forgot about it.

Christmas and the holiday of 1987 arrived and we had now been married for about four months. I'm sure we had Christmas with Martha's parents, because we never did anything with any of my relatives, even though my uncle lived in Bellevue, but he and his wife were usually with their kids on the holidays anyway. Martha wanted to do something fun and different for the New Year rather than just be boring and stay home, so she decided we would stay downtown Seattle in a hotel with some friends and go to one of the local comedy clubs which was showcasing Howie Mandel. I didn't know how I was going to be able to afford the hotel much less the dinner out, the drinks and comedy and whatever else I was sure I would have to chip in for. But I didn't wonder for long. I quickly learned the art of writing checks at grocery stores for cash over the amount. I knew that this wasn't the best thing to do (you could actually call it wrong or illegal), especially when the money in the checking account was nowhere near enough to cover the entire check. But a desperate man does what he has to do, is the only justification that I could come up with. I ended up going to four different stores writing a check at each one for $50 over, so I ended up with a nice sum of $200 cash to play with for the weekend. I wasn't really proud of how I got the extra cash, and I knew that once the fun was over, I was going to be in even bigger trouble with more bounced checks, but at that point, I was only thinking about the short term.

I remember the comedy club pretty well, because one of our friends got up to go to the bathroom during the show, and Howie stopped his act and singled her out as she was heading toward the door, making her feel very self-conscious about her having interrupted his act because she had to go pee. Then while she was gone, he had our section trade places with the opposite section so she would have no idea where her seat was when she came back. It really was quite funny and we all had a huge laugh as she stumbled around, finally catching on to his prank. The next morning Martha and I were nursing severe hangovers and all we wanted to do was get home and vegetate on the couch until we felt ourselves again, but I was having a problem finding the entrance to the freeway. Finally Martha became so tense and agitated she finally pounded her fists on the dash and told me to "find the fucking freeway now!" I almost wanted to pull over, get out and tell her if she was going to be a bitch about it, she could drive herself. Did I do that? Of course I didn't. I did not have the balls to

136

perform that deed, but luckily when I turned a corner, I saw the big green sign that said I-5 N next left, and it was not soon enough we finally got back to the apartment. Of course a couple of weeks later, I got the bounced check notices in the mail for each of those checks I had written.

At some point, I had been talking to my friend Barry, who worked down in the print shop at the Company, and we were talking about money and I remember asking him what the odds would be that we could actually print money ourselves. He thought it was a pretty interesting idea, but there would be no way we could print anything that would look like real money because the presses were just for newspaper and were not near the quality that could print 'real' money. Besides, the paper would be different and we wouldn't have any plates or prints to go off of. I told him I was just kidding anyway, as surely we could get in serious trouble for doing something stupid like that. But I kept thinking about it and I went to the public library and started to look at books about money. In one book, I found a good picture of a ten dollar bill in roughly the same size as a real bill, with clear photos of both the front and the back. I remember checking the book out and taking it to show Barry. He looked at the pictures and asked if he could keep the book while he was on his shift. He wanted to try some ideas he had just come up with. He worked the overnight shift, so he didn't have to worry about anyone else looking over his shoulder at what he was doing. I had to get home before Martha started wondering where I was, so I told Barry I would see him the next day.

I stopped in to check on Barry before I left work the next afternoon, and he pulled me aside and told me he wanted to show me something. He gave me a folded piece of paper and when I looked at it, saw a great replica of the front of a ten dollar bill. He told me he had tried a lot of different things the night before, and didn't go into the finer details of what he did, but he was able to print a pretty good duplication. To make a long story short, more for shits and giggles, we printed a whole mess of ten dollar bills. How he could do such a good job was something I never questioned, Barry was great at what he did. He was always a great employee and never put out less than quality material in everything he did for the Company. Anyway, I had seen movies that dealt with counterfeiters, and they would put the finished product in clothes dryers with poker chips, so bingo! I thought that was what we should do. I don't know how many bills Barry printed up, but I took lots of them home in a box one day when Martha was out with her friend at a home Seahawks game and spent a couple of hours playing with the money, poker chips and the clothes dryer. You think drying tennis shoes in the dryer makes a lot of noise? Try 40 or so poker chips with paper and see how much of a racket that makes! Martha would have had a cow if she had heard all that clatter and I don't think any lie that I could come up with work with her, which is why I had to wait until she was gone for a while. After the bills went through the dryer cycle, they didn't look anything like the ones in the movies, and I don't think I was anywhere near serious about actually spending them, so I gave them all back to Barry and said we needed to get rid of them. Barry agreed with me. We didn't think it would be wise for either of us to be caught with any of those bills, risking our careers for possessing items that could put us in jail for the rest of our productive lives! What were we been thinking? After I gave all the bills that I had back to Barry, I never saw them again. Well, I never saw them for at least another year anyway.

Have we lost count on how many things I had been keeping from Martha yet?

I don't remember the exact circumstances, but right before the Memorial Day weekend, I pissed Martha off again pretty bad, and she once more told me to get out, she didn't want to see my face again, so that time, I did leave. I told her if she wanted me out, then fine, that is what she would get. I put a few things in a bag and left the apartment, got in my car and drove to see my friend Mike. Mike was a great friend from work, who I had talked to a lot about my problems with Martha and he was one of the guys who had always been one of my biggest supporters, always telling me how I should stand up for myself and take control of my life (which of course had always gone in one ear and out the other), but when I showed up, he happily told me I could hang with him for the weekend. Mike himself was living at a friend's house, and I think was renting the room he was staying in. He had access to the kitchen and cooked some steaks for us that night. Then we went out to the bar where I drank a lot of beer, played pool and commiserated about my sad life and consequently got drunk. I remember we woke up and I was sitting in Mike's easy chair and started watching some cheesy horror movie and even though it was only around 8 am, I popped open a can of Coors and started drinking. Mike was a little concerned at how early I had started, but I think he felt that under the circumstances, it was somehow justified. That weekend, thank God it was a 3-day weekend, was pretty much a 3-day drunk for me. I remember at some point one during one of those three nights, I drove by the apartments just to see if Martha was out partying and was actually surprised to see her car parked under the car port. Of course now that I think about it all these years later, she still may not have been home, one of her friends may have picked her up and taken her out the same as I was out with Mike. I don't know if I was truly upset about being kicked out, or whether I was just using it to be away from Martha and enjoy my freedom and getting drunk. But I do know that by the third night it took a little extra work to hit that plateau and get lost in the beer and the pool and darts and enjoy because I knew the next day I would have to go back to work and face the real world. I would have to go deal with the Martha situation.

I was sitting at my desk (I must have brought work clothes with me to Mike's place) and I had been avoiding the print shop and avoiding at all costs running into Martha, when my phone rang. I picked it up and it was her. She sounded very quiet and reserved, but after all, we were at work. There was no anger or fire in her voice. She sounded subdued, almost beaten and said she was sorry for what had happened. I said I was too, and I think I actually meant it. I asked her if she had told anyone what had happened, her parents or anybody, and she said she had not. I told her the only one who knew what happened was Mike, but that I trusted him not to spread any rumors. Martha asked if I wanted to meet her for dinner and talk about things, and I said I did. I had a coupon for a free dinner I had gotten for Christmas that I told her we could use and we agreed to meet after work that night. This would be the perfect time for me to get everything out in the open and tell Martha all of my concerns, my problems, fears, but when we got together, it seemed like such a romantic reunion and we held hands and looked at each other with goofy eyes and I couldn't say what I wanted to, so again, I kept everything inside, but I agreed with her that we needed to stop fighting and work together and keep the marriage working in a positive direction.

Of course, by then, I was getting bounced check notices in the mail, and I would try to get home before Martha everyday so that I could prevent her from seeing those letters. She did get some and started wondering what was going on. I told her that the credit union had made a mistake and that I was on top of things, but I think she still had her suspicions. It got to the point where I cringed every time the phone rang when Martha was there because I thought it would be a bill collector and I didn't want her to pick up one of those calls. I got lucky one morning when I had stayed home sick from work and the phone rang after Martha had left. It was my uncle wondering when I was going to send him the next check for payment on the loan. I think I put him off for another month, I was just happy that Martha did not get that call, remember I had not told her anything about that loan.

Things were getting really bad and I had bounced a rent check and put that off for another month and now my stress level was out of control. I was shaking a lot, frazzled and not eating. I was drinking more every night, though very careful to get rid of the evidence of drinking after Martha went to bed. I was asking everyone I knew if I could borrow money and making a complete fool of myself. I had even sold the bed I had before I got married to the neighbors for some extra cash. I told them to keep that a secret from Martha and they said they would.

Then the fateful Friday night came. I remember this night as if it happened yesterday. I had driven to the video store and gotten a couple of VHS rentals so that Martha and I could have a nice relaxing Friday evening watching a couple movies and enjoying each other's company. When I got home and opened the door, I saw Martha standing in the kitchen with a strained, stricken look on her face. On the table was a notice she had found taped to the door when she had gotten home. It looked like one I had found the month prior after bouncing the second rent check. Yes, it was another eviction notice and this time Martha had found it first, not me. It was a three day pay or vacate notice. It was done. I knew from the look on Martha's face that it was over. She was not yelling at me or throwing things or pacing or anything that a woman in rage would do. She quietly but with conviction told me to get out, that that was the last straw. She was done. I was absolutely speechless and I could think of nothing to say. I mean, what could I say? The evidence was there on the table right in front of Martha's eyes. I couldn't hide things any longer. I think I said that I was very sorry and then I went upstairs and packed up some clothes and things in a suitcase and when I came back downstairs I said to Martha that I guess I would see her later, or something totally lame and stupid like that. What else could I say? I think she was crying and I may have had some tears, I don't remember. I think I was just numb. That's the best way I could describe it. It's like when you are caught red-handed by your mom with your hands in the cookie jar after she has specifically told you no and you did it anyway... like a deer in headlights. I felt complete and utter numbness. For some reason I made sure to take the VHS rentals with me when I went out the door, after all, I was pretty sure that they would not be watched and I wanted to make sure they were returned.

I left the apartment and drove to Mike's apartment. He had just recently moved in with another friend of ours from the Company just a few blocks from work. But I first stopped at the pub that was also near work that was a nice hangout where I had been with Martha when we were first going out—there were pool tables and darts and a few pinball machines I liked. I sat at the counter and had beer thinking about what had just happened. I didn't really know whether to laugh or cry. My emotions were in such a turmoil right then, but I think I was feeling relief more than anything. It was a Friday night and my plan was to get drunk and celebrate my being single again, because I pretty much knew for sure that there was no going back this time. I guess I could say I knew for *sure.* After my beer, I went to Mike's and pulled out the pint of vodka that I had had stashed under the driver's seat and walked to his front door. He opened it and saw me standing there holding the vodka out in front of me and he instantly knew what had happened. We had discussed previously that if I ever showed up on his doorstop with a bottle of vodka that my marriage was over. And he had said that if that ever happened that I was more than welcome to stay with him for a while. He gave me a big hug and asked me if I was okay. I think I said that I was better than ever and went inside and we got drunk.

Having said all that I have about my marriage, I really don't want to portray my wife (ex-wife) in too much of a bad light. Though I know it takes two to tango, there was no way that we should have ever gotten married. I don't think I was in any way, shape or form ready. This is, of course, easy to say now, but I know I was not emotionally mature enough, I was certainly not financially stable enough, and it is my belief that the union was doomed from the start. I should have called it off, or at least postponed things when Mom asked me about things that afternoon when I was home and she had said that if I had **any concerns, any doubts,** that was the time to take a step back, regroup, examine if things are going the right way. It is so easy to think about those things in retrospect. All I can do is take what I have learned and try to use that knowledge in better ways. I did love Martha, I know I did, but sometimes I don't think love is enough.

And so that's the end of my story and everything after that was so much better, no problems, no heartbreaks, no dilemmas. So why is there so many pages left, you might wonder? Am I perhaps lying again? Just seeing if you are still reading, seeing if you haven't gotten tired of all my pathetic antics and wondering if I am ever going to wise up and do things the right way. Well, I wish I could say that is what you will find when you read on!

So I moved in with Mike and that weekend I called my parents. When I told Mom that Martha and I had split up and that things were over between us, she sounded relieved. She told me "finally I have my son back!" I remember those words. That meant a lot to me, and I knew then that she must have known things were not right, but had never wanted to say that to me out loud. Like I have said before, I am a firm believer that mothers always know things! She asked me what I was going to do and I told her that I was staying with Mike for a little while, until I could get back on my feet. She told me to call her if I needed anything.

It was kind of weird with both Martha and I working at the same place, but we really didn't bump into each other a lot since we worked on different floors. I remember one time I had to talk to her on the phone for some reason and I caught myself saying "hon" and then immediately said I was sorry, that I was so used to saying that. I knew it bothered her, hell; it would have bothered me to hear my ex call me an endearing name as well. I did get a lot of sympathy from my immediate co-workers in my section of the office, because most of them could tell that I had changed and lost way too much weight and was always on nerves and shaking, and they could see that I was now different. I remember that when Martha and I got engaged, I was almost 180 pounds and when we split up I weighed 132 pounds and my waist size had gone down to size 32. I hadn't been that size since I was a little kid! But soon after that, I gained the weight back; if not some extra I'm sure. I think I got reprimanded shortly after my breakup and told that I was letting too many personal things interfere with my work, and that I needed to take care of things, leave personal things at home and be professional while at work. I took no offense at that, and told my supervisor that I would do my best at my job.

It was around the latter part of July 1989 that I was going back to Boise for my ten year high school reunion. It couldn't have had happened at a better time, as I could get away from where I was and have a little vacation from all my problems. Just because I no longer had to worry about having to hide finances from my wife, did not mean I still did not have financial problems, though they were a bit easier to handle since I did not have monthly rent or utilities for a few months. Thank you Mike! My folks had told me that when I came back home they wanted to help me go over my financial status and make sure I was okay. I knew I would be embarrassed to show them how bad things were, but I supposed that it would be for the best, and if they could do anything to help me, they would. So I gathered all my bills, past and present and put them in my briefcase and took everything with me for a long weekend.

I flew back home and was excited to see Mom and Dad. They welcomed me and gave me big hugs and said that I looked great, though they thought I needed to put on a little weight. It's kind of funny because I think that's the last time they have made that remark to me; now it's always I need to lose some pounds, exercise more, watch what I eat. I was able to borrow their car and go around and do errands for them and enjoy no longer having to worry about what someone else is thinking, criticizing how I drive or anything like that. I also was drinking more. I was drinking a lot more and not just beer anymore. I think I just wanted to get that buzz, get that good feeling and celebrate my newly acquired freedom.

I remember going to *The Little Dutch Garden* which was a place I had seen forever and always wondered what it was like. It was a little house that had been transformed into a pub. I don't remember that they had anything on tap, just cans and bottles. It was nothing fancy, but it had a nice atmosphere and I had a few beers there the afternoon of the reunion dinner. I also had a pint or two of vodka in the car with me so that I could enjoy some liquid refreshments while driving. I remember when I got back home to change before going to dinner I unlocked the front door and set off the house alarm. I didn't know the code to reset and silence the alarm and looked around for the code, or some note from Mom that would tell me where they had gone to. I found nothing and meanwhile the alarm was still ringing loudly. I started calling their friends, hoping to get lucky and catch them so I could turn off the damn noise before the police arrived. I'm sure if that happened, the great buzz I had going would rapidly go away and I didn't want that to happen. I finally got a hold of Mom and she told me where to find the code, and then there was a sweet silence after I punched it in. Luckily, no police or security showed up to check things out.

I drove downtown to where the reunion dinner was being held and it was great to see a lot of my old classmates, the majority I had not seen in ten years. Surprisingly, everyone looked pretty much the same, except most of the guys had gained weight or lost hair, and most everybody had children. But what did I expect? Ten years is a long time, a lot can happen in that many years. Most everyone that I thought would be married was, and even some of the girls that I couldn't have imagined ever getting hitched were in fact no longer single. There were two people who couldn't attend the reunion due to the fact that they were no longer living. One good friend of mine had taken his own life shortly after we had all graduated and another girl who I didn't know very well was also gone, though I can't remember the circumstances now. But otherwise, pretty much the entire class of 90 some people were in attendance. Even our English teacher, who had been very demanding but extremely well liked by all of us was there (he had adamantly stated at graduation that he would never attend a reunion, not that he did not like us as students, but that he hated reunions). There were some speeches by our class president and the class Valedictorian, and then the dinner. And cocktails were present I think. I was prepared even if they were not serving booze. There was talk about having a 20-year reunion, but I never made it to that one. We'll see about the 30 year. That's still yet to be.

After the dinner was over (it was probably about 10 or 11pm), the festivities died down and people started saying their goodnights. We would all be seeing each other one last time the next day at the Sunday picnic, and most people had to get home to take care of their children. I don't remember if I actually had made plans with some of my buddies to

144

meet at a local hangout for beer, pool and pinball or not, I may have concocted that story or that may have been the intent of what was, but that is what I told my parents what the plan had been. Is that what happened? No, not even close.

The next thing I remember is it driving on what appeared to be a dirt road and I had no clue as to where I was. There were trees on both sides of me and the only illumination was from the headlights of the car. I started to hear a "whump-whump" noise and it sounded as if one of the tires had gone flat. Now not only was I lost but I was driving on a flat tire. All I wanted to do was find a phone and call Mom and Dad and get some help. I was driving very slow, as that is what one is supposed to do when you have a flat tire, and then I think I heard a popping sound, and I remember stopping and getting out to see what that noise was. I now had a second flat tire, and had not the foggiest idea of where the hell I was! My mission now was to find any damn phone booth and call home! Ahead, I saw a sort of clearing and wait... there was a paved road beyond a concrete post barricade! Salvation was at hand! I figure the car was a compact vehicle and could make it between the post and the concrete side, but as I slowly inched up there, I found that I had misjudged things. I was not going to make it to the other side. I stopped the car and when I looked out the windshield I saw two police cars parked on the other side of the road, both drivers leaning with their hands folded over their chests, watching me with obvious interest. "Oh, fuck," I think I said, maybe even out loud to no one at all. There was nothing that I could do and I just put my hands up like they do in the movies when a gun is pointed at them.

The next thing I remember is I was at police station (I don't have any recollection of being given a field sobriety test or being driven to the station at all) and being told I could make my phone call. I don't know how many of you readers have had to make that call, but it was the hardest, most embarrassing call I had ever had to make up until that time. When Mom answered the phone, I don't think she had any idea that I was in trouble. She asked where I was, and I told her that I was at the police station; I had been arrested for drunk driving. I remember she paused and then asked if I wanted them to come and bail me out right then. I told her that she should just go back to sleep (like that was very likely after that call) and just worry about me in the morning. I said it was my fault I was there and that I should just stay in jail overnight. Mom didn't sound as pissed or as upset as I thought she might, more worried than anything else. I hung up and was taken to a larger cell with a lot of guys already in there, most sleeping. I recall it looked like a large dormitory room but all the beds were already taken. I was given an army cot and I had it put together in a few minutes, put my sport coat on top of me and was asleep in probably a few minutes.

I think they gave us some cereal for a breakfast, and then Mom and Dad were there to bail me out. I know they had to be very disappointed in me, but they did not show it—I think they could tell how much I was already upset with myself, but I knew I would hear about how they felt sooner than later. We were taken to our car, which had been towed to impound so I could get any of my other belongings that I had left behind. Mom noticed an empty pint of vodka in the back seat and asked me if I had been drinking that while I had been driving. I said I probably had been. I couldn't lie about that, the evidence was right there. I saw the two flat tires and then noticed all the scratches on one side of the car, from all the bushes and branches I had driven through. Somehow, Mom figured, I had gotten off of the main road and ended up on the greenbelt of the Boise River. How I had done that, Mom had no clue, though I recall her saying at a later time they had actually figured it out. All I knew was that it was a complete miracle that I had not crashed the car, whether into a tree or another vehicle and that I had not hurt or killed someone. I must have been driving on instinct or with an angel watching over me.

At the picnic that afternoon, everyone was pretty subdued, no wild rowdiness or anything like that at all. Maybe everyone was suffering hangovers or maybe it was just how they acted now that they were all out of high school, adults with responsibilities. No parties like in the old days. I don't recall having a huge hangover, though in light of how much I had had to drink I certainly should have. There was only one other person at the picnic who had black ink around the finger tips like I did. My friend JT had obviously been fingerprinted as I had. As it turned out, JT had been arrested the night before as well, but where I was more creative, he was more blatant. He had made an illegal U-turn on the one-way street in front of the capital building. However our arrests occurred, the result was the same, and we figured it was odd we hadn't passed each other in the holding cells.

Our family attorney was called and it was agreed he would represent my case without my having to be there, though I kept in constant contact with him by telephone after I had gone back to Washington. My parents never really laid into me for being so stupid and careless like I thought they would, or maybe I have put that out of my memory because it was so bad. I think Mom figured that I was just so relieved at being done with everything: my separation and Martha, that I just celebrated too much, and she left it at that. I think she could tell that I was already being really hard on myself and knew I would not do something stupid like that again

We went over my finances before I left and my parents were pretty dismayed by what they saw. They decided there was no way they could (or would maybe) loan me the money to pay everything off, and after another consultation with the attorney, it was recommended that I should declare bankruptcy. Mom told me that no one in the family had ever had to do that and it was a good thing that my grandfather was no longer alive, because he would have been so very upset with me. But I was too far into debt what with credit cards, wedding bills that I still had not paid, back rent of the apartment Martha and I had shared, and I'm sure there were other things as well. I told Mom I knew of someone who had gone through the same thing and I would call the company he used for filing, which I did when I got back to Bellevue. Mom added the money to get the bankruptcy rolling to the tab of attorney fees and costs related to my DUI.

I had to take some tests at a local alcohol assessment company once I got back to Bellevue, and I think I must have conned them pretty well, because it was determined that I did not have a problem with alcohol at all. I was just a normal social drinker and they did not recommend any further treatment. Mom to this day still tells me the policemen told her when she came to pick me up that morning said that I was an alcoholic, that I had such a high blood alcohol count and the fact that I could still drive would lead them to that conclusion, but my assessment test proved that theory otherwise. Today as I write I know that assessment tests can certainly come to incorrect conclusions when manipulated correctly.

The outcome of the whole Idaho vs. Me was titled a "withheld judgment" which probably would never have resulted in that if it was in

2008. How do I know that? We'll see. But back then, the DUI laws were not as strict as they are now. I had to turn in my driver's license and not drive for six months, and if I was arrested for drunk driving again in 3 years or something like that, the withheld judgment would revert to a DUI with the consequences that come with that. I abided by those rulings and did not get into any trouble during the specified time, and I was able to get my driver's license renewed after the time had elapsed. I was not proud of my adventures in Idaho, so I told no one but my closest friends, and even they did not give me a huge ration of shit, which was cool, though they did show their concern and was glad that I was okay.

Before I could go and do anything about declaring bankruptcy, I was called to go see the person I had dealt with at the credit union. It had come to her attention that I did not have any car insurance on the Ford that I was financing through the credit union. I played stupid and said I guess not. She asked me if I knew that car insurance was mandatory in the state of Washington. I looked at her and said that I had not known that either, which might have been true as I don't think I did, seriously, but regardless, I knew when I got the car, no one had mentioned the subject of car insurance, so I had not pursued it. I told her that when we included the car in the loan I had gotten prior to my wedding, she had not said anything then. She admitted she had assumed that I had had it. The gist of that conversation was that insurance would be added to the loan retroactively, so in other words, I now owed a lot more than I did earlier in the day. It was just my luck. Were things going to get any better? Let's see.

I was sitting at my desk at work, inputting price changes into the computer at around 2:30 one Friday afternoon, when my phone rang. I picked it up and gave my usual Company greeting and I heard Barry, my buddy from the print shop on the other end. He sounded like he was crying and I asked him what was wrong. He said that he had been fired and that I was next, they were going to be coming to get me. I asked him what he was talking about. He told me they had found out about the money, the money that we had printed up. For a second I had no idea what he was talking about. Then I remembered. I asked him how could that be, we had gotten rid of it, hadn't we? He didn't have a lot of time to explain things to me on the phone and I could hear his wife yelling at him in the background. He would talk to me later; he just wanted to warn me of what was coming. I had a horrible feeling in the pit of my stomach now, knowing that someone was coming to get me.

Sure enough, about ten minutes later, the Company security man came to my desk and told me to go with him down to the security office. I did so and once we got there, I was sat down in front of the desk and saw a couple of other men with suit and ties in the room. The door was closed. I was interrogated for about a half hour by someone who identified himself as from the United States Treasury Department regarding my involvement of counterfeiting ten dollar bills. It seemed pretty surreal thinking back on that afternoon. It's hard to describe accurately exactly how I felt, I remember that I was trying not to panic, and I that I knew that I could conceivably be going to prison for a very long time. I don't remember all that I said, but rambled on about the whole thing being just a lark, we were just playing around and wondering if it could be done at all, we weren't planning on spending any of the bills. The main guy reached into a box that was on the floor beside the chair next to him and pulled out a ten dollar bill and showed it to me. He said it was the best reproduction he had seen in a very long time, and was surprised that it was made on a printer such as the one the Company had. I don't remember if he or Barry eventually told me that the money was found buried in the mountains nearby by a hiker and everything was traced back to us because of shredded coupons found with some of the bills that had been shredded. I was told that the only reason we were not outright arrested and jailed that day was because intent to spend was not shown due to the fact the bills had not been buried in plastic bags. That was our only saving grace. He asked me if we had spent any of the bills at all, and I said no—that was not a lie. He asked me if we had ever intended on spending any of the bills, and again I said no. I was asked why we had printed up so many, and I told him I didn't know, which was true. I never knew why Barry had printed as many as he did. I think it was close to $500 grand worth of bills all said and told. Before he left, the agent told me that I would need to go downtown Seattle and get finger printed and sign some documents and that it would be a good idea to secure a public defender. He gave me a letter with details of what I was supposed to do and then left the room. The Company security man still remained in the room and I asked him if I was fired. He looked at me like I was stupid and then said that I was and that I was to go back upstairs and get my personal belongings and would be escorted out. We went back to my desk and I grabbed some things and my jacket and as I walked by my manager's office, Mike (my boss—same name as my friend I was staying with) looked up and asked me where I was going. I told him I could not talk to him, that I had to go. He told me to wait and go in and see him, and I was allowed to briefly step inside. I told Mike that I had been fired and I had to leave, that was all I could tell him. Even that was hugely difficult to tell him. He looked at me stunned and I turned and walked out of his office. I think that was the last time I saw him. I was escorted to the front door of the Company and told I was no longer permitted on the Company premises and that I would be subject to trespassing charges if I did. I said fine, and went to my car and drove back to my friend Mike's apartment. I don't remember if I cried, but it would not have been unlikely if I did. Too much had happened in such a short period of time. To this day I still wonder how I survived all of that and did not develop severe mental problems or require the need of a psychiatrist. The thing I had to do now, was tell my parents I no longer worked at the Company, but what I feared even more, was telling them *why* I had been fired. I mean, they were bound to ask, but there was no way I could tell them the truth! I would have to blend some fiction in with the facts to make it seem more reasonable. But I would wait for a few days, clear my head out, think things through. I thought about Barry and wondered how he was fairing, he had even more to lose than I did, after all, he had a wife and three children, and now no job. I wondered what he was going to do now. But all I could really do right then was to begin what I was good at, so I grabbed a can of beer from the fridge and started drinking, to dull the pain. Mike (my friend) got home an hour later and I filled him in on what had happened, and he just shook his head in disbelief. He had known about what Barry and I had done, but like me, he had forgotten all about it, as that had been so long ago. I think we went down the corner pub and got drunk.

I didn't want to wait for Mom to find out about my being fired by having her call and ask for me at work, so I finally got together enough balls to call her myself. That call was almost as bad as when I called from jail that weekend I was home. I told her that my friend Barry and I had printed up some fake bills for a Halloween party and that they had been so realistic that when some were found after we had gotten rid of what we had made, that the authorities got involved and we were let go for printing money on Company property. Pretty much what had happened expect for some of the more intricate details. I don't remember any more specifics of that phone conversation except for her saying that I had better get my head put on straight and buckle down and get serious about my life and put a lot of things behind me. She was sorry that I had lost my job, as she knew (I did too) that it had been a good job, one that could have lasted a long time. I know she chastised me on my stupidity and again, that hopefully I had learned a valuable lesson from things. She said too much had happened to me in a short time and that I needed to get serious. I agreed and promised that I would be looking for a new job and would let her know what I found as soon as I did. I think we put an indefinite extension on the loan repayment at that time (I remember it took me a very long time to pay it off, but I did).

So I guess you could say that I had started another chapter in my life. I was jobless, wifeless (though *that* I was not exactly crying about) and without a place to call my own. I had a place to live for the moment, and now my goal was to get serious and find a job and get my bankruptcy on track and get my life back together. The End. Okay, maybe I should say: the beginning. The New Beginning!

THE NEW BEGINNING

So now I was starting over, and once again I was back to Kelly Services trying to get some part time jobs lined up to earn some kind of income. Meantime, I had gone to a legal service company that my friend Mike had been to before and recommended. I filled out all the necessary paperwork for the Chapter 7 – Full bankruptcy. My parents paid that fee and of course it was added to my loan with them. Fantastic! Even more money to add to the bankruptcy total, and it was a moot point they would be paid back. I was granted the bankruptcy in 1990, so that added to my fresh start. One thing the attorney for the big B told me at that time was that I could add on my student loan to the deal for an extra $275 and for whatever reason I declined that offer (now of course any federal loan cannot be declared—and I kick myself for not taking advantage of that recommendation back then, as I am still paying off that loan today!).

My first couple of jobs through Kelly Services included working at a lumber warehouse in Kirkland (2 days) and helping to set up a bookstore on the main Microsoft campus in Redmond (1 day. I just never went back and didn't even bother to turn in the time slip). Then I was sent out to a home-care medical supply warehouse for a data entry position. I liked that job and the people I worked with were very friendly and supportive, they made me feel like part of the team.

Now after I had gotten that temp job I had moved from Mike's place to an apartment on Beacon Hill in Seattle, staying with another friend I had met playing darts with at the local pub we hung out in near Mike's. Andrew told me I could stay there for something like $50 a month and he would be fine with driving me to work every morning as long as I took the bus back after work. That worked out ok for a while.

Andrew loved to party just as I did and we would sit in his apartment for hours on end drinking beer and playing backgammon. We did this pretty much every night. There really wasn't anyplace near his apartment that was nice to go to, as Beacon Hill is not in a particularly nice neighborhood. I wouldn't recommend living there and raising children. Of course, that is just my opinion. After a while, I would find myself chugging a beer or two in the car on the way to work and just eat some pepperoni sticks right before going in to mask the breath, why? I have no clue. Could it be possibly because I could perhaps? That made absolutely no sense. I think they could smell the alcohol on my breath, though they never came out and said anything. One day shortly after that, I was told they were going through some downsizing, and that my position was being phased out. To be fair, they were giving me a couple of weeks' notice so I had time to look for something else. It never occurred to me to equate that with my drinking. I'm sure if I had I wouldn't have been too far off the mark.

After that home-care job was over, I was no longer making any money, and of course, Andrew didn't want me living at the apartment much longer, since I was no longer contributing anything financially to the kitty. Once again, I had to move. I ended up finding a room to rent in a house back in Bellevue. It was a big room with my own secure entrance and private bath. I had kitchen privileges and the use of a separate refrigerator. As luck would have it, I found a job at an AM/PM gas station a few blocks away, within walking distance from the house. It was more or less perfect at the time. If you can call a minimum wage job at a self-serve gas station "perfect" but, hey, it was a job and it was bringing in some money, so who was I to complain? I could have been worse off, though. As you remember, I might have been in prison—but at least then, there would have been free room and board, for a very long time…

I've often thought that having too much time on one's hands and watching late night infomercials along with some extra money can be a bad thing. Especially if one's judgment can be called into question. I can safely say (and this is something I have proven by my past—I am not necessarily proud of this, either) that the producers of these programs know exactly what they are doing and how to put on a good show that makes people buy their products. Anyway, I was watching this show on how to start your own business. It sure sounded like a good idea and looked easy to do. There was a huge instruction booklet, cassette tapes, and the best part were the technical support specialists available 24 hours a day—it was such an organized deal that sounded fool proof! "Send in your payment now of only $499 plus shipping and handling, and you too can own your own business." And if I missed any details about what the program was talking about, I just had to watch late night TV the next night or the next, and invariably it would be on again! There were so many testimonials from people who had made a ton of money, that I thought that it would be a cinch for me to do that also! I called Barry up and talked to him about it. Part of the program included setting up your own 900 numbers for astrology, chat, and a sport's line. You could do your own advertising, it stated, but that should be a cinch. I figured I could put up flyers on bulletin boards, check into classifieds, I mean, how expensive could that be? Just advertise wherever you wanted to and you would get a profit off of each call. Barry was as excited as I was, after all, *everybody* called 900 numbers all the time! Hell, I was proof of that! Barry told me he couldn't go in on the initial investment, but that he would help me anyway else he could. I had recently received $1000 after my grandmother had passed (my two brothers also each got the same), so I had money to spend, and I thought it was a wise investment (yeah, remember my wise decision to go into coupon mailers?). I ordered the program.

When all the information got to me, it looked a bit harder to set up than I had previously thought. The cost to advertise the 900 numbers would be expensive wherever you advertised, whether in the local newspaper or in magazines. I remember putting some flyers out, but not much more than that. Suffice to say, I don't think there was any profit from the 900 numbers at all. The other part of the program had instructions about going into business arbitration. After reading through all the details involving that, I thought that would be interesting, after all, I was pretty good at dealing with people, and didn't really have a problem talking to people (surely I must have forgotten about my shyness with selling radio advertising). I remember going downtown and obtaining a business license and did whatever else we needed to do. Then all we needed was to find some clients so we could start making some money. That was the harder part. Finding people that needed business arbitration wasn't easy unless you were able to advertise, and I had spent the rest of the money from my grandmother on things like a phone with a second line for the business, paying the rent from the last month that I was behind on, as well as things that I'm certain I didn't need, and suddenly there was no extra money left. I was back to barely keeping my financial head above water. I remember Mom asking me once what I had done with that $1000 and I told her and she just shook her head; I don't think anything fazed her about what I did any more.

That job and housing situation lasted throughout that summer and when it became evident that I was going nowhere and fast. I did spend some quality time on the computer at the house that I was allowed to use and totally re-wrote a stage play that I had been toying with for some time. The woman that I was renting from and I would have coffee from time to time as I was writing on her computer, but I think she soon tired of me. I'm sure I told her more than many times that I would soon find a great job and be more on time with the rent (she had let me pay late for the last couple of months), but of course that never seemed to come to fruition. Sometimes I was so low on cash that I had to be creative to get my party beverages. I remember one night my landlord was having a party in the main house with her relatives and there were two huge boxes of wine located near my fridge. This was way too convenient, and I couldn't let this opportunity pass by. I filled a large plastic glass up about 5 or six times and crashed in my room that evening. I figured they wouldn't mind or even know, because it would be too hard to monitor the wine level in a box.

I had still been in contact with my friend Barry (formally of the print shop at the Company, former compadre in 'crime') and he had eventually gotten a really good job with a plumbing company. He had turned into quite an efficient plumber, able to learn quickly and do a great job with very few comebacks. I went with him on some of his calls every once in a while and we would talk about old times and I would tell him how shitty my life was compared to his. He told me about the house he and his family were renting in Maple Valley. He and his wife, Carole had been talking about my situation and wanted to help. I had always figured Carole would be holding the longest grudge against me because I know she felt it was my fault Barry had been fired from the Company. But he *did* have a great job now, and was making better money, so she figured maybe everything had worked out for the best. Anyway, they were offering a room in their place for me to stay rent free while I looked for a better job. I considered the fact that Maple Valley was pretty far out from the city (Bellevue, Seattle, anywhere) but they would help me get a car—as my Ford had recently bit the dust –something had caught fire in the engine before I had moved out of Mike's apartment, and it had never run since then. Well, what could I lose? Free rent, help with a car, rides to interviews, it seemed like a good idea at the time. So I accepted their offer, since I felt I was getting closer to being asked to move out of the room where I was currently staying anyway (I don't know, but I think I still may owe her my last month's rent). So I packed everything up and moved out to Barry's.

I spent about a month being lazy and not doing much. I would help out with chores around the house and help Carole when she had things to do and would help with watching the kids—they had three children, two girls and a boy I think between 5 and 10 years old at the time. They were all pretty well behaved kids and Carole was always good to them and home-schooled them. Carole's mother also lived at the house and helped out. I didn't do a lot of drinking, it seemed I was more relaxed and had cut back to just weekends, when Barry and I would go out and shoot some pool or play darts and have some beers. Barry and I would occasionally smoke some weed, but we were never really into raising hell or getting in trouble. Carole seemed to have a tight rein on things with Barry, which I will never disrespect her for. They had been married for a long time and though they fought like cats and dogs quite a bit of the time, I could tell they were very much in tune with each other and cared deeply for one another.

Back to the arbitration business once more, I remember when Barry and I were playing pool one afternoon at the bar (gee, I go to the bar a lot, don't I?) we overheard someone talking about how he was having a hard time getting a company to pay him for the equipment that he had installed for them. We started talking to him and ended up telling him we were in business of arbitration. I remember actually putting on my suit and tie and going to the Ocean Spray juice headquarters on his behalf one afternoon. After all was said and done there, left with my tail between my legs as they had told me I didn't know what I was talking about. I hung up my jacket and left that business to gather dust. Well that was good money wasted, so much for my bright idea once again.

I ended up with a job at the Motel 6 in Issaquah at the front desk working the afternoon shift and sometimes as the weekend night auditor when needed. It was not a hard job, and I seemed to do pretty well. The pay was minimum wage (seemed that's all I could get lately) but like I said before, it was money. And I *was* able to help out with some bills with my new income. The one bad thing about that house was that it was not very well insulated, and when it started to get into fall and winter, the electric bills began to double from what they were during the summer. We had to have heat, because I remember it was extremely cold winter, colder than most previous winters. What could we do?

I got to know most of the employees at the motel and they were all very likeable. One housekeeper in particular I found myself very attracted to and though it seemed she liked me as well, it was one of those 'as a friend' likes (funny how that happens). Clara and I did flirt a lot, and I remember one Christmas I gave her about 8 presents wrapped in newspaper, all items from the motel break room. She thought that was sweet, and she really enjoyed the attention.

I also became good friends with a married couple, Rosie and Bob, working at the motel. Bob was the maintenance man and Rosie was a housekeeper. They lived in a quaint little house in Issaquah and invited Clara and me over for barbeque many times over that next summer and never asked us to bring anything except for ourselves. They always supplied the food and all the beer. Bob and Rosie were big beer drinkers which did not bother Clara or me in the least. That meant we always have free beers whenever we went over to visit them, which became quite frequently.

I had met the owner of the plumbing company Barry worked for a few times, and Don seemed like a pretty likeable fellow. He invited me along a few times when he took Barry out to lunch and we seemed to get along well enough, One day Barry told me that Don had a line on a car that he thought would be great for me. I don't remember what the make and model was but it was an older four door sedan, not the best looking vehicle I had ever seen, but it did start every time and ran well enough to get me where I needed to go. Don ended up buying it himself and then sold it to me for $100 and let me make two payments. So now I had wheels and a bit more freedom, which felt great, let me tell you.

I remember one weekend, it was a Saturday because the liquor store was open, and for some reason I had parked in front of said liquor store in Issaquah. I didn't have any extra cash, so there really was no reason that I can remember doing that, but I recall when I opened the driver's door to get out, I noticed between my car and the car to the left of me there was a twenty dollar bill folded in half with a paper clip attached to it laying on the ground. I didn't know if it belonged to the guy in the car next to me, so

I pretended to look for something in the glove compartment to give that occupant the opportunity to retrieve the cash if he had dropped it. I heard the car back up and drive away and smiled when I saw the cash still sitting there. I couldn't believe my luck! Free cash! I picked up the $20 and it felt thicker than a single bill folded in half. I took off the paperclip and found five twenties and a five all together. What a great day that turned out to be, suddenly I was $125 richer than I was when I woke up that morning.

Now this is where I found out about my greedy side of myself. I did go into the liquor store and I think I bought about twenty bucks worth of vodka or bourbon or both and went back to the house and stashed my booze in my room. I didn't want Carole to know I found the cash, because I figured she would want me to donate more to the household bills and for food and those kinds of things. But my contention was that this was *my* windfall and there was no way in hell I was going to share it! I walked to the bar near the house later that afternoon and was playing pool and drinking beers and just enjoying my day when Barry came in. They had wondered where I was as I had not told anyone where I was going. Now you have to know that Barry was a great friend of mine, and I couldn't keep secrets from him very well, so I told him I had found the money and why I hadn't told anyone, and he did understand. I bought him whatever he wanted that night at the bar and we got home later than we had intended. Carole was pissed, more at Barry than at me. We just told her that we had been playing pool and were winning a lot so other people were buying the drinks. That seemed to placate her. I don't think Barry ever let on to Carole about my bonus discovery.

Our house was right on the Cedar River, which was known for flooding whenever it rained very hard or for many days in a row. It was right around Thanksgiving that the rains I just mentioned did occur. The river did in fact overflow, and flooded into the basement. I was lucky that I worked at the motel, so I was able to get a free room there for three or four nights, Barry and his family rode out the weather at the house, to make sure they could stave off any further damage that they were able to. On the second afternoon, Barry brought me back to the house to show me how bad things looked and I was dismayed to find all the stuff that I had stored in the basement pretty much destroyed. It wasn't much, some luggage, pictures, not really anything of true value, but some sentimental things none the less. He took me back to the motel and I watched some TV and went to bed.

The next day, I started my shift about one in the afternoon, and then started to feel somewhat feverish, and sweaty. I didn't think too much of it but about an hour later, I was dizzy and nauseous and called my manager out of his apartment that was attached to the office. He came out and told me that I should probably go back to my motel room and take the rest of the afternoon off. I thought that was just fine, so I left and went back to my room, turned on the TV and thought I might try some beer, to see if that would make me feel better. I think I took one sip and reclined on the bed, and dozed on and off for about an hour. I woke up and I was covered in sweat and was feeling worse than I had earlier in the day. Food did not sound good, beer sounded even worse. I called Barry and told him it might be a good idea to take me to a clinic or something, maybe I was coming down with something. Barry showed up about a half hour later and I was glad to see him. He asked how I was feeling but after looking at me he told me I didn't have to answer. Barry had to help me to the car, as I was feeling pretty weak and he ended up driving me to Overlake Hospital in Bellevue, to the emergency room. The triage nurse took my temperature and told me that they were going to set me up in a room, because they wanted to hook me up to an I.V. right away. Barry told me later that I said that was fine but if they were going to admit me, please do it before 8, because the TV show *Thirtysomething* would be starting then. That is the last thing I really remember until a few days later.

I recall bits and pieces of blood tests, doctors coming in and out, I heard that my Uncle from Bellevue and his wife visited me, Barry and Carole came by a few times. Finally I was becoming more coherent and the main physician tending to me said I was seriously lucky that I came in when I did. He said if I had waited another 24 hours I might have died. I looked at him with my mouth open. What was wrong with me? It turns out I'd gotten a blood infection. They told me when I was at the house during the flood, something had gotten into my system through an open sore or something (I have dry feet and sometimes I get cracks under my toes) and that I had developed Cellulitis, which is a very bad blood infection, which if goes unchecked can cause death, hence why I was admitted right away. I thought how lucky I was that Barry got me there when he did. I remember the person who handled insurance issues came in to see me a couple of times to get any information she could, but I told her that I had not worked at the motel long enough to qualify for anything yet... I think I had to be there for a year before I got insurance, or maybe I had never signed up or maybe didn't want to pay the extra or something stupid like that. So she had me fill out all kinds of forms and papers to see if I could qualify for welfare assistance (I never thought I would be in that position, but at that point, I was grateful there is that program!).

I spent a total of 8 days in the hospital I think and that was the first time since I had been a smoker that I had gone that long without a cigarette. That was great in itself! I thought that maybe it was a good time to quit, especially since I had a good head start. Nah, that didn't last. Sheri picked me up from the hospital (yes, she was still around, though I just hadn't seen her that much, every now and again) and I lit up a smoke in the car on the way back to Barry's house, which by that time was dry and put back together. I recuperated for about another week, as they didn't want me to walk much. One of my legs had swelled up so much with infection and needed time to heal itself, which was fine by me. That just meant a week of relaxing and doing nothing except watching TV and goofing off. The hospital bill came to over $10,000 and welfare ended up paying for most of it. Overlake wrote off the rest of the bill as a grant. I do remember I wrote the hospital a thank you note expressing my gratitude for them having basically saving my life, and thanking them for the grant to cover the cost of balance that Welfare had not paid for. I never received an acknowledgement for my letter, but that was okay, I was still sincerely grateful.

After about a week of being lazy, I became bored with all the hard work of doing nothing, so I called the motel and asked them if my job was still available, and I was relieved when they told me that they had not yet filled my position, and I was welcome to come back. Sometimes it is good to know you are liked well enough to have a job held for you while you are hospitalized. I went back to work and it felt great to be back with all of my friends from the motel. I quickly got back into the swing of things, and then about a week after that, we got new managers. At the Motel 6 it was not uncommon for managers to stay at one location for a little while and then be transferred elsewhere. When Del and Sandy arrived, I found that they were the nicest, most caring managers that we had had yet. Del would sometimes sit in our break room during lunch or before the housekeepers went home and chat with everyone or just sit by the window and play his guitar. He was very open and genuine. Every once in a while he would ask me when I was going to ask Clara out. I asked him what made him pose that question to me. He laughed and said it was obvious.

Bob and Rosie knew well that I liked her too, and would often try to play matchmakers for us, but Clara was stubborn and just wanted to keep things as friends. As frustrating as it was, I really have to admire her determination. It sometimes is true that friendships can suffer when they move past the friend category and then something happens to the relationship. Often you can never go back to being just friends. I think she had been there one too many times and maybe didn't want to risk it.

One day, Barry's boss stopped by motel and wanted to talk to me. I took a break and met him in the parking lot and he offered me a job with his company. I told him I knew nothing about plumbing, but he said it would be more taking care of a property he owned outside of Issaquah. It was an old hospital that he wanted to convert into some rental units. He told me that I could live there and earn a wage by performing upkeep on the property and the building, cleaning the place up and getting it ready for conversion. They were willing to pay a dollar more an hour than I was getting at the motel, and I would get free rent to boot! I talked to Del, and he told me that he would understand if I accepted the offer. He also told me that if it didn't work out as I hoped it would, he would let me come back again if there still was a position open. What did I have to lose? I think I have said that before. I probably will say that again. So I called Don up and told him that I had thought his offer over and that I would take the position.

I moved into the old hospital in North Bend and did odd jobs around the building, making myself productive and useful. I cleaned up all the rooms on the first floor and organized all the plumbing supplies that were stored in the basement. There was one section of the basement I opted to stay away from all the time. That was the old hospital morgue. Even in the middle of the day, it was very creepy and I always got the feeling that there were lingering spirits or something down there, it's hard to explain. And I never went down to the basement for any reason at all at night. You couldn't have paid me enough money. Maybe I had seen too many horror flicks in my time, but the fact was that I lived in an old hospital where people had died and their bodies were stored in the basement morgue -- that was creepy enough. I will never say that I saw any ghosts, but one day I was outside mowing the lawn and when I went back inside, there was a door in the main hallway that was standing open, and I know for a fact that before I had started my work, all the inside hallway doors were closed, and I was the only person who was there. That made the hairs on my neck stand straight up. I think I sat outside and had three or four beers before I was able to calm down enough to go back in. That was the only "supernatural" experience I had there.

I was still hanging around with Clara a lot, and she and I were maintaining a solid friendship, though I knew that if she had just let her defenses down, maybe even just a tiny bit, she would be able to admit that she was attracted to me as well. *Bob* and *Rosie* could see that Clara liked me; otherwise I don't think they would have tried as hard as they did to get us together. I remember one night we were all sitting at the pub we all liked to hang out at. We were eating appetizers and talking about the day's events. Clara was sitting next to me and the next thing I knew she took hold of my hand under the table and squeezed it tightly. It shocked the hell out of me. She leaned over and whispered in my ear that she really liked me too and wanted to be my girlfriend. I think that is what she said, it might have been more subtle or direct than that, but I recall being so uplifted and happy that you could have slapped my face and I still would have laughed.

Clara moved in with me at the old hospital and we lived there together for a few months until it became apparent that maybe Tom had become dissatisfied with me or my work, I don't know, but I was told one day that I would need to start paying rent the next month. I could deal with that, but the price he wanted me to pay was way more than the room offered. Maybe he somehow knew I had been smoking inside my room when he had told me there was to be no smoking inside and that pissed him off (that I could understand, that was blatant disregard of rules by me). I never found out what the reasons were, but after that I didn't feel welcome anymore. I had gone to Del at the motel and asked if my job was still available and he gladly welcomed me back to the front desk.Clara and I made arrangements to get an apartment together downtown Issaquah. We gave no notice to Tom and moved all of our belongings to the new place one morning and then we were done with Tom and the old hospital. That was no skin off of Barry's back, as he had always felt that things didn't seem right with that whole situation anyway.

Clara and I got along well together. We had a lot in common: we adored each other, we liked beer, we both smoked pot, and we both worked at the hotel. At one point we even considered applying for a manager's position with Motel 6 as a couple, but were told our chances wouldn't be all that good because Clara had quit and come back several times, so there would be a concern about that with those that made decisions about management.

As time went by, I think she may have grown tired of me or maybe our relationship I think because we were too laid back, always doing the same thing, working, drinking, seeing the same people, we were as predictable as they come. But when you don't make a lot of money and want to keep all the bills paid and make sure things don't fall behind, you have to make sacrifices. We just didn't have a lot of money to do a lot of different things. I remember one night Clara asked me if I minded if she went out and shot some pool by herself. I told her that was fine, I never wanted her to think that I owned her, or that we *always* had to do things as a couple, so off she went. I felt fine about it, but I think it was a sign of change in how things were changing between us.

Bob had a heart attack one day and had to be hospitalized, which left Rosie pretty devastated, so I stayed at her house for a few nights to keep her company and make sure she was okay. I didn't mind, because they always had an ample supply of beer at the house, and they also maintained tabs at a couple of the local pubs in town. So we went out for the next couple of nights and drank which seemed to keep her from a little distracted from her worries about Bob. Of course, I was always telling her that things were going to be okay, which he was, and he came home a few days later. He did have to stay home and recuperate for about a month before they would let him come back to work which I knew was very difficult for him.

I had been filling in for Bob in the maintenance position at the hotel while he had been gone, and somehow he had gotten it into his head that I had used his heart attack to get myself promoted into that position. I had been wondering why he would not talk to me and he would just glare with daggers in his eyes. Rosie eventually got that sorted out, and I was glad of that, because I loved both Bob and Rosie and couldn't bear going through any period of time with bad feelings. Besides, there was no way that I could ever fill Bob's shoes competently—my own mom had told as a child I was creatively inclined, not mechanically inclined.

Clara told me one night that she did not want to be a couple anymore. This came from out of left field, after we had been watching some TV together and having beers. I was kind of dumbfounded and didn't say anything. I don't know if I was too buzzed to understand or not, but I think I chugged my beer to the end and put it down and told her if that's what she wanted, that was fine with me. I don't think I said it rudely or crass, just matter of factly. Then I got up and walked out of the apartment and went on a walk. I had no idea where I was going, it was late at night but I just needed to get out of there. I was halfway down the street when I saw Clara's Mustang back out of the parking lot and pull into the street. I was thinking that wasn't too good of an idea. I doubt that either of us was sober enough to drive. I heard the tires squeal and then the car took off.

Clara eventually came home, as did I but we no longer were an item and she eventually moved out and got her own apartment in Renton. We did part amicably, which I thought was good, because she was a friend before, and I know she had been skeptical about the whole relationship thing for that exact reason, so I was glad that we were able to remain friends after we broke up.

So then it was just me in the apartment, well, except for the cat. I had gotten us a kitten a month or so back, thinking it would make a difference in our relationship when things had started to flounder. After Clara left, money became even tighter and I remember a time when there was nothing to eat in the place save for a can of Spam, that wonderful mystery meat product, which not even the cat would touch. I think I may have ended up at the food bank to get some supplies, not that I qualified for the food bank, but even *I* had to eat.

During the time I had the cat it went through at least two of its nine lives that I know of. The first was when Clara and I still lived together in the Issaquah apartment. There was an interesting frequent guest of the

Motel 6 that I had become acquainted with on a somewhat friendly basis; we had talked enough for me to know that he had led an interesting life, what with his failed marriage, some businesses that he had been in, his drinking, and I had told him that I was a writer, or a "writer-wanna-be" as it was. Somehow along the way, we got the notion that I could interview him and write a story about his life. Harmless enough, yes. So one Friday night (it could have been any night though, now that I think back) he came over to the apartment (probably not a good idea) and we got comfortable with some beers or whatever he was drinking, and I had paper and pen ready to jot things down as we talked. I remember Clara was gone somewhere so it was just the two of us, and the cat around somewhere, wandering as usual. We hadn't gotten too far into the interview when Clara did come through the front door and when she saw Mr. McCarthy, she looked at me and asked who he was. I told her and explained what we were doing. She looked a little rattled, probably because there was a stranger in her abode, and I hadn't told her what I had planned. Anyway, I have no idea what the cause was—what instigated what happened next. It could have been that she had been drinking. It could have been Mr. McCarthy had been drinking, hell, we all had been drinking, but something was said, and the next thing I knew, Mr. McCarthy had the cat in his hands and threw it at Clara. The cat missed her, but not by much. I remember the cat hitting the wall behind the chair and then disappeared. Clara became enraged and ran towards the door, screaming: "Get the fuck out! Get the fuck out NOW! I am going to call the cops!!" Then she slammed the door behind her. I was kind of stunned—you know how you feel when things become sort of surreal and dreamlike? That's how it seemed. Maybe I was just really buzzed and that helped the feeling, but I think I told him it might be a good idea to leave, that Clara was *pissed*! Mr. McCarthy did go. I don't remember if the police came over and talked to me, but Mr. McCarthy spent about 5 or 6 days in jail and then was evicted from the hotel. I think the moral of that little ditty is do not bring strange hotel guests home from work. Now, let's get back to my story.

Things got better between Clara and me, not to the point of getting back into a "thing" but she knew my money was tight and I don't remember the exact circumstances and I could be wrong about the exact order of things, but here is ultimately what happened:

Clara was seeing a new guy and planned to move in with him in Seattle. She was going to move out of the Renton apartment, where the rent was about a hundred dollars a month less than what I was currently paying. So she moved to Seattle and I moved into her apartment in Renton, taking over her lease. At the same time, I had come to really enjoy the hospitality business, and I figured that if I was going to try to make it a career, maybe I ought to get myself into a place that might be somewhat classier Motel 6, not that I disliked the company in any way, it was a great place to start my learning.

I saw an ad somewhere for a front desk position at a hotel in Kirkland, so I went and applied there. It was a smaller, really nice hotel in the Clarion luxury chain. A few days after I had applied, I was offered a job there working at the front desk and I accepted. It was a little difficult leaving Motel 6, not only because I had been there for close to 3 years, since 1990 but also because I had gotten close to most of the people who worked there. They were for the most part like my second family. But they were all pretty happy for me and they threw me a going away party, which was quite touching, as they didn't do that for many other people who left.

So I went to work at the Clarion (I don't think it has kept that name, but I heard the same people own the hotel) for about a month or two but apparently it was not a good fit for me with the owners and their ideas and goals for that hotel. I also felt that what was expected of me and the training I had received were not equating well together, but I do not regret the short time I spent working there. It had given me a taste of what it was like working in a different class of hotel than a Motel 6.

I happened to be in Bellevue one day on a weekday off from the Clarion prior to my leaving there and went into a smaller downtown Bellevue hotel and on a lark, filled out an application. They told me there that they currently were not hiring, but they said that I really should go over to their Redmond location and give the application to the manager there, as he might be interested in talking to me. So off I went and spoke to Todd, the manager who was awesome. He seemed excited to chat with me and I think that afternoon, I was asked when I could start. That was a good day indeed! I went back to the Clarion and gave my notice and at 31 years old, I was ready to start my hospitality career.

THE NEW CAREER

Working at the new hotel was a great new experience for me. It was a faster paced than Motel 6, but a lot less stuffy than the Clarion, so it felt to me to be the better of both of the worlds I had come from. I felt that I had made a correct decision in making the move that I had, which was a nice feeling because, as you know, some of my prior choices have left me in less than desirable positions. I really hoped that the new people I would be working with would be as cool as everyone was at Motel 6, and so far I had not been disappointed. Todd, my new manager was outgoing and seemed pleased to have me as a new addition to his team. I met Julie, the girl who worked the swing shift and there was one other girl whose name I can't remember, but they were both genuine and pleasant to get along with. We used a totally different system in reservations and the phone rang more times in ten minutes than it did at either of the prior places. I was quite overwhelming at first, but I picked up on things pretty quickly with the help of my co-workers. After a couple of days, I truly felt like a welcome part of the team. I think that is important, because after all, you spend more time with the people you work with than anyone or anywhere else.

Home life was pretty blasé as it was just me and my cat living in the two bedroom apartment. There really was more room than needed for single guy, but who was I to complain? It was cheaper than any place that I might have found on my own and I had been very fortunate to be able to take over Clara's lease when she had moved to Seattle to live with her new boyfriend. She and I had remained great friends and she came back over to visit me from time to time, and on one occasion introduced me to the bar that was across the street from the apartment, *Foxy's Bar and Grill* (I think it's a Christian bookstore and supply now).

Foxy's was a quaint little bar, which I thought it was more of a pub It wasn't the classiest of places, but certainly not the down and out dive, either. It had pool tables, dart boards and pinball machines, and Olympia on tap (which was my favorite beer at the time). I think they kept Olympia beer on tap mainly because of me because that's all I would drink when I was there—not only because it went down so smoothly, but it was also a dollar cheaper per pint than Bud or Coors. I almost cried when they finally took it out of the draft selection. But *Foxy's* to me was just like *Cheers* because it got to where the people who worked there knew me well enough that they would call me by name and I became somewhat of a regular, not that I necessarily should have been proud of that fact, but it is nice to be recognized. I got to know the guy who cooked in the grill, Gavin, and after a while, I would often order the "Gavin Special" to go. It was special because I never really knew what it was until I got home, but it was always good and for $5, it was a great deal—like a double cheeseburger with all the works and fries, or something like a Monte Cristo sandwich deluxe. I was never disappointed, I will tell you.

There would be dancing there on the weekends and one Saturday night it was confirmed that I was a horrible dancer. I heard that two different girls who did not know each other both had commented that I had no rhythm and hoped that I would never ask them to dance ever again. I thought that was funny, but also a little disheartening at the same time. But it was nothing that I did not already know. I just hope that one day I will find someone who will look beyond my idiotic awkward looking dance moves and teach me rhythm, have the patience to make me into a prince on the dance floor. But that is not a deal breaker.

The big blue car that I called the wobbly beast finally developed alignment/suspension problems so bad that anymore I was afraid to drive it, because I never knew if I would find myself in the opposite lane or just lose my steering capability all together. Clara must have been a psychic because I got a call from her one day. She was getting a newer car and wanted to know if I wanted to buy her Mustang. I couldn't have had better luck if I had purchased a twenty dollar scratch ticket and got a huge winner. I told her about my car and she said she'd give me a good deal on hers: $300, payable in 3 monthly payments or something like that. It was a deal that no sane man would pass up. So after thinking about it for about a second, I happily told her I would take it! I think I got a ride over to Seattle with Barry and drove back to my place in my "new" car. It was a yellow two-door Mustang that was in great shape and I drove it forever. Well, at least until one fateful day, which I will tell you about shortly.

Work was going very smoothly and I learned the swing shift and started training part time on the night audit for the weekends. We used a big book where we would physically write down in the big reservation book on the line that corresponded to the room number and the date. It was actually a good system because one could instantly see how things were each day and could pick the room at the time the reservation was made. If things were done correctly, mistakes were minimal, but it was necessary to use a pencil with a good eraser when using the book because there were always changes being made. Of course computers are used now, but it is fun to think back as I write this how much simpler things were back then.

It had been a while since I had had any decent sexual encounters so I remember trying out those free chat lines that are always found in the back section of the *Seattle Weekly*. I ended up talking (it was actually trading messages until a live chat was accepted) to one sexy sounding girl and she asked me what my fantasy was. I told her that it would be to have a sexy young woman come to my hotel one night when I was working graveyard and be wearing a long coat covering a scantily clad body, seduce me and then have passionate sex with me. She said that was a cool fantasy and that maybe someday it would come true. I had to agree, I hoped it would come true as well, but I knew it was only a chat line and that every guy must have that same fantasy.

One night about two weeks later I had just finished my night reports at the hotel and a girl walked in and asked if I had any rooms left. I looked and told her I did and she asked what the rates were. This was not an unusual occurrence, so I thought nothing of it. She told me she was just interested in the hotel business and we ended up sitting on the couch together in the lobby and talking about things for a little while. It was a nice diversion and I had a lot of free time. It was only about 2 am, and I didn't have to start getting the continental breakfast ready for a couple of hours yet. She then asked me if there was a more private place in the hotel where we could go. I asked her what she meant, because I seriously didn't have a clue what she was going for. She asked me if I remembered talking to someone about fantasies on the phone before, and then I think my eyes opened wide and I my jaw almost went to the floor. I asked if she was the girl I had talked to on the chat line and she smiled. I must have silently thanked any powers that be for this great surprise and for just a brief moment the thought occurred to me that this was wrong to be doing something like this at work, but at that point, there was not a lot of thinking going on in the big head. So I took her in the back and she took off her long coat and I saw a slender body covered in lingerie. I told her I really had not been prepared and didn't have any protection; she told me not to worry. She said she had just had some surgery done, so it was okay, but because it had just been done recently, she asked if I would be gentle. She undid my pants and sat me down in the chair and then sat on top of me and that was one of the wildest unexpected surprises I could remember. When we were done, she got herself together, kissed me and thanked me. We exchanged numbers, though I was pretty sure I would never hear from her again. She left and then I scrambled to make sure everything was in place as I was starting to feel a little guilty about what I had done so I wanted to make sure there would be no evidence of our encounter. I thought to myself that things like that happen only once in a lifetime so I should just enjoy the memory—I could always use that as lighter fluid whenever I was going to "barbecue alone." Turned out that she did call me up a few more times for a few more encounters, always out of the blue but I always somehow seemed to be ready for the unexpected.

Clara had really been into the band "Nirvana" and really took it hard when Kurt Cobain committed suicide, and I saw her drinking a lot more, trying to drown her pain over the loss of one of her beloved musicians. I remember going to see her a few times, trying to console her and ended up drinking right along with her, both of us ending up getting hammered, which I really didn't mind. But after a while, I think Clara realized that she was headed down a bad path, and decided to start going to AA. I remember she talked me into going to a meeting with her, maybe she thought it might do me some good as well. It seemed to be okay, but all I got out of it was a bunch of people sitting around a bunch of tables drinking a lot of coffee and smoking a lot of cigarettes. They talked about how drinking and alcohol had affected their lives and that they were glad to be there and share their stories and their camaraderie to help them stay sober. I wasn't really paying too much attention anyway, because I was just there to support Clara, I had no reason to be there myself, after all, I wasn't an alcoholic. I remember after she and I left and I had gotten home, I couldn't wait to pop open an ice cold beer! But I also knew that if Clara really wanted to quit drinking, I would support her as best I could.

I mentioned earlier that my cat had gone through two of its nine lives, so I now I'll tell you about the second time. The cat used to love to sit on the window ledge in the living room and stare out onto the parking lot two stories below. Occasionally I would open the window to let fresh air in, and I was pretty apprehensive when the cat would sit there because I didn't have a screen on the window. I think sometime before I had moved in, it had fallen out and was never replaced. Anyway, occasionally when it got overly stuffy or hot in the apartment, I would open the front door to let the cross breeze blow through the apartment which cooled things down rather quickly. One time when I had done that, I was in the back bedroom looking for something and I heard a loud screech and then I some scraping noises and then silence. Then I think the phone rang, and forgot about the noises. About 10 minutes later when I realized I hadn't seen the cat I began to get a bad feeling. I went to the living room window and pulled the billowing curtain aside and started to look out, dreading what I thought I would find. There was my cat lying on the pavement below, appearing quite motionless! I ran out of the apartment and down to the back parking lot below the window and when I reached the cat, I saw his chest moving, so I was relieved that he was alive, though his breathing seemed labored. I gingerly picked him up and he seemed to be okay, pretty dazed and his nose was scratched up. I took him back up to into the apartment and set him on the floor. He ran into the bedroom and went under the bed and I didn't see him for a while. After a few days, he came out and apparently was hungry as he went to his food dish and ate and drank his water and seemed to be back to normal, though I never saw him sitting on the window ledge again.

I had a couple of different roommates while I was living at the Renton apartment, the first was Ray, a friend who I had met at Motel 6 before I had left there. Ray was hired at the front desk, and we had gotten to know each other quite well in a short period of time. He was laid back and I remember that he didn't drink alcohol, but he smoked cigarettes and also liked pot same as me. He had just broken up with a girlfriend I think, and he ended up needing a place to stay, so I asked him if he wanted to share my apartment with me—it would benefit us both, sharing the rent and utilities, and he agreed and moved in.

I had been calling the chat lines more and had been talking to one girl quite a few times, and we started having fun with phone sex. To me it was kind of exciting because she had such a sexy, seductive phone voice, and it really was a turn on. She seemed to be having just as much fun as I was. I was totally discreet about the whole thing, not doing any of those actions when Ray was around, because of course, that would just be wrong, not to mention, totally embarrassing. There was one time when she and I were heavy in the middle of our seductions, if you get my meaning, where the phone was being held with only one hand, when I heard a key in the front door lock. I don't think I have ever moved so fast to cover myself up with whatever was closest to me, thank God there was a blanket or a towel already on the couch (what the hell was I thinking doing that in the living room, anyway), and then Ray walked in. I hoped I didn't look as pathetic as I felt... I am sure that he must have had an idea of what was going on, nobody is *that* stupid, but he did not give any indication of noticing. I may have told him that I was talking to a special friend and he told me that I should just invite her over, or go meet her, or something. He thought that talking on the phone all the time was one thing, but if there was the possibility of meeting and getting something for real, why not go for it? He was right, of course, but I wanted to do that when I was ready, and for whatever reason, I was just more comfortable with talking to her on the phone...maybe I was afraid that the face and body would be totally different from the sexy voice, and I didn't want to face that disappointment. Having sex on the phone with a fantasy vision in mind is one thing, but if in reality she was huge or unattractive, then that could make for an ugly situation.

One morning, I think a Saturday, I woke up to the sound of my bedroom door opening. Ray came in and he had a smile on his face, and his excitement was obvious. He told me not to be mad, but he had wanted to surprise me with something he thought was nice. I asked him what it was, looking at the clock and noted how early it was (9 am?) and he told me just to come out into the living room and I would see. Ray wouldn't take "no" for an answer, he was just too excited, so I threw on some jeans and a t-shirt and followed him out into the living room. I saw a girl that I didn't recognize and Ray introduced her as the girl I had been having phone sex with for the past month or so. I was quite shocked that she was there, sitting in my apartment. Now, ordinarily, I would think I'd be happy to have a girl show up who was willing to have sex with me on the phone and because wouldn't she also be willing to have sex with me in person as we had talked about? Instead, I took offense that Ray had taken it upon himself to arrange this whole scenario for me. I cannot remember any specific reason that caused my anger, I mean, the girl was not ugly, she was not fat, she didn't have pimples or crooked teeth that I could see. The only thing that was the least unappealing about the girl was that she looked like she had just gotten out of bed and her hair was unkempt and a little oily. I managed to smile at her and shook her hand as I introduced myself formally to her and then made up some quick excuse as to why this was not a good time for her to have come over and that maybe she could come back another time. The problem was that she had not come over on her own. Ray had gone to pick her up because she did not have a car. I ended up driving her back to her place over in the University district and then came back to have a talk with Ray.

I don't remember what I said to Ray, but he told me that she had called while I was asleep and she and Ray had talked for a bit, when Ray suggested that he could drive over and pick her up, bring her back and surprise me, and she had apparently liked the idea. I don't know if it was because it hadn't been my idea, or maybe I thought that the whole thing was an invasion of my privacy by him conspiring with her, or what exactly set me off, but I think that changed the whole course of our friendship. I remember that we did not talk to each other for about a month, though not out of his effort, Ray did try to smooth things out in that time, but I was so bull-headed and would not let go of my grudge. He eventually moved out and soon after got married, though I did end up warming up to him a little before he left. The last I had heard, Ray was managing his own Motel 6 for a while and now relocates RV's across the United States for a company. What a cool job that must be!

After I had been at the Redmond location of the hotel for a year, I had obviously made enough of a good impression to the powers that be that I was asked if I would like to transfer to the downtown Bellevue hotel and help to establish a better running front desk. I thought that would be a good move, as that location catered to more of a business clientele and might give me a more professional experience to add to my resume. I happily consented to the transfer and made the move.

The atmosphere was indeed a little more stiff than I was used to but I was able to acclimate my personality accordingly with relative ease. The front desk staff was just as friendly and easy to get along with as the

Redmond location, so I seemed to blend in pretty well and make friends quickly. I was now working more in the morning and early afternoon hours, so I was able to become more acquainted with the housekeeping staff than I had at the previous location, which I liked. I found myself becoming quite attracted to one housekeeper in particular, and she must have felt the same way, because it seemed like every time I went out to the back of the hotel to the designated break area to have a smoke, Luella was always not far behind and we would sit and talk about the hotel, life, just about anything. The more I talked with her, the more I got to know her, I found out she was an amazing lady, a very hard worker and a wonderful asset to the hotel. I had noticed a ring on her ring finger, and asked if she was married, and she said she was, so I made sure our little flirtations did not go beyond any questionable level, as I had decided I was done doing anything with married women.

We went through a few front desk agents during the time I was there, but one of the new agents we had hired was a young lady with gorgeous auburn hair and a pretty smile. Her voice was pleasant with a little nasal twang, and we seemed to get along fine. Rachel had a boyfriend, but the way she acted around me, I figured they were not serious or they were going to be breaking up soon. Rachel never really said anything good about him during any of our conversations as far as I could remember. I thought that was too bad for him, but then again, that would be cool for me, because maybe she would go out with me if I asked her. I think it was a couple of weeks later that I did muster up enough courage to ask her out, and she told me no, that she did not date people she worked with. I told her I understood that, which really, I did. I wish in retrospect that I had not been so damn persistent in my pursuits. A couple of weeks after that, I don't know whether it was a date, or how it came about, but Rachel had come over to my apartment in Renton, and I think we had a beer or two there (she wasn't quite of age to get into the bars yet, though I think I got her in once across the street at the pub). We watched a little TV and we started making out on the couch. It got a little heavy and she stopped us, saying we shouldn't be doing this and again mentioned her rule about dating guys from work. I don't know what I said, but this is what I remember. We ended up on the living room carpet (the curtains were closed I am sure) naked and having hot wonderful sex. I don't remember that we used anything but nothing came back to haunt us. We talked about things afterwards and there would be no attachments or anything, it was a pretty much no-strings deal. I was fine with that, but I hoped that we could do that again.

My older brother was living in an apartment complex that was close to both locations of work, and we had been talking before about the possibility of me moving in with him so that we could both save money on rent. It would also benefit me in that my work commute would be cut in half. Before I hadn't taken that conversation seriously, but now I wondered if it wasn't such a bad idea. I knew it would save me money on gas, not to mention the wear and tear of the Mustang. He and I never gotten along particularly well when we were kids, but now that we were both adults, we seemed much better—guess that just has something to do with growing up. So we talked again about rooming together and he told me that his young son could sleep with him and I could use the second bedroom for myself. The more I thought, the more convinced I was that it just might work out. So I gave notice to my landlord, and packed up all my things and was able to slowly make the move to Bellevue.

I usually had Tuesdays and Wednesdays off from work, and I remember one Tuesday afternoon around 2pm, I was driving back to my apartment after taking some of my boxes to my brother's place. I was heading south on I-405 and I remember there was almost no traffic to speak of. I had just gone through the tunnel north of the I-90 interchange and there was a small Mazda pickup truck about 6 car-lengths ahead of me. All of a sudden the pickup jerked and swerved to the right and then to the left, and I remember thinking that was odd, it seemed a bit early for somebody to be driving drunk! Then I saw a huge tire attached to a wheel bounce over the Mazda and instantly I knew what had caused the driver's quick maneuver. And then my eyes went wide as I realized it was bouncing straight toward me! The only thing that I had time to do was to quickly try to veer to my left and then there was a loud crash and it sounded as if a stick of dynamite had exploded inside my car. The back window blew out and the front windshield shattered, but did not completely break out being it was comprised of safety glass. I opened my eyes and realized I was still driving, though my head was tilted left towards the side window because the roof had been caved in. The wheel had hit my car dead center of the roof. I looked down at myself to see if I was bleeding and all I saw was glass shards all over me and the front of the dash, but there was no blood on my shirt or arms. I looked to my left and saw a car pass, its occupants staring at me in open gaped wonder. I could only give them a bemused smile and shrug. I was about two exits from where I had to get off the freeway and then my apartment was only a couple of minutes from there. So since I was still able to drive, I was determined to make it home. I parked in a stall and turned off the engine, got out and surveyed the damage.

There was a huge skid mark in the middle of an indentation in the center of the roof and as I looked at that I realized had I not made that quick jerk to the left, the wheel would have hit exactly right above my head. I sincerely doubt I would have survived that blow. It was then that I realized that I had once again almost died and I thanked my higher power profusely as anyone would have had they gone through what I did. That was the last time I drove the Mustang.

I got on the phone and called the police and told them what had happened and asked them what I should do, They told me that I needed to file a report with the Washington State Patrol, that since I was on the freeway it would be their jurisdiction. So I called them and they started to tell me that I needed to call the police. I was getting irritated and just a little pissed off that I was being given the runaround. After all, I could have been killed and sounded like they gave a shit! I called the state patrol back and told them they were who I was supposed to file a report with. I gave someone all the necessary information and they did call me back within the hour. They said that a trucking company had reported one of their trucks was missing an entire wheel and it hadn't been noticed until the truck stopped at a weigh station. The wheel had apparently come off while the truck was travelling northbound and bounced over the median into the southbound lanes, where it had struck me. The driver had not noticed anything because the truck was empty, so when the wheel came off, it did not cause any difference in the way the truck handled. The state patrol searched the entire area around where I had reported the accident and never did find the missing wheel. I told them there was no possible way I had made up the story, and I had taken pictures of the damage.

After all was said and done, I was finally contacted by the trucking company and they offered me a settlement check of $500, which I thought that was quite an insulting paltry amount considering what I had gone through. I asked the guy I was talking to on the phone how he would feel if his son or daughter was in the same situation…would he feel that was enough compensation? There was a silence on the phone and then he said he was not authorized to answer a question like that. I told him that was fine, he just answered my question. I hung up.   My brother had me talk to an attorney friend of his and I don't think I was very satisfied with my results of that conversation. I don't remember getting any sure fire advice of suing the trucking company so I did not go back to see him again. My brother was sure I could get more from that company and said I should wait and not cash the check. He said if I did, there would be no way to open the case back up. My brother was kind of miffed when I told him I had already deposited the check into my account. Hell, I figured that $500 was better than nothing, and the extra money would come in handy for something. I just wanted the whole thing to be over with. I did get an extra $50 from a company that bought cars "as is – running or not" and they even came and got it.

A couple of weeks later after I had moved in with my brother, I ended up getting another car for an amazing low price from a neighbor of his that had to move unexpectedly, I think like $50. It was a 1982 Mazda GLC (afterwards known as the Glick) and I had that for a number of years. It had a standard transmission, but that didn't bother me…there were no hills to speak of in Bellevue so I would not have to worry about that. I cannot drive a stick shift on steep hills…I tried that once in Seattle with the Mustang and while trying to back into a slanted parking spot on a hill, I panicked and cars started honking behind me and I finally stopped the car, put on the e-brake and said "Fuck it!!" and made a friend who was with me handle the parking.

So now I was sharing an apartment in Bellevue with my brother and his young son, who I think was no older than about 4 years old or something like that. Things were okay and work was fine and things were getting better with Rachel, too.

I had been told before that it was not a good idea to form personal romantic relationships with those you work with, and I believed that to be true. Certainly I had learned my lesson with the Martha debacle, but I knew that with me and Rachel things were different. Besides, we were just starting to get closer, we were not getting married and I would be careful not to let things interfere with my work. At that point, we were just friends anyway, though with occasional benefits, that was all.

Rachel was living at her father's house and had told me several times that she wasn't happy there. She said he was too strict and demanding, always wanting to know where she was and wanted her home by certain times. She did not want that. This all seemed normal enough to me, she was just a young woman, wanting to get out and find her own space, start living her own life, that's all. What could be wrong with that?

I don't know that there was ever an official statement or anything about how things were between us, but at some point, we were pretty much hanging out with only each other, and we seemed to be comfortable with that. I knew at least I was. I had brought her over to the apartment and introduced her to my brother, and I got the feeling that he was comfortable with Rachel, which made me feel good, not that I needed his approval certainly, but it was nice. After all, he was my brother and his opinions did seem somewhat cool to me.

I came up with an idea that I thought would help Rachel with her situation and would be beneficial to me at the same time. I asked her what she thought about moving in with me and my brother and his son. Then she wouldn't have to worry about the demands and problems with her father. She thought about that and said she was okay with that, though she didn't think her father would be too keen on the idea, but that if things were cool with my brother, she would worry about things on her end. After I got home from work one night, I broached the subject with my brother, and he thought about it for a little bit and then told me that things might be a little tight, space wise anyway, but if that was what I wanted to do, it would be okay with him. I told Rachel and she seemed pleased and then life seemed all the better. We ended up going to her father's and got a lot of her clothes and things she needed and then she moved in.

The work situation was such that she and I never were there much at the same times, as I was mainly covering the night audit shifts so at most I would see Rachel for an hour or two, then I would be solo for the remainder of that day's (or nights as it were) hours. I think we had the same days off, so we had time to do things together. Like I said previously, we really got along so well together and I felt more comfortable with her than I had when I was dating Martha, so I thought that was a good thing... it was different and I took that as a good sign. And the sex we had together was amazing! The weird thing was that she chose to sleep on the couch in the living room, which at the time didn't really bother me too much, after all, though we were seemingly in an exclusive relationship, that didn't mean that we had to sleep every night together in the same bed. I didn't want her to think I was so demanding that I thought she *had* to be with me every night, I didn't want to come across as the overbearing and demanding type of guy that I had seen of some friends that I knew. Besides, she had gotten enough of that from her old boyfriend and from her father, as she had told me.

Rachel's birthday was coming up, and it was her special one, she had said. I asked why and she said she would be legal. I guess I had never really paid attention if she had told me how old she had been before, because I remember being a little surprised that she had been under 21, not that that would have made a difference; it actually made me feel kind of good, here I had a much younger woman who was interested in me... that's always been a guy's dream, to go out with a younger woman, anyway. But the bad thing was that I had to work that weekend and I would not be able to go out with her and celebrate. Rachel seemed to be disappointed, but she told me that it was okay, she understood. I don't know if it was my idea or hers, but it was suggested that she could go with my brother, he would make sure she had a good time and got home safely. I don't think I saw Rachel until the next day or after, just due to my work and sleeping schedule, but when I finally caught up with her, she assured me she had a great birthday and was glad my brother was there, though she wished of course I had been there too. I don't know what it was, but it seemed like after that, Rachel and I were starting to spend less and less time together, even though we did hook up for great sex from time to time, and for some reason, that always seemed to make things better, at least for me, it is such an intimate bonding between two people and that closeness has to mean something, doesn't it? Anyway, I thought so.

I was asked by a friend who worked at the Redmond hotel if I would spend the weekend at his apartment and watch his cat and dog while he went out of town to visit his parents and I told him that of course I would. I asked if he minded if I had Rachel over, as I thought that might give her and I some quality time together without my brother or his son around, just some Steve and Rachel time where we could do whatever we wanted with nothing to bother us. He said that would be fine. I had that weekend off, so it sounded perfect to me. She worked during the morning shift so she could come over after she got off and I could make us dinner and we could cuddle and whatever. I don't think she made it over the first night, something came up and I thought that was okay, it was kind of cool just being in a new place that was quiet and not cramped like things were in my brother's apartment. The second night Rachel did come over and it was pretty nice although she did spend a lot of the time on the phone, talking to some friends and then to my brother. I wondered why she would be talking to him, but I think she said he just wanted to know what time she would be coming home for some reason. They ended up talking for over a half hour and I spent a lot of that time out on the porch smoking cigs and watching her, starting to feel jealous. We may have ended up watching some TV and then I remember we went to bed and did have what I thought was the best sex we had ever had. I was so spent that I had collapsed and she finally pushed me off and said not to take offense, but she didn't like the feeling of soggy rubber inside. I think that was the last intimate moment we shared together.

I sensed things were going south after that, and not just with Rachel. There were a few times that I think I asked my brother if he wanted to have a beer, or maybe go to a movie, but he always had to do this or that, and I was getting the feeling that I was getting the run-around, or maybe just the brush off. He seemed to be giving Rachel more time than me, his own brother. Then one night Rachel was complaining about not feeling well, and when I asked her what was wrong, she said she had a bad yeast infection. I went down the store and got what I could to help her out, to make her feel better, even though it was almost midnight; I thought that might show her that I still cared and would do anything for her. Ultimately I don't think it helped much. That infection seemed to last for quite a while, but what did I know about female things, really? My ex had never had one of those as far as I could remember. I think one night Rachel came into the room and she actually started making moves on me, though I think it was more to make me feel less neglected rather than out of true affection, and to this day I still remember what came out of my mouth instead: "what about your infection?" She pulled herself off of me and said, "Oh, yeah, that's right." She then tucked her shirt in and left the room. There were other indications that a change needed to be made, as I was starting to really feel less and less important around that apartment.

I started to hang out more and more in the bedroom by myself, I just didn't feel up to watching TV or playing computer games sitting on the couch with Rachel and my brother, and going out to the bars alone seemed to be expensive, so I would buy a 12-pack here and there and just party with myself watching the little color TV next to the bed in my room. I had started smoking in the bedroom, even though I had told my brother that I would only smoke outside, but I figured that if I kept the window open and blew the smoke outside, maybe light a scented candle or two, he would never know. I kept a stash of beer in the closet hidden behind my boxes of personal things that I had no room to put elsewhere and would just empty out the trash after everyone went to bed or when I was home alone. I don't know why I didn't want them to know I was drinking alone, maybe I didn't want them to care, or maybe I thought it would hurt more to find out they didn't care if they knew.

After a couple weeks went by, I had already started looking at cheap apartments; I was trying to come up with a contingency plan because I knew that the day would come when I would need a place to go. I remember one of the most embarrassing moments when I was just overwhelmed with how things were falling apart. Rachel had come in and we had somehow come to the realization that things were just not working out between us and all of the sudden it became apparent to me that we had just broken up. It all seemed to happen so fast, and I remember she left the room and I may have popped open a beer and drank it, probably did. My brother came in and asked if I was all right. Funny now that I think about it, he must have known what had happened otherwise why would he ask that? Anyway, I told him that I was not really. I told him that I had been thinking about moving out and when he asked why, I told him that I just didn't really feel welcome and that every time I asked if he wanted to do something, he always would tell me he was too busy. I suppose right then I was reaching out for my brother, reaching out for some kind of support, but I never got it. All he told me was that he **was busy**; he had a family to look out for and support. I told him that I thought I was family, and I don't remember what he said to that or if he did, but I remember that I started crying, I don't know if it was outright sobbing, but I think I told him that he could get out now, I didn't want to be seen like that. He left and that's all I really remember about that. I know that I found a little one bedroom apartment in a complex on 156th in Bellevue close to the mall and moved out the next week. It was the middle of February, and I remember getting a hell of a deal: I think I got a half off the first full month and they waived the deposit.

That first week after I moved into my new pad, I got drunk pretty much every night, I know that wasn't the best way to be living, but it sure made the nights easier to handle. Otherwise nights were the worst. My ritual was simple. I would buy a half rack of whatever beer was on special and then at a certain point during the evening, I would switch to vodka somethings or bourbon somethings. That was pretty much my nightly routine for the first week. I remember one morning during one of the more pronounced hangovers trying to get into the shower tub and I slipped and sliced a nasty cut between my toes. That is really the worst place to try and keep a Band-Aid secure, let me tell you, and it also hurt like a mother fucker! As you probably have seen by now that I don't swear a whole lot in my writing, but when I think back at how that felt that is the first term that comes to my mind.

I had some good friends from the Bellevue hotel that would come over and console me and help me with my grief and kept me from getting too depressed. One girl worked at the front desk with me and I think was using that excuse to spend more time with me because she really liked me and never really had a chance to tell me or let on because I had been so stuck on Rachel, but I still never picked up on that because of my state of mind. There's more to that story, but we'll get to that in a little bit. I was just glad for the company, believe me, it is better if you are going to drink to do it with people. But with others or not, I was getting good at escaping into my little world with the liquid help.

We had a new maintenance chief start at the Bellevue hotel, and I was told he came with a lot of good experience and that he would be a great asset to the hotel. Before Rob started there, I don't even remember who the person was that he replaced. Anyway, when I met Rob, I found him to be a very pleasant person who was funny, yet serious, seemed very knowledgeable about things without sounding boastful. He was easy to become friends with and I remember there were three or four of us from the hotel that went out one weekend and by the way we were interacting, it seemed as if we had had known each other for a long time. We soon became the best of friends. We still are to this day.

I was out back in the smoking area one afternoon enjoying (what else-- A smoke) when one of my co-workers came out and joined me. I had been doing a lot better the last couple of weeks in coping with the Rachel thing and had seriously cut back on the drinking, and seemed to be back to more of my normal self and I could tell that my friends really appreciated that. I was glad that Rob had not known me during the really bad times; he just came in at the very end of the recuperation – but anyway, I can't remember her name now, but as we talked, she said that she knew something that she had been wanting to tell me for a quite a while, but had just never know when would be the best time. I know I was very curious and asked her what the news was. I could tell she really didn't want to tell me and she admitted to that. She said that she didn't want to hurt me, but thought that I should know.

She went on to tell me that she had overheard Rachel bragging to someone about some great night that she had had the night of my birthday (I worked night audit that night). That had been months ago and Rachel had told me that she hadn't planned on doing anything because I wasn't going to be home, and she wanted to celebrate it with me. I thought that was odd... but I told my friend to keep telling me what she had heard. Apparently Rachel was telling that person how that was the first night that she had slept with my brother. I remember being in shock, I couldn't believe what I had just heard. I asked her if she was sure that was what Rachel had said. She said that unfortunately that was what she had heard, and I had no reason to believe that she was making up the story. All of my friends had been very supportive of me, though some I am sure were dying to tell me the "I told you so" thing and that's why you don't date someone that you work with. My friend told me that she was sorry, that she probably should not have told me, but I assured her that it was okay, it was most likely something I would have found out about sooner or later. I remember going home that night and skipping the beers, heading right for the hard stuff. I knew Rachel was working that night so I called her at work and told her that I knew what she had done and she said "oh, God, I am so sorry…" I don't remember exactly what I said in return, but I'm know I didn't blow up anything, I just hung afterwards feeling empty. I then thought that if I called her out on the deal, I shouldn't leave my brother out, so I called him as well. When he answered I said "I know what you did with Rachel." There was a pause and he said, "So?" I couldn't believe it…it just sounded so cold that it truly caught me off guard and all I could think to say was "you are no longer my brother" and hung up the phone. A minute later the phone rang and I saw on the caller ID that it was him calling back so I didn't answer, I just let it ring. There was no message left and I then proceeded to drown my sorrows in my booze.

I don't know how I was able to deal with everything but somehow I did, thanks to copious amounts of booze and also by disassociating myself from everything. I am sure that my work performance suffered, and the next few months went by pretty much in a blur. I did get a letter from my younger brother soon after, as he had heard what had happened from Mom. It was very supportive and said under no circumstances should I even think about taking Rachel back, not even if she begged for my forgiveness, that I should just forget about that part of my life and move on. He told me it wouldn't be easy, but he had been through bad breakups of his own and he got through things, so I could as well… life does go on. He was right, but I think what made it different was the unusual situation of what and how things had happened. Mom wanted me just to forgive and forget; just to get things back to the way things should be with my brother, and I knew that although eventually I could forget, forgiveness would be much harder. All I ever wanted, ever needed was just to hear the words "I'm sorry" from him and that would begin the healing and help to let things go.

For a while, even though I knew it was idiotic and insane, I really missed things the way they used to be with Rachel. We still worked at the same place, so I had to see her, not every shift or every day, but she was always around, which made forgetting more difficult. I had it in my mind that maybe we could put what happened behind and get back together,

184

regain some of the closeness that I thought that we shared (how quickly I had forgotten what my younger brother told me in his letter). I sent Rachel flowers once and even went to a psychic to see if she could get us back together. I was acting like a crazy person. Of course the psychic did not make a difference. Of course the flowers did not make a difference. I was dealing with a young girl who didn't know what she wanted in life, she wasn't ready for anything steady, nor should she be! But then I tried a new strategy, maybe if I could get her to feel sorry for me, she would come back to me. I thought that if she knew what emotional turmoil I was going through, it might make a difference, so I would leave the yellow pages open at work, to psychiatrists or therapists, in hopes she would see that and put two and two together, maybe ask me about it or start some form of communications. But of course I had forgotten who I was dealing with and of course that did nothing but probably cause me more embarrassment. I think I just got tired of things or just plain gave up, whichever the case, she was let go from the hotel not long after, not because of what had happened, but something unrelated. Then it was out of sight and out of mind. She did live with my older brother for a while after that, but sooner than later, I had heard she had moved out of his apartment and I have no idea where she is to this day. Well, actually now I do, and perhaps that will be highlighted in the second "Steve's Story" book.

I still had been keeping in touch with my friend Mike who I had lived with after my split with my ex-wife, and one Saturday afternoon, he called and asked me if I wanted to go with him to where he got massages and check it out. I thought that sounded cool, since I was not working that day and so he picked me up and we drove to a house pretty near where I lived. It was an older, smaller house, on a side road, not at all a "Street of Dreams" home, but not a total fixer-upper either. I looked at Mike and asked him if this was really the place, as there was no sign or anything advertising it as a place of business. He assured me it was the place. We went to the front door and he knocked and a moment later the door opened and an older lady looked out. She obviously recognized Mike as she smiled and opened the door wide and told us to come in. She looked at me a little skeptically, but Mike told her I was cool. He said I was here for a massage as well, and I think she had me write my name and phone number on a card and I was then given a little ticket stub, like you get when you purchase a raffle ticket. Another girl, younger and cuter than the first lady came out wearing spandex pants and a robe. She smiled at Mike and she escorted him out of the main room into the back. I was told to have a seat and wait for a little bit. I looked and saw some old magazines on the coffee table and before I was able to get into any articles, I heard my name called. The lady that called my name was okay looking, nothing to write home about, but she was also wearing something tight with a loose fitting pullover. She took me into a back room that had a massage table and a small dresser with a boom box stereo and some lit candles next to it. She told me to take off my clothes and lay on my stomach and she would be back in a few minutes.

I was a little caught off guard by the disrobing command, but I thought that maybe that's the way they did things there, so I complied and got on the table on my stomach. She came back in and placed a sheet over me and started the massage. She didn't really massage me as much as run her hands all over my back and legs and then I felt her using what felt like a feather duster as she slowly pulled down the sheet. It was very strange, but exciting at the same time. The music was some Middle Eastern exotic type and added to the atmosphere and I found myself getting pretty turned on, in spite of my trying not to. She then told me to turn over on to my back, which I was completely embarrassed to to do, since the first thing that she would notice would be the tent that my happy friend was causing. She told me it was okay, not to be shy. So I thought what the hell and did. Then it occurred to me (why it took so long I think I am just dimwitted sometimes) that this was not your ordinary type of massage parlor. This was a "happy endings" massage place! And that is exactly what she provided. She was pretty thorough and nicely cleaned me up and before she left the room, she asked me if I had enjoyed my massage. I said that I thought that was certainly obvious. She told me to take my time, relax for a few and then when I was ready to come on out and close the door behind me. From that day on, I dubbed the place the "Sixty Dollar Place." It soon became the "Eighty Dollar Place," and I had my share of massages, though I was not as much as a frequent flyer as Mike was. I think after about the third time I had been there, I was told about the unprinted menu which contained other items for higher prices, all negotiated by each "waitress." I read in the paper some 10 years ago that the place had been busted by a bunch of men in black Chevy Suburban's and everyone inside was arrested. I actually considered myself lucky, because I certainly could have been one of the people inside there at that unlucky time.

At some point after I had learned of the massage place, I was looking towards the back of one of the weekly free Seattle newspapers once again and scanned passed the phone sex lines and began looking at the personals advertising escorts. I wondered what it would be like to call one to come over, and I remember asking Mike if he had ever done that, and he said he had not. I got brave one night (where did I get all this money?) and called one of the numbers. I think I was asked a few questions regarding what type of girl I was looking for, age, hair color, etc. I don't recall exactly what I asked for other than someone under 25 or so. I remember being nervous about what I was doing, and I probably had a few drinks or beers while I waiting. The girl got to my apartment and she was young and very pretty and after she told me what one hour of her time was worth, I agreed and we got the business out of the way. It was much like the massage place, but slower and more relaxed and after about 45 minutes, she asked me if I wanted to get another hour. I couldn't believe how fast the time was flying by, and so I agreed and she made a phone call. I think she ended up staying a total of about three hours and before she left, I ended up having great sex with her, with protection of course. But don't let me fool you here, sex with escorts is fine, but it is nothing like doing it with someone you know or even have gotten acquainted with for at least a little while. I was spent and then after she left I was lonely. I was done with my escort experiments. For now.

A few months later I was more to my normal self and things were better, I was happier and life was better as well. Luella (that amazing housekeeper I mentioned earlier) and I were still talking together a lot and the flirting seemed to be getting more intense, not in a bad way, but more playful and more often. Our conversations began to take on more sexual overtones and were fun because it was something that we both knew we should not be doing, and therefore made it more exciting. I remember one afternoon I saw her go into the linen room on the second floor and I went in after her, saying I needed to get something for the front desk. It is hard to explain, but the air was charged with something, and when she and I looked at each other, I knew something had to happen, was going to happen. I locked the door from the inside and we embraced and then kissed and it felt like it was the first kiss I had ever had, it was so tender and exciting at the same time. It started softly and then became such a needed passionate exchange of emotion; I can still remember it right now like it happened just five minutes ago. We parted and we were shaking and looking at each other in a new light, it was like we didn't know what had just happened, but then again, we knew exactly what happened. I unlocked the door and before left the room, we embraced and kissed again, then I left, very light headed and very happy.

We didn't talk about that kiss for the next couple of days, but every time we passed in the halls at work or saw each other, we would always smile and we knew what it was about. The next week we did talk together while out we were out back having a break and admitted that we wanted to see each other outside of work, we wanted to take things a step further. I so wanted to be with her, but I was also fighting that urge and I knew she was too, because of her marriage. I think, though, our emotions were getting the better of both of us. Luella was not getting attention from her husband and she couldn't get enough of the attention that I was giving her, the compliments, the smiles, just everything. If I told you that she and I both stood up to our morals and did not take things any further than that kiss in that linen closet, I would be lying, and that is not my intention in writing this. Luella came over to my apartment twice, both times before going to the hotel for her morning shift and we made love each time. I say it that way because it seemed more than just sex, there was more feeling and passion behind what we did. I think at that time with how things were between her and me, things could have really gotten out of control and I know that I had to be careful because I was not ready to be in a relationship right then, there would just be too much baggage on my side and I didn't want to be involved in causing the breakup of a marriage when there were kids involved, especially when we worked together, it was just adding up all wrong no matter which way I looked at it. I wanted to be sure that we remained friends as well; she was too important and too sweet. Now I don't want to come across as the good guy here, for all I know she may have been the one to initiate stopping things, but I know we did stop our intimacy and remained good friends and I remember that she even set me up on a blind date with a friend of hers. That was the first time

I had gone out with a girl who spoke absolutely no English and we ended up seeing an "The Lion King," as that was the only thing she nodded her head at when I was asking what she wanted to go out and do, but I digress.

The longer Rob (maintenance chief) worked at the hotel, the better friends we were becoming. He was living with some friends of his down in the Kent area which required at least a 45 minute drive or longer if traffic was bad. We talked about him moving up to Bellevue and we could get into an apartment together, the same type of deal that I was supposed to have with my older brother, but I felt that this would be a much better situation. Rob thought it was a good idea as well, especially the idea of saving time and gas, and he ended up moving into my small place while we looked for a bigger apartment. It was more than a little cramped, but we made do until we found better accommodations. Meanwhile, I was starting to spend some time with Carley, the girl from work who had the crush on me, but I wanted to just keep things on the fun side and not let things get serious, because I didn't want to fall into any type of rebound relationships.

Rob and I ended up finding a great apartment downtown Bellevue for an amazingly low price considering the size of the place. It was a two bedroom, two bath with a wet bar and washer and dryer. With those amenities, it was really a steal, and we thought we would be really stupid if we passed up on that deal. So we signed a year lease and moved in together. We had a great housewarming party and invited all of our friends from the hotel and had a great time with lots of booze, chips, music and of course, hangovers the next day.

Having a roommate that I actually got along with was something that I had not had since after G and I lived together. Rob and I got along so well, we were almost like brothers ourselves. But after the first couple of weeks together, I found that we were different in as many ways that we were the same, but this was not a bad thing. I seemed to make friends easily and had more than my share of them, while Rob was new to the area and wasn't as comfortable meeting new people. He was more down to earth and had gone through tough times with finances and was good with bills and finances while I was quite the opposite. He could be quite quick with his temper and raising his voice where I was more introverted and calm and would never raise my voice in anger. I can say that as time went on, we helped each other immensely in each of those areas. The one thing that Rob told me that really kind of made me feel good was that in all the roommates that he had had over the years was that I was the first one that he truly felt he could trust, the only one that he could truly call his friend. I really took that to heart.

Carley and I started becoming more of an item, but not in the real boyfriend/girlfriend sense, at least on my side of things. I know she really liked me and had for a long time, and if I even had the thought of asking her to be my girlfriend, she would literally jump at the opportunity, but I never was ever near that state of mind. I enjoyed the attention from her and enjoyed our sleeping together and the sex was good; we were always careful about using protection, of course that was without question. Carley was a really sweet person and very likeable, but she was also very clingy and opinionated and she and Rob would sometimes clash in their views of things each with their own convictions. I sometimes got so uncomfortable that I would just grab a beer or two or a cocktail while they were arguing and leave the room so they could do their bickering in peace. Other times she would just clam up and sit by herself and would not say anything for hours on end, it was as if she was in her own world and did not hear anything that was said to her, ignoring any questions we would ask her and then later she would snap out of it as if nothing had happened, and would wonder why Rob and I would be so perturbed.

One day she started acting really strange, much weirder than normal and was very quiet around me, almost like she was embarrassed to be with me, or like she was hiding something. I kept asking her what was wrong and she would say nothing, nothing at all, but would still act like something was. I started getting some eerie feelings and I just had a gut sense that I knew what was wrong. I don't know what made me think that I did, but I asked her to look at me and when she finally did I asked her point blank if she was pregnant. She didn't say anything and I repeated the question, but I knew the answer just by the way she was not giving me one. Finally she said yes she was. Now I know I had gotten a girl pregnant once before, but had only found out way after the fact, so this was all new to me, and you may think that what I tell you I did all wrong, was overly insensitive, and you are correct, and maybe (if there ever is a next time) I will be better in handling a situation like this. I asked her if it was mine.

She looked at me like that was the stupidest question she had ever heard. I told her I thought we were always using protection and she snapped back at me that of course we were, that she was on the pill. Now part of me was thinking that maybe she wanted to get pregnant so that I would feel that we should get married, and I know that is a typical male thought, but it had crossed my mind before. I then asked her—maybe told her I wanted to see her birth control pills and then she screamed at me something that I couldn't understand and I thought she was seriously going to hit me, but then she turned around and stormed out of the apartment. I called after her, realizing I shouldn't have said what I did, but I couldn't take it back now. She didn't come back.

I was pretty much speechless after that, and then Rob came home and could see that something was wrong and asked me what was up. I told him what Carley had told me and he started to get pissed at her, then said she was probably making it up (he had also verbalized his concerns about her doing crazy things to get me) and I said that I thought maybe she really was serious, and I told him what I had said. Rob told me I had better go find her before she causes some disturbance in the neighborhood. I told her she left and he said her car was still in the parking lot. I said I needed a shot of booze first (any reason for booze was a good reason) and so I took two shots and then went outside looking for her. I found Carley sitting on the sidewalk a couple of buildings away from ours and she told me to go away. I tried to talk to her and ask her what she wanted me to do and she looked at me with such hate in her face and said that I obviously didn't want it so she would take care of it. Then she got up and left before I could say anything. I probably should have gone after her and tried to be more comforting, but I had nothing to give. She had really caught me off guard and I had not been prepared for any of it. I thought she might come back in an hour or call, but she never did and that was the end of our relationship. A few weeks later she did call me and asked if I would at least go to the clinic with her, which I did and that was the last I saw her. I think I heard that she has since gotten married but I have no idea where she is to this day (actually as of the time of re-editing, I do know she is happily married with children and living in Colorado).

At work I had been training for the Lead Guest Services position, and was supposed to put together some training manuals, but apparently had been taking much too long to do that, and my manager finally called me into the office for a chat. He told me that my performance as of late had not been what he had been hoping for, and that he was demoting me back to just a front desk agent, but that he was giving me a raise, which then made me the highest paid front desk agent in the company. I couldn't see the reasoning behind any of that: a demotion and a raise? It gave me a headache trying figure that out, but what I was beginning to see that maybe I was getting burned out in my job. Maybe the hospitality industry wasn't for me. I had been working at various motels and hotels for about 6 years now and was still just a front desk clerk. Of course part of me says that is my own fault for my lack of effort, that if I had followed through on half the things I should have and taken things more seriously that I may have been further along, but that has always been a problem, hasn't it. Anyway, I decided it was time to start looking for something else that I could do, maybe some other career or something I could get into that I could get excited about. I just had no idea what that was.

So on my next weekday off I went to one of the other placement businesses and did some tests and talked to a counselor and she was looking at what I had done with the night audit position and asked me if there was accounting work involved in that. I told her that I had to balance the money taken in with the rooms rented, and account for all the cash and checks and credit card transactions, so I said, sure, there was some excellent accounting experience. She then checked to see if there any entry level accounting jobs open or available and told me there was a position currently available at a local car dealership in Bellevue and if I was interested, she would set me up with an interview there. I thought about it for a minute and then said, sure, what could I lose? I currently had a job, so it wouldn't hurt to check this new one out and see what it was all about. I went in for two separate interviews, the first with the person who the candidate would be working directly with and the second with her supervisor. It didn't seem like it was totally different, "really," from what I had done before, except that it was in a different industry, I mean, accounting is accounting, right? I was thanked for coming in and then went back to the agency. My counselor told me they had called her and gave a good report on me and that now it was primarily a waiting game and she would let me know by the end of the week whether they would

192

want to hire me. I had been keeping Rob appraised of what I was doing of course, and he was keeping his fingers crossed. He knew what it was like to be changing careers and he sensed that I was kind of excited about this prospect. A couple of days later I got a call that they were willing to try me out. Now I figure one of two things had happened. I had done a good job in the interviews and they were confident that I could do the job or I had snowed them completely and had no idea what I was in for. I think it is closer to the second of the two scenarios.

The particular job the agency had found for me was not one where the employer paid the agency fees, therefore I was liable to pay the agency if I was to accept the position, and since it was something that I really wanted to take, I called my parents and told them all about my interviews and what the job was about, they offered to help me with the loan. At least this time they felt that I was making a more sound decision in something, as there had not been much of a hesitation in the offer. Once again, I was going to be making monthly payments to the parents, but it was at a much better interest rate than a regular bank (zero—the best rate of all), that's for sure. Now it was 1996 and making a fresh start.

ANOTHER NEW CAREER

I found out fairly quickly that I didn't know nearly enough about accounting as I had led on during the interviews with the dealership. I did ask questions, as any new employee in a new company should, as that is expected, but I was asking too many questions, and I was getting flustered that most were questions I had asked more than once, so apparently I was not retaining the answers I had been given. Though my supervisor never said to me outright that she was not thrilled with me, I could tell that was exactly the case. It wasn't that I was making any serious mistakes; it was more that I was taking much too much time to do the simple parts of my job, and I was supposed to be taking the burden off of my supervisor. The problem was, that was not happening. She was ending up taking too much of her time to help me. But after a few weeks, I had gotten competent enough that I was finished with my work early, so they had me assist in the service department to help out with the cashiering. I really didn't mind doing that too much, I felt that any knowledge I got in any department couldn't hurt. It got to the point that I started spending more time in the service department than I was in the business office.

After I had been at the dealership for a month, I was called in to my supervisor's office and she told me that there had been some downsizing in the accounting department and they were no longer going to need me as her accounting assistant. She said, however, that they had been very impressed with how I was doing helping the service department out and they wanted me to replace the cashier who was leaving. I asked about the pay and was told that my hourly wage would remain the same. I also asked her what would happen if I didn't take that position. Would I be out of a job and she slowly nodded and said, yes. That was the deal. So I said that I would love to be the cashier. And so that was it for my career as an assistant accountant. Actually, I was more or less relieved, as there seemed to be way too much stress in that business office, and the women were always complaining about this or that, and it seemed as if I was learning more about their personal lives than I needed to.

I remember telling Rob about the change of job title at work, and he thought it might be a better place for me, that it sounded like I was getting in way over my head. He said that there had to be too much difference between hotel accounting (at least what I had done) and the car dealership accounting and I would digging myself into a hole. He was right about that. I did stay on at the Bellevue hotel on a limited part time basis on the weekends at the front desk for a few months after I started at the dealership, and it was worth it getting two paychecks, as it was getting close to Christmas time, so the extra money was going to be put to good use.

Rob worked at the Bellevue hotel for a while after I left and then he thought the long hours and low paychecks just were not balancing out. He had been doing research and was finding that he could be making more money at any of the larger hotels in the area, so he started getting his resume out and going on interviews. He ended getting a job at a great hotel in Lynwood, which was part of a major chain that had locations all over the world. It was a great move for him and he did start making more money than he was where we worked before. It was also more of a challenge for him because he basically had to put a maintenance department that had been in shambles for a long time completely back together. He ended up spending a lot of time at work, putting in much longer hours than he anticipated, so often times when he came home he was tired and moody. I would make us cocktails so he and I could unwind from our days.

Rob didn't have a lot of friends in the area because he wasn't from here and didn't have a lot of time to make friends, and he relied on me a lot for company, for companionship, as it were. It was fine, really, and I thought it was great to be able to be there for him, because like I had also said earlier, we got along so well and were more like brothers than my older brother and I were. But at times it seemed that Rob and I were always doing things only with each other. If I went somewhere, he wanted to go and if he went somewhere, he wanted me to go. I got the to the point that if I wanted to go somewhere alone to see a friend, I would feel guilty if I didn't invite Rob. Please do not get me wrong, I enjoyed spending time with him, I considered Rob to be my best friend, but I also didn't want to think as if we were like a married couple and had to spend every minute outside of work together But sometimes, more often than not, that is the way it felt, and I hated to feel that way as it made me feel uncaring, unappreciative of him. I never told Rob any of this, and I know that I should have, but I wasn't sure at that time that he would have understood.

He had gone through some very rough times with roommates, as I am sure everyone has; he had people steal from him, take him for granted, move out unannounced and leave him with all the bills… it was very hard for him to put trust in someone, and since he had put that in me, I didn't want to do anything to show him that I was or would be like any of those other roommates were.

There were times that I could hardly wait until he went to bed so that I could have my own "Steve time" and sometimes I would make extra cocktails for myself or doubles so that I could get a nice buzz and then I could tolerate things easier. I know that in retrospect, it was not Rob that caused me to do that and I am not blaming him for that, I had just found that it was what I had done before to help me cope with stress and things I didn't want to or didn't know how to deal with. That's what I did when I lived with Martha and it worked then.

In writing I am finding out a lot of things about myself and learning what I should have known back then. When one has a roommate who is a best friend is one needs to realize it is also a give and take relationship and there has to be communication and trust and I know I said I wasn't ready for that with my marriage and perhaps I was not ready for the kind of roommate situation that I was currently in at that time with Rob. I should have been up front and told him about how I was feeling, but instead, I only did what I knew best…kept it all inside and not say anything and instead just talked to my booze. But it wasn't an every night thing with the drinking. Not at that time. Not for a while.

As the cashier in the dealership service department, I answered the phone and transferred calls to the service advisors, which wasn't always as easy as it would seem. Most of the time they were all with customers or would not respond to my pages, so sometimes I would have to keep the callers on hold or take messages. Sometimes I just blindly transferred the calls to an advisor if I saw they were ignoring my pages, which didn't always make them happy, but what was I to do? The other tasks I had was getting payment from customers when they came back to pick up their vehicles in the afternoon or whenever the car was ready. Sometimes I was the receiving end when they were frustrated at the total of the bill or if it was different from what the advisor told them it was going to be. But it was never dull working there, and for the most part, all of the people I worked with were very friendly and more than willing to answer questions for me if I asked, and I was always treated with respect. It was like being a part of the family, which I was not feeling when I was working in the accounting department.

The first Christmas party at the dealership was a lot of fun. It was held in the showroom after the dealership had closed and there were a lot of people there, from all the departments. I remember I was surprised when the owner came over to me and shook my hand and wished me a happy holiday and used my name. I was astonished that he had known my name as I had never met him before. It made me feel good, as I wasn't used to being treated like a person. I was more used to being just a number in pool of employees. There was no alcohol served at the party due to problems with drinking at some prior parties, but having been a Boy Scout I was prepared for that. I remember a couple of times going out to my car and having a libation or two and then going back in to the party, always using the excuse of going out for a smoke.

I worked as cashier for almost a year, and found myself learning a lot about people and their cars. One of the things I found interesting was that a lot of vehicle owners were very stingy about spending money on their cars. There were times when the technicians noted that the brakes were very near worn out and that it was recommended that they should be replaced before they damaged the rotors as well. Of course when the customer would decline the repair they would come back screaming at the service advisor about the huge replacement cost of replacing both the pads AND the rotors when the brake had gone metal to metal. Customers were hesitant about replacing water pumps, air pumps, anything that would not cause the vehicle to stop running immediately, because they wanted to save money. They just didn't realize what the term "preventative maintenance" really meant. I learned more about cars and how they worked than I had when I was 16 and studying for my driver's license back in Idaho. I remember barely passing the classroom tests. The technicians were easy to talk to and seemed happy to answer any questions I asked, no question seemed stupid to them. I would also listen intently to the advisors when they talked to the customers and soon thought that it would be fun to actually be a service advisor. It didn't seem to be that difficult as far as I could see thus far. When the advisor was unavailable, I started reading over the paperwork with the owners when they came in to pick up their cars so they would know what we did and give them an opportunity to ask any questions. I remember later getting a huge compliment from the dispatcher who had overheard me doing that. He said that I sounded just like an advisor and that I knew exactly what I was talking about. He was truly impressed.

Most Friday's after work, a lot of the technicians and some of service team would go to the bars and unwind, drinking and playing pool or darts. I was invited out to join them one night and from then on, I knew that I had been accepted as part of the group, the family, as it were. It was very different to see the people I worked with outside of the job. Outside the workplace, he guys that I thought were most laid back and quiet turned out to be the wild, crazy partiers! I always had a great time. I remember bringing Rob out to one of the outings, and for the most part he had fun, but he really didn't feel he fit in, probably because he didn't know the guys well.

Rob had more fun planning for vacations and he did finally get me fired up about going to the Oregon coast after I had gotten my first week of vacation accrued from work. It was a great trip and we actually spent two weeks on the road (I took one week unpaid, but that was okay, it was well worth it), and I learned where the best places to camp were, where the best state parks were, and no offense to Washington State, but I think the Oregon State Parks are so much better for camping.

I had had an addiction to nasal spray after bad cold years before had stuffed up my nose so bad and I used the spray for so long, that the passages would not stay open unless I kept using it. I can't even begin to calculate the amount of money I had spent on the damn stuff, but I know that I had tried almost every brand, and at the end, was using a private label only because I could get the special two-pack (for the price of one). Rob never could understand that particular addiction, but I told him that it was just a personal thing; I had to be able to breathe through my nose. If it clogged and I had no spray, I would panic. I'm sure I would not die, but I had just gotten so used to my "fix" that I always had my stuff, even if I had to use the "five finger discount" to get it, I always had my nasal spray.

When Rob and I were driving to Boise that vacation to see my parents, I was so irritated with his consistent nagging that I should quit the nasal spray, how I didn't need it, why couldn't I just quit, etc. etc. that I just rolled down the passenger window and threw the stuff out. I did it more just to shut him up than anything else! I think he had been on me for about half an hour and I just didn't want to hear about it anymore. It was kind of a weird thing though, I was really worried about the nose stuffing up and I would be really wishing I had my stash to squirt up the nose, but for whatever reason, it never happened. I don't know if it was mind over matter, but my nose never clogged up again, and I can honestly say that ever since that day, I have never used nasal spray again. I may have used a saline solution once or twice, but never the actual stuff that I had used for years. Rob never did say "I told you so" like I was expecting, but I know that he was pleased that I had finally listened to what he had said and had followed through.

Sometime during the summer of 1997 I think, I had mentioned more than once to the service manager that I would like to be considered for a service advisor position if one became available. I had the support of the other advisors and most of the technicians, who had watched as I learned and they felt that I should at least be given the opportunity. I remember one advisor told the manager that it would be a shame to waste my talents because as good as ambitious as I was, I wouldn't be staying in that position forever. I heard about that statement after the fact, and I was really proud that I had made that much of an impression on the people I worked with. Soon after I was given my first "official" performance review since I had been with the dealership. I remember walking into my manager's office and before I had a chance to sit down, he extended his hand to me and said, "Congratulations, you are an advisor." That is the only thing I remember about that review, except for being completely shocked, yet ecstatic at the same time. I couldn't wait to get home after work to share the news with Rob. I think we celebrated with cocktails of course!

Rob had been going through some good things at his job as well, and had been nominated for Chief of Maintenance of the Year for Western Region and was extremely surprised when he found out that he had won the honor. He was flown to Chicago for a few days where he received the award. I was thrilled for him, of course. But it also meant that I had the apartment to myself for a few days, which I enjoyed, because then it felt like I was a bachelor living on my own. I know that sounds weird, but when you have lived with people for most of your life, it is great to be able to have your own space, and I had gotten used to that when I had moved out of my brother's place into my own. I just felt freer, I didn't have to do the things we did all the time together, the usual evening routine of cocktail, dinner, TV, cocktail, popcorn, not that any of that was dull or boring, but if I wanted to skip the dinner or popcorn, there was no one to raise an eyebrow or question if I had two or three drinks and then a snack, or maybe make some mac & cheese and drinks or whatever I wanted... I don't want you to think that all I did was drink, but it was something I did, it was just a part of my daily routine. It was a stress reliever, and I liked my booze. I drank more on the weekends but at least a few nights (sometimes more) during the week. I didn't drink to excess and get drunk every night, that would be wrong, and I had a job I liked.

When Rob and I had visited my parents in Boise, Mom had given me her old computer, as she had upgraded and purchased a new one for herself, so we had installed the computer in the living room. Having internet access at home was a new thing for me, and I had installed AOL and was able to surf the net through the then modern dial-up service and when Rob was not at home, I could look at whatever I wanted to. I am sure that he would think that if all I looked at was the porn websites he would think that was a waste of time, and I am sure I would have if I had really thought about it, but I just liked to check things out. It wasn't just porn that I was looking at, I remember becoming a regular visitor to the chat rooms. What a great invention that was, being able to chat instantly to people all over the country and the world, right on your computer in your living room. I would have fun in the local chat rooms and try to "pick up" girls or see if I could get any girls to get interested in meeting some time. So you can see how this was all easier to do when someone is always there looking over your shoulder at what you were looking at or what you were doing.

I did start a kind of long distance "relationship" with a girl from the Minnesota area, and we talked online for a couple of months, often late at night, and our chats went from casual stuff about our lives to of course sex stuff and then the possibility of meeting sometime. We exchanged phone numbers and I remember calling her a few times on the weekend when

Rob would be at work (all this secretive stuff hidden from Rob). This girl finally told me that she was willing to pay the airfare to fly me out to meet her. She said she would pick me up at the airport and put me up in a hotel near where she lived and we would have a wild night of sex and fun. I figured I had to tell Rob because if I was going to fly off for a weekend, he would find out, so I filled him in about the girl and what the plan was. I expected him to tell me I was nuts and why would I want to waste my time. Instead he said that it sounded like a lot of fun (I think he was patronizing me and seriously he thought I was nuts) and hoped it actually panned out. I remember I had to go to the store and told him she would be calling when she purchased the plane tickets and asked him to answer when she called. Of course she never called and I never flew to Minnesota. I later found out she was married and I got a very nasty email from her husband, who threatened me with serious harm if I ever talked to her or sent her any further emails. I stopped immediately. Rob never said anything about the incident, but I wouldn't have blamed him if he had.

Soon after I had gotten promoted, there was a new guy who was hired in the service department to replace the cashier who was leaving. I remember when I met him I reached out to shake his hand and introduced myself. When I was just about to tell him who I thought he looked like—he cut me off and said "don't say it!" I asked him what he meant, I was just going to tell him that he looked a lot like Jon Lovitz He yelled at me that he told me he hated that and he hated me now. Jeff never said another word to me for a couple of weeks. He later told me that for some reason he has always despised being compared to Jon Lovitz and really didn't mean to come across as so mean to me the way he did. That has always been an inside joke between Jeff and me to this day. Jeff and I became great friends after that.

As I think back on living with Rob I think ultimately it was a very positive experience. I did learn a lot from him, and as I think I have mentioned before, he was able to discover new outlooks on his life through me as well. Sometimes though, I felt that I needed to do things by myself, I needed change from the same things we would do together day to day, sometimes week after week. I know Rob got "cabin fever" from time to time, but he always wanted the two of us to go camping for a long weekend, or go to a concert, or plan a vacation together, which I did enjoy, but I felt guilty because I didn't want to always go places and do things with only him all the time. It was nothing against Rob, I just needed my individuality and I suppose if I had tried to explain that to him, he probably would have understood. But sometimes it was just easier to go ahead and do things with him because he was enjoying the companionship that he had never had with such a good friend before. And I didn't want him to feel that I was abandoning him. Best friends do not do that.

But then the day came when Rob was called upon to help a troubled hotel in New Jersey and help the management company with a change of leadership and staff there. They wanted him to fly out and spend about three weeks during the introduction of the new management team and help oversee the transition. Not only did I think that was a great opportunity for Rob to show how important he was to the company, but I also knew that I would have the apartment to myself for the time he would be gone! I was so much looking forward to this. I drove Rob to the airport and wished him a safe flight and then stopped at the liquor store on the way home to buy myself some booze for my own personal consumption. I didn't want to drink from the house supply we had because I might forget to replace that and I didn't want Rob to know that I was drinking too much and having too much fun without him.

I think that first time Rob was gone was when I decided to check the free Seattle newspaper ads for the escorts again. I ended up finding a service that had a website where you could view actual pictures of their girls. It was the only service that I ever used that truly followed through on what they advertised, and believe me, in my time of experimenting with escorts, I found some that would come over and would take the money and then tell you if you wanted them to do more than just sit there on the couch, you had to cough up more cash. That to me was deceptive advertising (but what am I talking about? Prostitution is illegal anyway) and would so I would stick to the service I knew that always came through for me. The sad thing about that is the amount of money I ultimately spent on escorts over a 6 month period was incredible and embarrassing. I keep thinking of all the constructive things I could have that money on. It truly makes me want to cry. I think during those first three weeks Rob was in New Jersey I probably spent over $500, and that was just on escorts. But I never looked at the financial aspect of things back then. I just looked at me being able to take advantage of "Steve's time," and I had to make good use of my time and do all the things that I normally would not do when Rob was home.

I think the last week of his New Jersey trip was when I delved into the 900 numbers again. It was probably the last weekend before he came home and I needed something to shake things up. So I was drinking my cocktails and making the calls, pressing #3 to move to the next message and then I came upon a particular girl's message that must have intrigued me and made me connect live to her. Had I passed up on her message and never spoke to her, my life would probably have been a lot different, but that's life, isn't it? It did happen and so I have the story to tell. Was that a good enough build up?

Anyway, I talked to Libbie live and somehow through our chat, she agreed to come over and see me. I don't recall the specifics of our conversation, but I gave her my address and phone number (this was before I had a cell phone and people still had land lines) and then I waited for her to arrive. I probably had several drinks before she got there because I am know I was nervous. Waiting for an escort from the service was different because I knew more or less what to expect, but with Libbie, I had no idea what I was getting myself into, I only had to hope that how she described as herself was what was going to be showing up at my door.

She wasn't bad looking, probably a little older looking than I imagined she would be, but right around my age (38ish—she was probably five years or so younger, but who am I to guess ages, I have always been horrible at that), and short. She was not Black, but not White either, but pretty in her own way. I invited her in and had she sat on the couch. I didn't have all the lights on, I guess I wanted to make the place seem a little cozy and more likely to lead to some action. Libbie pulled a small glass tube from her coat that was attached to a little rubber hose and asked me if I wanted to try something. I asked her what it was, as I had never seen it before. She asked me if I had smoked anything before, and I told her cigarettes and pot. She asked me if I had smoked anything else and I told her I had not. She wanted me to try what she had, that I might like it. She said it wasn't anything bad like LSD or heroin or anything like that. I didn't want to seem like a prude or anything, so I thought sure, why not (remember how good I am on some of my decisions, yeah)? She told me to put the rubber end in my mouth and when she lit the end of the glass tube she was holding, told me inhale and hold the smoke as long as I could and then blow it out slowly. I was more than a little nervous, but I did what she said, and as I exhaled the smoke, the most unique feeling came over me, one I had never felt before, and it was great! It was like my entire body came alive and all of the sudden I was tingling all over and when I looked at Libbie I felt such a sexual charge surging through every part of me. It was as if I was immediately hornier than I had ever been in my entire life. At that moment all I wanted to do was to have both of rip our clothes off and start romping together naked and having wild sex right then, right there on the couch, it felt so fucking good! I asked her if I could have another hit and she told me to wait until she had one herself. I think she gave me one more after she did, and it was all I could do to wait for my turn again. I wanted that feeling again and I wanted it now! It was like having your first orgasm that felt so good that you just had to have more and more! I'm sure a lot of you might know what I had my first taste of, and for those who aren't sure, it was "crack" cocaine. I had never heard of it before, and in a lot of ways, I wish I had *never* heard of it, much less tried it. I can tell you that it is exactly what they say, very addictive because once you have had it, you want it more and more.

I think Libbie knew what she was doing, by introducing me to crack. She told me after my second hit that she didn't have any more, but then after making a call, she said her roommate could get more, but that they needed money. Well, of course I would help her. By all means! Then after I offered to give her the cash for the crack, she then told me that they were behind in rent and she needed some extra money for that and would I help her with that. Thinking that she would be more willing to get more crack I agreed to give her extra money for her rent. And I was still hoping that there would be some sex involved that night, as that was the original reason that Libbie had come over in the first place. I remember we waited outside for the roommate to come and pick her up so that she could get more, and finally he arrived. I went along since I had to get cash for them and then we went to their apartment about ten minutes away. I waited in the car for a long time for her to come back out, and when she finally came out to the car, she said that she wasn't able to get anymore that night. It was about three in the morning by that time, and she suggested that since it was so late, we could get together again another time soon. I was tired and more or less frustrated by then, so I said that was fine. They drove me back to my place and then left, leaving me about $300 poorer in the end. She got what she wanted. I didn't. The end. But it was not the end, by any means, not with her or the crack.

I will say right now that though I enjoyed my "freedom" when Rob was gone or out of town, I should have begged him to not leave any more. Why? Every time he was gone out of town for the weekend or even for a night, whatever, I always had a lot less money than before he left, and sometimes, lots to cover up, due to my wild escapades.

My birthday rolled around that November, as they do once a year, and the gang at the dealership wanted to celebrate it with me at the local hang out. Though it was on a Friday that year I had to work that next day, but that didn't stop me from planning for a night of drinking and fun. I drove to Jeff's place to enjoy some pre-drinking festivities, and when I found that he had already left, I took several pulls off my fifth of vodka that I had brought with me and then walked to the bar from there. Everyone was waiting for me and I had a lot of drinks purchased for me since it was my special day. I don't remember how many I had after that, but I know I had way more than my share. The last thing I remember was that third double vodka tonic and then I woke up on a floor somewhere, feeling like a truck had run over me, not unlike how I felt the morning after my bachelor party. Then it dawned on me I was at Jeff's place, as we had planned. They had half carried me to his car and somehow gotten me inside his apartment onto the air mattress that he had set up. I splashed some water on my face and put on my pants and work shirt (the same ones from the prior day's work) and drove to work, feeling like I was still drunk (quite sure I still was). I know that I had to have reeked of alcohol, but most people knew that I had been out on my birthday night, so no one said anything— probably the only time I wasn't told I smelled like booze when I did. Somehow I survived the rest of the work day and when I got home after work and think I slept well into Sunday, needing the sleep to recuperate from the festivities.

Rob and I had been planning a Christmas road trip that year, made reservations at all the places we were intending to stop at, and then about a week before we were set to leave, I checked with my manager in regards to my time off that I had requested. Somehow between when I had put in the request until then, it had been lost, or maybe I had never requested the time off. After all, that was certainly possible, though I was pretty sure I had. So when I told my manager about the dates I needed, he told me that I would only be able to take a few of those days. I asked if he could reconsider, work with me, as I wasn't asking for a lot of time, but he said that there was just no way he would be able let me go for the whole two weeks I needed. I was starting to sweat, I knew that Rob would be devastated, because we had spent so much time in preparation, and he had been looking so forward to getting away for Christmas and New Year's. I had not a clue how I was going to get myself out of this predicament. He was going to be pissed off, and I was going to be the sole reason for it. I asked my manager what would happen if I just took the entire time off anyway (I knew what that answer would be already) and he said if I did, I would not be coming back to that job. I went through a whole pack of smokes, trying to think of something, anything I could do to salvage the situation, and finally, I realized it was hopeless.

It was the day we were to leave on the vacation that I came home and told Rob that I couldn't go, that someone had called in sick and needed me to stay and cover, as there was no one else to do that. He blew up as I expected and I don't think he was cursing at me so much as cursing my work and how could they do that when the had been requested off so long ago and why did this always have to happen to him and why couldn't I just stand up for myself and tell them to honor the request. All I could do was let him rage. I couldn't tell him that it was probably my own fault that it had come to this; I thought it was just better to lie and put the blame on something other than me. I felt like shit for a long time after that, as I saw how much this hurt my best friend. Rob finally did calm down and I told him that he should just go on the trip without me, as we had already put deposits down on several hotels and he should at least enjoy the trip even if I couldn't go with him. He almost didn't go but I think he really needed to get away even if just for himself. I told him I would be okay and that I would call him on Christmas and New Year's and make sure he was okay and having a good time. We took all of my stuff out of the car and then he left. I half expected him to come back in the door, but after about a half hour went by and he hadn't come back, I relaxed a little and had some drinks to calm my nerves. Rob did really have a good time on the trip, though he did miss me and my companionship, but he said the time alone actually did him some real good. I didn't get in to too much trouble while he was gone (that I remember), but I did have one escort visit me on Christmas Eve and gave me some good 'ol holiday cheer.

At work, we had gone through a few too many service managers as well as service advisors, and one advisor, who was not well liked and who had previously been transferred to a satellite store as manager was going to be returning to our store as service manager. This was a shock and all of us in our department knew that nothing good would happen when he was back. We were told to keep an open mind and that maybe things would be different from when he was with us before.

Meanwhile, I had been given the job of organizing our courtesy car program, so as to better keep track of the loaner cars. I drafted up fairly strict rules that we all had to abide by because we had lost track of a few vehicles in the past, and now when an adviser gave a car out to a customer, he or she would be responsible for the car's whereabouts, or face being written up or possible termination. This program worked out pretty well, as no one wanted to be fired due to a loaner car screw-up.

I myself had to deliver one of our cars out to a customer's house while we had their car they had just purchased return with a gas tank problem (we had just repaired it the week prior). I figured that the customer merited a courtesy car for their inconvenience and I wanted to deliver it myself to show our good service and good will. I drove it to their home and left the car (locked) in the driveway with the keys and the paperwork under the front door mat of the house. That was all fine and everything was great until they did not want to pick up their car or return the courtesy car. They felt they no longer had trust in us, our repair, or their car. By this time the general manager was involved and he asked where the loaner car paperwork was, as it would have the necessary signatures and the "return by date" on our copy. I was not able to find our copies because I had left them all with the customer. This created a huge problem and I was told that the company attorneys had become involved and I don't remember if we were going to take the customer to court over our car or what the deal was. What I do know was that I was called into the manager's office with the dealership general manager. I was grilled about the paperwork and they let me know in no uncertain terms that they were not happy with me. All I could do was sit there and apologize.

I was accused of lying to cover up my involvement and that there never was any paperwork, that I had just delivered the loaner car incorrectly. I was in the right, but of course I had no proof of it. A week had gone by since my reprimand and I thought things had calmed down, but that Friday afternoon, I was again called into the general manager's office and when I saw a woman from the human resources office sitting in one of the seats as well, I knew it was not a good sign, not at all. I had a very bad feeling about things. I was told that my association with the company was terminated as of that moment. They presented me with a three page report with incidents where I had supposedly been previously written up about a stolen car (that was untrue—I had heard about that afterwards but I was not involved) and that I had lied twice to the general manager, which was also untrue. I still believe to this day, that I was set up. The only thing they truly could fire me over was the loaner car paperwork. In a perverse way, you could say I was nailed by my own rules. But I also believe things may not have happened like that had the guy no one liked ever returned from the satellite store as manager of our service department. He never liked me. I honestly don't know what I ever did to him to cause him to feel that way. I certainly didn't care for the guy, but no one else did either. I may not have been the model employee, but I did my job, I liked what I did and I made good money. I had been at that dealership for over four and years and I was well liked and respected by those I worked with as well as many of the customers we had. Sure I may have been a drinker and come in to work smelling of booze from time to time, but a lot of people who worked were the same from time to time. I wasn't *that* much different. I was told later that they had to have a special meeting with the department employees to explain why I was no longer there. I would have loved to have been a fly on the wall during that meeting!

So what does one do when he is fired? Well, when his roommate Rob is gone for the night (I don't remember where he had gone that time), and one has some cocaine that he has gotten from a friend, he makes his own crack and smokes it and drinks booze. Rob came back the next afternoon after I had been out all day looking for a new job, and for all he knew I had just gotten home from the dealership. But I did finally tell him that I had been let go and I don't think I held back too much of real details of what happened. Naturally he was upset for me especially since I had been there for so long. He told me to keep my chin up and just get back out there and he had no doubts that I would rebound from this just fine.

I remember applying for unemployment insurance but I was denied because it was reported that I was fired due to my lying. After only two days of filling out applications and going to dealerships and a few interviews (I made much more of an effort in job searching this time than I ever had before) I did get hired at another dealership on a trial basis, but I wasn't thrilled about working there because they used a computer program that I was not used to and it was a much faster paced service department than I was prepared for. I was drinking more and I remember most of the three or four days I went to work there, I was tired and hung-over each day. The second day I was there I was sent to take a drug test but I really wasn't as concerned about that as I should have been because it had been about four days since I had smoked the crack. I had heard that it only stays in the system for about 3 days. But of course I tested positive and I was let go before I even really started. I wasn't heartbroken about that job because I didn't really like it to begin with. I told Rob that things hadn't worked with that company, and not the real reason why I was no longer there—he did not know about my crack smoking at that time.

I was called by an automotive placement agency that had gotten my resume from another dealership I had applied at. That dealership had been impressed with my credentials and would have hired me however they had no positions available, so they faxed my information to the agency. I was told there a dealership in north Seattle that was looking for a service advisor and they sent me to interview there. I drove up and spoke to the service manager and was hired the next week. The computer program they used in the service department was the same one I had used at the first dealership I was at, so it was easy to make the transition to a new car line. The staff and technicians were just as friendly as the ones I had known before and it was easy to fit in and I knew I would do okay at my new place of employment. This dealership specifically dealt with American-made vehicles and I found out that the majority of the car owners I dealt with really wanted to take care of their vehicles. I remember one older gentleman who was faced with a rear end rebuild or something like that and he said if it needed to be done, to go ahead and do it. He said that he was retired and it would take a huge bite out of his fixed income, but he needed it done. I don't remember any customer at my last dealership that would have authorized that same kind of repair!

Rob had been promoted to a project manager position for the management company that owned the hotel that he worked at, and was then responsible for numerous of hotels they managed in Washington, Oregon and California and therefore did a lot more traveling. He now had to oversee projects such as property renovations, handling staffing or internal engineering problems, and the like so he was gone a lot more of the time. One of those times was a month or so after I had started at the new dealership. Somehow I had hooked up with Libbie again, and ended up going to see her where she was currently staying (I don't know that she ever had a permanent place that she could call home in all the time I knew her). Of course she had crack there and was actually pretty generous with sharing it with me. She never was really interested in doing anything sexual with me, but she had a porno tape and magazine that she let me look at while smoking the stuff which suited me just fine. With me, porn and crack seemed to go hand in hand. Somehow during the course of things, she ended up with my credit card number. I probably gave it to her because she said they needed food or something—she knew that with crack, she could get anything from me. The bad thing about that night was that I ended up staying up all night and by the time I realized what time it was, I was mortified to find it was after ten in the morning, 3 hours after I was supposed to be at work. And I was supposed to drive down to the Oregon coast to meet up with Rob and his girlfriend that weekend. I finally called work at four (there were several messages on my cell phone wondering where I was) and gave them some lame excuse that I had not been able to sleep and had taken sleeping pills and then realized the power had gone out and messed up the wake up alarm I had set. My boss called me into the office the next Monday and gave me the third degree about the situation and of course I gave him the best snow job I could think of, though deep down I don't think he believed me. But the issue was dropped. Soon after that, I noticed several charges on my account that I did not recognize and I was pissed because I knew that Libbie's friends had used my account and racked up the charges. She denied knowing anything about that but told me that she would ask them if they had used my card number. Of course she said they had not. I changed my card number immediately after that, but not after losing over $500.

I had cashed out my 401K from the first dealership I had worked at and after taxes had been taken out, I got about $4000, which was a nice chunk of change for me. I hadn't had that much in my checking account in a long time. It was just sitting there and I was wondering what all I could do with it. As you can probably already thinking, I did the responsible thing. I called Libbie!! She was glad I contacted her and asked if I could help get a hotel room for the night in Seattle and the stupid gullible guy that I was said okay, but I also told her it was the last time I was going to help her out like that. I reminded her of how I had lost money before, and she swore that she would not let that happen, that she just needed the help for the one night. I met her at the hotel in Seattle she wanted to stay at and I filled out a credit card authorization form and was sure to check the box that I was only authorizing "one night" to be charged on my card. And then I told Libbie once again that I was only paying for the one night, and then she would be on her own. She said that was fine. I think it was about a week later when I got my bank statement I saw that I had a lot less in the account than I had thought I had and saw over $1000 charged to the hotel where Libbie stayed. There was no fucking way that was possible and I called the hotel and had them fax me over the room charges that were billed to my card. I found that there were three nights of room and tax, plus charges for pay movies and then page after page of telephone charges! I was furious. I had to get things straightened out! That was MY money! I left work early and drove down to the hotel and asked to speak to the manager. I told him I had only authorized one night's stay. He looked over the total bill and said it looked like there was something funny going on, and if I wanted to press charges, they would need to bring the police into the picture, as it looked like the actions of a prostitute with all the calls. I told him I had no idea what she was doing, that she was just an acquaintance that I was trying to help out. But the way he was looking at me I think he thought I was in on something with her and that I was just trying to get out of paying the bill. I told him I would try to contact her and that I would call him back with what I wanted to do. I drove away thinking that I was fucked. There was no way that I could get the police involved. I knew it would somehow come back to haunt me and I thought that would bring even more trouble to my life and my job, so I just told myself that I had fucked up once again and that I was through with Libbie! I would not deal with her again. Enough was *enough*!! I had lost way too much money due to Libbie and I knew that I didn't have a snowballs chance in hell to get any of it back. I had pretty much sailed through my entire 401K windfall I had received because of her and partying with escorts and booze and hell I don't even know what else. I never did tell Rob about any of that. I'm quite sure he would have had much to say to me and I was in no frame of mind to hear any of it. I was already pissed off enough at myself as it was.

I think about a month went by with nothing more exciting or unusual happening. Work was work and I was doing my best to try to get my life back to as normal as possible, not to mention trying to get a handle on my financial situation. I was drinking more than I used to, but of course that was because it helped me to cope with things. It made me feel better and less apprehensive about how I had been screwing up recently. I remember I had recently been keeping a bottle of vodka in my bedroom closet so I could sneak some swigs between the cocktails Rob and I would have during the course of our normal nights. One night Rob walked into my room and caught me taking a pull one before I could cover up, and became very concerned because it was obvious to him I was hiding my drinking from him. Rob assured me that it wasn't necessary to do that, if I wanted to drink, why should I feel the need to hide it, I should just do it. He told me about a few roommates who had had serious drinking problems and had been doing the same things I was doing—hiding alcohol in the closet. Those roommate situations did not turn out well because of the deception and he did not want our friendship to end up the same way. He told me he loved me like a brother and only expected me to be honest and open. I agreed he was right and I promised I would not hide booze anymore. I brought the bottle out of the closet and put it in the common liquor supply. The next day I brought home another bottle for my private supply. It wasn't that I outright wanted to defy him; it was just that by then, it didn't feel right to be without my own stash.

Now I know that I said just a few paragraphs back that I was done with Libbie and I meant it when I said it back then, but I am only human and intentions are just that. I don't know exactly how it happened, Libbie must have called and sweet talked me or told me she was sorry, but whatever she told me, I ended up going to visit her down near the airport in a motel she was staying at. Maybe she told me she was going to pay me some money, I don't know. All I know is that I was down there and we had been talking for a bit and though she didn't have any crack, she did have a pipe which she told me I could scrape to see if there were enough resins to make a hit from. I managed to get one hit out of it when there was a knock at the door—this is where things got really weird. What happened next seemed like it was all in slow motion and was like a scene straight out of *Cops!*—the police show on TV. Libbie opened the door as I put down the pipe. Three or four guys came barging in and said something about being the police or detectives and I just about shit my pants right there. I heard the door bang against the wall and saw two of the guys take Libbie into the bathroom area and the other two came over to me. They had me up and off the bed I had been reclining on and sat me down in a chair. They tied my hands together with a plastic strap behind my back. They proceeded to ask me how I knew Libbie and what I was doing there with her. I told them that I had met her from a 900 number some months back and I was just hanging with her or something like that. I was so sure that they were going to take me to jail and I was going to lose my job, and my life was over. End of story. The two guys who had been talking to me conferred with the guys who had been questioning Libbie for a few minutes, and then came back to me. They said it appeared like I was telling the truth as she had given them the same story about me. They told me that they were taking Libbie in for outstanding warrants and they were going to let me go. They removed the restraints from my wrists and told me to go home and they then advised me to stay away from Libbie if I knew what was good for me, that all she was good for was trouble, she was bad news. I remember looking at them in disbelief that they were just going to let me go. I asked them if I was in any trouble and was told just to get out of there, to go home. I did as they said, still not quite comprehending what had just transpired. I was sure that as I walked out to my car that I was going to be surrounded and arrested, but I made it to my car without incident. I was so very paranoid all the way home, making sure to keep right at the speed limit, always keeping an eye on the rear view mirror. I got home and there were no cops waiting for me. I was thanking the good man above and everything else I could think of that Rob was gone and not there to see in the state I was in. Once inside, I locked all the doors, made sure all the windows were closed and locked and then gulped down several shots of booze. I didn't sleep well at all, dozing on and off, and when I finally did drift off for a longer period, it was only due to the high quantity of alcohol that I by that time I had consumed. I was half expecting the cops to come pounding on the door all night. Again I vowed that I would not have anything to do with Libbie again, as my luck couldn't hold out much longer. Not that I could call anything that I had been through with her as luck—though somehow I had escaped going to jail along with her, but I am quite positive they could have nailed me, really. How could they have missed the fact that I had a crack pipe in my hand? I am sure that I would have failed any field drug test they could have given me. If the preceding wasn't more conclusive evidence that what I'd been doing up until then was absolutely, stupid, unwise, unhealthy and ethically wrong, I don't know what else was.

There had been a new girl, Julie, who had been hired on as the cashier at the dealership. She was cute and quite the flirt and I enjoyed talking to her and did my share of flirting right back. I figured that was as far as I would be taking it, as Julie did not have the body type that I was normally attracted to, but she did have a great smile and also seemed to give me a lot of attention, more so than any of the other advisors or staff at the dealership. At some point we exchanged email addresses and then began chatting with each other on the computer at night. I loved getting to know her that way because it seemed impersonal enough that we could talk to each other about anything at all and not be embarrassed by actually vocalizing our thoughts or seeing the looks on each other's faces when we asked questions or made comments to each other.

We talked that way for about a month about anything and everything we could think of, and of course, as chats normally tend to go to over time, the subject of sex came up and it seemed the later into the night it got the more open with each other we became. We talked about what we liked to do in bed, if we'd ever smoked pot, all sorts of things. We found that we seemed to have a lot of interests in common and that both of us enjoyed having sex after getting stoned, as the high really enhanced the orgasms. Then the question was posed if we ever wanted to meet sometime and do more than just talk about it. After a couple weeks of toying around with that topic we worked up the courage and agreed that we shoule get together and do it.

Of course, at work we were very discreet; we never talked much about those things there. At the dealership, we tended to portray ourselves as clean cut normal friends, with casual talk, we were very careful not to let it get out that we were carrying on with wild talking on the computer at night. Rumors were spread much too easily at a dealership as it was.

After going back and forth on when the best time to hook up was, we came up with the idea of meeting up after the office Christmas party that year and getting a hotel room. We were both planning to attend anyway and would be in separate cars, so it would be easy to meet up after the party. The hotel that Rob used to work full time at would be the perfect place for the rendezvous and I asked him if he could get me a good rate and he said he could; I told him that I was going to hook up with a girl from work after the party. I hadn't gone into all the details of how we had been talking for months on the computer or wanting to get stoned together. That didn't seem to be necessary. He seemed happy about me getting together with anyone as it was. He had booked me a room at the employee rate and I checked in early that Saturday and got things ready for that night.

Now you remember when I got that bad infection all those years ago and almost died? Well, I was told that I always had to be very careful not to let any open sores on either leg get out of control because my immune system had been damaged back then and I would always be prone to infection. Well, I had developed a sore on my lower left leg just above the foot, and though it had scabbed over, it didn't seem to be healing as fast as I thought it should. I was treating it myself with the usual over the counter antiseptics and also used hydrogen peroxide on it and always kept it bandaged. I remember making sure I cleaned that up after taking a shower before the party. I didn't want to have any open wounds or anything to turn off a bed partner when it came time for that action.

215

The Christmas party was okay, not anything to write home about, but it was cool to socialize with my co-workers outside of work. They were not the rowdy, rambunctious guys that I had gotten used to at the prior dealership or if they were, they were just not showing it at that party, but they were fun, nonetheless. If not for the alcohol that was available at the party, it probably would have been a bust. Julie was there as we planned, and we were cordial to each other, but we did not want to give anyone the idea that there was anything going on, or what we had planned for after the party, our night of fun and pleasure.

After the party ended, I drove back to my hotel room and made myself comfortable, mixing myself some drinks while I waited for Julie to arrive. I had called her from the car (I had a cell phone by that time) while I was heading to the hotel—I wanted to make sure things were still going to happen as planned and that she knew where she was supposed to meet me. She said it was all fine; she just had to go back to her place and take care of her two dogs, so she would be a little bit yet. That was fine. I had plenty of booze and there was cable TV there that would keep me occupied at the hotel.

It was about an hour later when Julie arrived, and she came in to the room and got comfortable. We had a few drinks together and sat next to each other on the couch for a while watching TV and making out and then we were both getting a little tired, so we headed for the bed. We did have great sex that night, and I didn't feel the urge to leave or ignore her the way I had with a lot of my sex partners in the past, so it was nice to just drift off to sleep with her. I think about an hour later, her cell phone rang and I heard her whispering into the phone and then she hung up. I asked her what was up, as it was about 4 in the morning, and she said it was nothing, that she just wanted to go check on her dogs. I thought that was odd, considering the time it was, but I didn't have any holds on her, so I really didn't think too much of it. She got dressed and put on her coat and told me she would be back in about a half hour (I have since learned to add at least another half-hour to an hour to whatever time she said) and then left. I turned on the TV and had a few more drinks and then drifted back off to sleep. I don't remember when she got back, but when I woke up in the morning Julie was asleep beside me.

Julie and I had another round in the sack before it was time to check out. I had locked my keys in my car (not the first time, not the last) and we had to find the hotel maintenance person to help us get into my car. This was not fun, because I remember it was pouring down rain and both of us were thoroughly soaked by the time we finally got the car open. We kissed and said our goodbyes and off she went. I went back inside and got all my stuff together and drove back home. Julie and I talked on the computer that night and agreed that we had had great fun the night before and that we should do it again! I said maybe she could come over to my place some night and we could smoke some pot and have sex like we had talked about. She thought that would be fun and we chatted for a little longer. I try to think back about what we could have talked about during all the countless hours we spent on the computer chat site and it just boggles the mind.

We did hook up periodically a couple times during the next few months at night. I would have my cell phone set to vibrate and she would call me when she was outside the apartment door. I would silently tiptoe out and let her in and we would sneak back to my bedroom and smoke the weed she had brought with her (as I remember, it was mostly me that would smoke the pot, I don't remember her doing it as much) and once we/I would get stoned we would have amazing sex…I have said before that orgasms when one is high are incredible. Then after we were done, she would sneak back out of the apartment and go back to her place. Why all the sneaking? Well, Rob had done his share of partying in his day and was done with drugs and all that. I knew he wouldn't have approved of my smoking so I didn't want him to know that was going on. I know this sounds under-handed and I fully admit I was deceitful and though I am not really proud of being that way, it happened. You may wonder about Julie; how she could just coming over, have sex and then leave—this was something she and I had agreed upon and though it sounds like I was just using her, I could say we were using each other. By that time I knew that Julie not only really liked me but liked me a lot, and would do whatever she could to spend time with me, and so if that meant coming over for only an hour it *was* spending time with me, too. We both profited from the arrangement, really.

When I had been working for the first car dealership in Bellevue, I had been making about $16 per hour and averaged about twelve to fifteen hours or more of overtime each paycheck, which was a nice chunk of change. When a person is making that kind of money, he gets used to that income and the lifestyle that goes along with it—the extra things you can buy and the more things you can do. It's all a reflection of what you make. After I had been fired from that position and started with the second dealership, I was making a lot less, and there was very little overtime, so the income was severely lower, but I was still trying to live on the previous budget, and that just wasn't working. Little by little the money in my checking account was dwindling. The foolish expenditures I made when Rob was out of town clearly didn't help that situation either. But though Libbie was a part of a lot of my financial woes, the only person I can truly blame is the one who *caused* those situations to happen, and that person was me.

I am sure Rob knew that I was making less, I know I told him how much I was making at the newer job, but I don't think I ever really let on how much of an impact the difference was causing me. I pitched in the same as usual when we would go on our road trips, when we went to concerts or out to the bars, but inside I was a nervous wreck. I suppose I should have given Rob the benefit of the doubt and confided with him about my personal financial situation, and together we might have been able to plan for any hurdles or dire constraints, but I was stuck with my pride, whatever you want to call it, so I would say nothing to him. I don't know if I could call that being selfish, because it certainly didn't help me in any way to keep secrets from him.

When it came to paying the household bills, we would always put the statements on the bulletin board on the hallway wall near the kitchen, so we would always know when the bills were due, and Rob would write me a check for his share and I would make sure the bills got paid on time. Sometimes, even though I had deposited Rob's share into my account, I would barely have enough in my checking account to cover the payment I sent in, or it would get paid into overdraft, causing an extra charge to my account. If I could count up the total overdraft charges I have incurred over my lifetime in, the amount would be staggering!! I remember one time when Rob was out of town, the check for the power company had bounced and I could not make arrangements to repay in time before the electricity was shut off. I had to scramble to first find the extra money and then get a money order to the payment site before Rob came home the next day. He would have flipped his lid if the power was off when he came back from an out of town trip. I have to tell you, those were very stressful days. You try to sell brakes and rear main seals while also trying to come up with a $160 money order and pay it before six o'clock—it's not as easy!. Such is the life. But somehow, I always found enough money to keep our liquor cabinet stocked, as well as my own supply of vodka.

Julie and I began seeing each other more and more, at first mostly when Rob was out of town because then we didn't have to sneak around at when we were smoking our pot at night. One morning though, I heard the front door open and close and figured Rob had come home a day earlier than anticipated. I heard him come down the hall and he burst into my bedroom to scare me, as he often did, for shits and giggles, so that I could welcome him home, but this time, the scare was on him, as he noticed Julie in bed with me. It was more than a little awkward, but he broke into a huge smile and said that he was glad to finally meet her, as he had heard me say so many good things about her. Thank God we had put away all the pot before we had fallen asleep. Rob and Julie got along quite well together and I was relieved at that. Now at least I did not have to sneak Julie over when she and I wanted to "play" together.

Although Julie and I were spending so much time together, we had not officially labeled ourselves as boyfriend/girlfriend; I was still really hesitant on doing that, I suppose, a lot of that had to do with my prior relationships going to shit, but I also didn't think she was my type as far as a girlfriend went. And though I had not slept with or had sex with anyone else but her since that night of the Christmas party, I still didn't think I was ready to settle down with anyone steady.

Rob had himself gotten a steady girlfriend and their relationship was going very strong and eventually they got engaged to be married. His fiancé stayed with us most of the time so it seemed like a good idea for us to think about moving to a bigger apartment and that way we could live together more comfortably and we all could share the rent on a three bedroom place. The third bedroom would be used by Rob as an office, since he was now working out of the house. We found a really nice apartment a ways north of Bellevue and made the move, which really didn't add too much more commute time to any of our drives. As we thought, splitting the bills up between three people made the finances much more bearable. As an added bonus, our place was closer to where Julie lived too so she wouldn't have as far to drive to see me.

The sore on my leg near the ankle was not getting any better, even though I cleaned and dressed it almost every other day. Over time the diameter of the wound had gotten twice the size as it was originally. I was starting to get more and more worried about it, but part of me thought that maybe I just wasn't using the right amount of disinfectant, or maybe I was changing the dressings too frequently. But when I would wait more than three days to change and clean it, the wound would start seeping puss out and the smell was really quite rank, not as it should be, or as I thought it should be... but what did I know about how a wound should smell? I think Julie told me finally that I needed to go to see a doctor about it. I told her that I would go if it didn't improve in a week, and she told me I shouldn't even wait that long.

After a week, I went in to the clinic that was covered by my medical insurance and after they looked at it, I was told it was indeed infected and the cellulitis that I had all those years ago had returned. I thought back to when I was advised to be careful about any open sores, that I was told I should not even try to treat them on my own. That weren't kidding around. The nurse cleaned it, disinfected it as best she could and gave me antibiotics to take for two weeks. I was told to return for a recheck after the medication was gone. The nurse also advised me not to drink alcohol while I was taking the antibiotics. I wasn't too keen on that idea, I had consumed booze other times I was on medication with no problems, no repercussions. But after the two weeks, it was obvious that the medication was not working (I can't be sure but it was probably the booze) and they ended up putting me on a portable IV that I had to wear for five days. That was a unique experience, let me tell you. It was easy enough to conceal under my work clothes, so no one could tell that I was any different at work, but it wasn't easy taking showers with the contraption and I had to be very careful when I slept so I didn't pull out the needle in my sleep. It worked out okay that time (yes, that time). When the IV solution was used up, I went back in to the clinic and for the two weeks following, I had to go in every four days so the nurse could clean out the wound, which gotten bad enough that it was eating away the skin around it. I was told that if I was not careful, and I let things get out of control, I could eventually lose my leg. After her digging and cleaning and putting on more powerful medications, the nurse put a soft cast over the entire leg. It wasn't really as painful as it might sound, except during the digging and cleaning process, but the real "pain" was paying the $30 co-pay each time I went in. But sometimes you have to do what you have to do to stay healthy. Too bad I didn't heed the first warning way back when about taking care of things.

Julie could be a jealous person, so I had to be careful about looking at or flirting with the other females I worked with at the dealership when she was around. She did smoke but didn't get the same break times as I did, so I was able to be with some of the other girls during my breaks. I knew that made her really jealous because she couldn't see if I was doing anything she figured I shouldn't be doing. I found that odd at the time, since we weren't officially dating. What could be wrong with a little looking and chatting? It's not like I was taking any of the other girls home with me at night. But it was easier to keep any of my flirting activities away from Julie's eyes and ears. For the most part though, things were going pretty smoothly between Julie and me.

I mentioned that the finances were better when there were three sharing an apartment and all the bills went three ways, but it seemed I was still having a difficult time with my own money. Somehow I always seemed to come up short at the end of every paycheck and things were getting stressful again in my own mind. Bear in mind that I still couldn't bring myself to divulge any of this to Rob; his job was already stressful enough as it was and I sensed that his girlfriend really didn't like the fact that she had to share his life with me. I know she didn't care much for me anyway, so I didn't want her to know any of my financial problems either. It got to where I started to call anybody I knew, old friends, acquaintances, anyone, to see if I could borrow a little chunk of money, really any amount, so I could get caught up on things and start to breathe a little easier. That didn't work too well. I think I burned all sorts of bridges in the borrowing department when I was married. I was starting to get desperate and then I found my solution—the answer to my prayers: a Payday loan.

I'm sure most of you have heard about these types of loans, and while I know they can be useful in the right type of circumstances, in the wrong hands, they can be hugely destructive, as was in my case. But I was grateful for the instant $500 (I had the checking account and the work paystub that was required) and it helped me pay off some things, and gave me some extra spending money for two weeks, but then came my payday. I had to take my paycheck and cash it, going immediately to the Payday loan place and pay that back (including the $75 fee), but that left me almost no money for the next two weeks so really I was still broke. I had to have money so I had to re-up and get *another* $500 loan. This went on for a month and then I had another idea: get a *second* Payday loan from another company (these ideas of mine were going to put me in the poor house for sure)! I did that and eventually ended up with a third loan from yet another company, juggling payments every two weeks and slowly losing money every time. Crazy, crazy times! I think after two months of that madness, I paid one off and just skipped out of the other two, figuring they would eventually catch up with me anyway and I would deal with that later. After all, my credit was already shot, so how could things get any worse?

During that time I remember changing banks twice, more due to the checks that I had on file at the Payday loan places. The lesson that I have learned is NEVER take out that kind of a loan unless there is NO other choice, but even then it wouldn't be a good idea. That is just me. I shudder to think of the trouble that I would get into if I did that now, especially now that the limit is $700 or even more.

After work was over for the day, I found myself involved in a regular afternoon routine. I would hit the liquor store and grab a fifth of vodka and either stop by Brad's place on the way home. Brad was my friend and technician I worked with at the dealership. I would have drinks with him while I watched him play his video games, or I would just take swigs from of my vodka right from the bottle followed with soda chasers as I drove home. It was easier for me to have a buzz by the time I got home. Things were stressful enough with my poor finances and the bills and knowing I could see no light at the end of the tunnel.

I remember some afternoons when it was almost quitting time at work after the manager and other advisers had left, I would go out to my car and grab my water bottle (of course secretly containing vodka) and boldly take sips right at my counter. I would always be careful to chase those swigs with pop and eat mints to mask the breath, since occasionally customers would still come in to pick up their cars. But I don't want you to think I did that all the time, just mostly on Fridays since I could justify doing that as it was the end of the week and I was just getting an early start on the weekend.

Julie and I had been having our ups and downs and I remember we had one huge blowout over something probably really stupid such as her clinginess and jealousy or something like that. I remember going over to her apartment that next day with a bag of her stuff that she had left at my place, and telling her that things were done between us. It was over. Talk about a scene from a soap opera, it was horrible. There were tears; there was screaming, pleading, such emotion! I never in my life had seen someone show so much passion for me. Even right now, it touches me and that was so many years ago. But that afternoon I was firm that we were done but she followed me out to the car and just would not let go. She hung on to me and it was all I could do to finally get my car door closed and drive off. The next day at work was very strange, I had thought Julie would have called in sick, too emotionally drained and embarrassed to see me after the outburst that she had shown. But she was stronger than I thought she would be, showing no sign of tears or letting on that such a devastating event had happened the day before. It was all show, though, I could tell. No one else however was the wiser. Over the next month, we gradually warmed up to each other and things started getting better; she was not as clingy as before, the jealousy was not as evident, and it was more pleasant spending time with her. Julie was not only generous with her affections, but also with money. She knew about what was going on financially in my life (I don't know why I could share that part of me with her and not with Rob), and she was happy to help me out in those times of need, making things easier. Maybe Julie felt that as long as she could help me out, I would remain in her life and that would be a good thing for her.

Rob and his girlfriend had finally set the date and gotten married. Julie and I had become boyfriend and girlfriend and soon it became the four of us living in the three bedroom apartment. At first it was good, because all the bills were split by four, but Rob's wife started to get perturbed (understandable) with never having the time alone to spend with him, after all, they were married! Thinking back, it was kind of kooky, a newlywed couple living with other people. But it was agreed that as soon as the lease was up on the apartment, we would all get our own places.

One Friday afternoon I was called in to the service manager's office at work (this seemed to happen a lot it seemed). I was a little nervous, but I couldn't think of anything I would be in trouble for. The first thing he told me was that I had nothing to be worried about, he was just telling me that as of the following Monday, I was going to be transferred to the sales department. I looked at him like he was crazy! Was he serious? I knew nothing about selling cars. He said the company was going through some reorganization, and the owners thought it might be better for the company and myself to work in sales. I asked if there was any alternative, why I couldn't stay in service. He told me that that's the way things were going to happen, he didn't have any choice in the matter. I said okay, because I figured if I turned that assignment down, I would be without a job, and that wasn't going to happen. Money was tight enough as it was. The only thing I was a little miffed about was that I had been given no warning, no time to get any shirts and ties so I could at least look like a car salesman. Not really knowing the real reason I had been transferred bothered me. I still wonder to this day if it had something to do with alcohol (more than once I had been told that I smelled like a brewery in the morning). I told Rob that I had been trying my hand at selling cars the past few weeks and had decided to do that full time since I could make more money doing that than in service. Again I made up a story about what had happened, for some reason, I wanted things to appear as if it had been my choice for the transfer rather than the company's demandment.

Selling cars is nothing at all like selling service, I soon found out. I had gotten to know quite a few salesmen in my time at dealerships, but I never knew exactly what they went through on a daily basis until I joined their ranks. It sure seemed like all fun and games, joking around and laughing, getting to drive around in the new cars, all that stuff, but the bottom line is if you don't sell cars, you don't make money. I don't know if it was beginner's luck or what, but I found that during the first couple of weeks, I actually did a pretty decent job of selling and was beginning to think that I might have something good going after all. I was making more sales than some of the guys who had been there for a while which made the sales manager happy but seemed to piss off some of the salesmen who had been there for a while which certainly didn't help out the camaraderie. I remember a particular two week period where my paycheck after taxes was about $3200, pretty much the biggest single check I had ever received. Julie was so excited to see that check too. That two week period had to have been a fluke, all the planets must have been lined up and the car gods were smiling because after that, sales slowed down and the amount of my checks dwindled rather quickly. I really think though, if I had been able to generate that kind of income every check, I might still be selling cars, but I don't think that was meant to be.

Julie's grandmother who had been living in a mobile home owned by her father had passed away recently. Julie and I had been tossing around the idea of asking her dad about the possibility of moving into the mobile, since it was vacant and it would be a lot less for rent and utilities than any apartment that we had found since we had been looking. After posing the question to her dad he agreed that we could move in. That was a clearly a load off of my mind, especially since I knew what the cost of putting down the first and last month's rent plus deposit just to make any kind of move, not to mention the credit check (I would fail for sure).

Moving day came and Julie and I moved all of our stuff into the mobile home and Rob and his wife moved into their new apartment (same complex, different building). We were still all close enough that it would never be a problem to keep in touch and hang out whenever we wanted. Best friends are hard to come by and just because Rob was married and no longer my roommate didn't mean we would end our friendship.

Once Julie and I were moved into the mobile home in a way it was almost like we were married too, but not in a bad way. We set up house and it was actually pretty cool. It was really like our own house: the kitchen was big; there was a living room, a computer room, a master bedroom with walk-in closet and bathroom and a guest bedroom, the whole nine yards. Having all that space made me feel so much more comfortable than I had ever felt before, and not having to hide booze from anyone was such a burden off of me. It wasn't easy to keep things secret all the time; I hadn't realized how much effort I had put into that task. Julie had known me long enough and she knew that I had always hidden my excessive drinking from Rob, though she too had always thought I should

225

be open about it with him, but I just never could. Remember that Rob had told me about his prior roommates and how bad some of them had been with alcohol and that he thought I was the best roommate and friend he had ever had, and I didn't want to ruin that image he had of me (are you getting as tired of that excuse as I am?). But Julie didn't seem to mind that I drank a lot, so it was a relief that I didn't have to hide things from her. She was so sweet, she loved me and accepted me for who I was.

I knew that Julie would have be overjoyed to hear me say those three words to her once we moved in together into a place of our own, but I still couldn't say them. I was open and frank with her about that and told her again that I in just trying to be fair to her, I would only tell her that I loved her only when I could say it and truly mean it. She knew about my past with my ex-wife and with Rachel and that had caused me to be really gun-shy about relationships and she told me she understood. Not only did I believe her I also really respected her so much for that.

We didn't have a lot of furniture, so Julie went to IKEA and bought three dressers, a coffee table and a curio cabinet and spent an entire next week putting everything together for us. Not only did she not ask me for any help, she didn't really *need* any help. I remember asking, but she wanted to do everything herself, which really was fine. My job, she told me was putting the computer room together, so I made myself busy with that. I would make my drinks and put back together the computer desk she had had in her old apartment and had been taken apart so that it could be moved. It was pleasantly different to get buzzed out in the open instead of sneaking swigs from the bedroom closet like I used to.

About a week before the move, it was apparent that that damn infection was not done with me, as a scab on my other leg got bad and by the end of our first week in the new house, it was out of control. So another trip to the clinic ended up with another soft leg soft cast and antibiotics so the infection wouldn't get as bad as before. The nurse that had seen me the first time asked me if I drank a lot of alcohol because that could affect my immune system and how the antibiotics would work, and I told her that I only drank socially (yeah, that was a lie), and that was no problem that I could see with that. I ended up taking a week off from work and surprisingly did not drink any booze for at least four or five days while trying to get rid of the infection. It wasn't easy being a couch potato in a place with no cable and only a few VHS movies that I had already seen before. Thankfully by the last day of being bed-ridden, the cable was finally hooked up and I had more diversions to help pass the time. By that following Monday and another couple hundred bucks of co-pay visits to the clinic, I was more than ready to go back to work.

As I mentioned before, car sales started slowing way down, and consequently, my checks started getting way small, which was no small comfort for either Julie or myself. I was getting discouraged and started to wonder if I should start looking for another job or concentrate harder on drumming up sales. Part of what they tried to teach me in sales was making cold calls, which I hated doing. Another trick I was given was calling up old customers and suggest to them they should think about trading in their current cars for newer ones. I didn't like that tactic and I hated taking any calls that came in to the sales department. I just didn't think I had enough knowledge about the all the different cars the dealership had available to be able to answer whatever questions I might be asked. I had been lucky to generate most of my previous car deals through the customers that walked on to the lot, and from some of my former service customers that had come in specifically to see me. But that just wasn't working any more, and I just I never developed the personal motivation to learn more and get good at the tricks of the trade. Maybe I was just lazy.

One day I got a call from a guy I used to work with at the dealership in Bellevue. He had been a technician when I knew him before, but he had left before I had been fired. He now was the service manager at a dealership downtown Seattle selling the same line of cars as the Bellevue store. He had called to tell me there would be an advisor position opening up there in a month and remembered I had done well at that before and would I be interested in working there. His call could not have come at a more opportune moment and I wasted no time at all in answering him in the affirmative. Two weeks later I went to Seattle and filled out an application and was interviewed. I felt very positive when I left and knew with all the recommendations that I had gotten that I should have no trouble getting the offer, as most of the people in that line of cars in the area knew me and they had all felt I had gotten a bum deal in Bellevue. I was still pretty respected outside of that Bellevue dealership. I told Julie about what was going on, and she was excited for me and the opportunity. She also figured that there if I got that job there would be a larger paycheck as well as a stable income. I think she felt that I probably would be happier doing something I was more comfortable with. She didn't want me selling cars anymore and I'm sure hoped that maybe I would then cut down on my drinking with less stress. I think I had that hope as well.

Finally the call came that I had been hoping for. I was offered the position and I of course said yes. They asked me when I could start and at when I said that I would like to give a two week notice I could tell that answer was not going to work. They wanted me start right away. The next morning, Friday, I talked to the sales manager and he told me it wouldn't be a problem with me making it my last day in sales. What a true relief that was. For once things were starting to turn around and work in my favor! I called my new boss up and told him I could start that following Monday. Julie and I celebrated that weekend with a barbecue dinner with friends and of course I had my vodka. A true celebration always needed some booze! Life was good.

I was not at all worried about going in for the mandatory drug test, as it had been quite a while since I had smoked any crack. I remember joking with them that I they would surely find alcohol in the results, but nothing else. They laughed and said as long as nothing illegal came through I was fine...so of course I passed the test with no worries.

It felt really good to be back working with cars that I was already used to, and I was looking forward to the possibility of seeing some of the same customers I had worked with before. I was starting at a higher hourly rate than I had been getting before and was also guaranteed overtime, plus performance bonuses, so money would be a lot better.

I was used to working in locations that boasted large offices, spacious work bays and lots of room but now I was faced with quite the opposite. We were located in a smaller downtown Seattle building and the service department was tiny and cramped. It was difficult to maneuver cars in and out of the work bays and not to mention around the parking stalls. It was very claustrophobic but there was not much that could be done about that. Most of the dealerships in the downtown Seattle area had to deal with the same circumstances as we did. It was just something that I had to accept and work with.

The atmosphere of the department was a lot stuffier than I was used to. The solidarity that I had come to enjoy working around was not there and the people I worked with were for the most part not as open and overly friendly with me. Maybe it was just me and I was too new. Everyone else had worked together for years and here I enter, an outsider to the group. From the beginning though, I really felt like a foreigner and everyone had their guard up. I had no idea how long it would take for them to open up and let me truly get to know them—at least that was how I felt in my first few days and weeks there. Ultimately there were only a few of the technicians that I did become pretty good friends with.

The guy who I had known from before left the company the week I started and after he was gone, I heard a lot of stories about him that were pretty negative. I found he was not well liked by his co-workers, which did surprise me somewhat, because I had always thought he was a cool guy, but then again, it had been several years since I had seen him and anyone can change in that amount of time. My service manager was a tough guy to really get to know. His demeanor was all business for the most part. It was very rare that I ever saw him laugh or even smile for that matter. He was nice enough, don't get me wrong, and he and his family lived up near where Julie and I lived, but I don't think that outside of work, he or I ever would have socialized much. He had his crew that he liked and had worked with for a long time and I felt like I mentioned before that I was the outsider coming in. I don't know that I ever felt like I was fitting in, truly accepted as part of the team. I don't know, maybe I had too many expectations of how things should be myself. I just wasn't altogether comfortable working there, something just didn't *feel* right. But the money was good, and I supposed I just had to be fair and give things a chance.

Now that I was working Monday through Friday, the same as Julie was, we had more opportunity to spend more time with each other and decided to take advantage of that and go on some weekend road trips together. The best trip we took was to Ocean Shores on the Washington coast. It was a three day holiday weekend so of course there was a scarcity of lodging, but we did end up with a Jacuzzi room in an older motel, which wasn't too bad. That was Julie's thing, the Jacuzzi, and while she lounged in the warm foamy bubbles, I sat in the chair by the TV with my little cocktail bar set up, enjoying my drinks. We had a lot of fun doing the usual touristy things, going to the antique shops (which we both loved), driving her car on the beach and even renting mopeds for an hour. That was a lot of fun, but when I got on the moped, I thought more than once that was I going to crash and burn—my coordination just wasn't as good as what I remember it used to be. I chalked that up to the fact that I was just getting old. As was normal I drank a lot woke up a hangover that last morning, but before we left, we had a most excellent lunch at a local Chinese restaurant and I then felt like myself again. All in all, we did have a great time together.

Working downtown Seattle at that dealership was really starting to depress me and I found myself really looking forward for when it was time to go home. To me that was the best time of the day, more important to me than most people would think. I did my job, and as far as I was concerned, I did it pretty well, but I no longer felt the satisfaction. I didn't get up in the morning and look forward to going to work. I just looked forward to getting off of work. Then I was free and it was *my time*, the time I felt the best.

My drive home from work was getting pretty predictable by then. I would either get out of Seattle and hit the liquor store near the house and buy my vodka and then go home or I would stop at the liquor store near where my old technician friend lived. Then I would drink with him while he played video games and tell me how things were since I had left and then I would go home. If I didn't stop anywhere after making my purchases, I would just take swigs from the bottle while driving home. I knew the best routes to drive where there would be less chances of being stopped by cops or anything. Besides, I never drank so much that I would have to worry about my driving. I had been having my little cocktails while driving for some time now and had never had never before experienced any problems. Besides, I never wanted to get home and be so sauced that Julie would be so concerned that and start questioning my drinking. She had been pretty cool things all this time, but I don't think she really know that the amount of booze I drank had been increasing. And I wanted to keep it that way. I didn't hide my consumption as much from her on the weekends, as she knew that I liked to drink to unwind, and though I could tell she was a little concerned about those weekend binges, she hadn't yet really harped on me about that.

THE DOWNWARD SPIRAL

Wednesday, December 1, 2004 was not a good day. It started out normal enough. I got up and drove to work, counting the hours until I got off and could head home. By that time I had been service advisor at the new store for about 5 months and I was actually looking forward to attending the Christmas party with Julie that Friday. She was excited about the party as well She was looking forward to meeting all the people I worked with and finally put faces to names I had been talking about. She had really wanted to see if they acted all snobby the way I had portrayed them.

I left Seattle around 6 pm and headed up to North Seattle where my friend lived to have some shots with and to pass some time before getting home. I stopped at the liquor store first and bought a fifth and as well as a pint of vodka and when I got to my friend's place and parked I poured the contents of the fifth into a large water bottle so it wouldn't be obvious when I took my driving swigs. I then tossed the empty bottle on the passenger front seat, thinking I would toss it out somewhere before I got home. Why I didn't take it in and throw it in my friend's trash, I have no clue. I went in and we drank and I watched my friend play games on his Play-Station. I remember thinking that there was no way I could ever learn to play like him, I just didn't have that eye/hand coordination that he did, but it was fascinating to watch him. My cell phone rang and scared the shit out of me; I answered and it was Julie, wondering when I was coming home. I was surprised to see it was close to 7:30. I told her where I was and that I was just leaving. I think I had killed off the pint and was into the big water bottle before I left. I remember my friend asking if I was okay to drive and I said of course. Not a problem. I thanked him for the video lessons and headed for my car. It was cold and crisp outside, pretty normal for December, the fresh air was invigorating, and seemed to perk me up a bit, as I was tired from the long day at work and I had been starting to feel somewhat drowsy. After I started the car, I lit a cigarette, took a swig from the water bottle and looked forward to getting home. The Wednesday night comedies on CBS were going to have started before I got there, but that was okay, I had seen most of them already anyway.

I took all of the back roads and shortcuts that I normally did and began the drive up the hill toward our turn off that led to the mobile home park where we lived. For some reason, I decided I needed to make a stop at the AM/PM that was further up the hill and get some soda, so I drove past our road. All of the sudden I looked in the rear view mirror and my heart stopped when I saw the flashing red and blue lights behind me. I remember hoping that maybe, just maybe they were after someone ahead of me so I slowed down, hopeful the lights would move past me, but then I saw behind me headlights flash from normal setting to bright and then back to normal again, and I said, "oh ***Fuck*** me!" Why the hell did I have to think I needed to stop and get pop? Why didn't I just make my turn and go home? But then again, I don't know how long the cop had been behind me, either.

I'm sure a lot of thoughts were whirling around in my head right then, and I couldn't tell you what they all were, but I knew that I had to pull over. By that time, I was at the AM/PM parking lot and I turned into a stall, the cop parking right behind me (like he really thought.I was going to back out and trying to get away). I did think I for just a brief moment that there might be that slim chance that I could get out of a ticket if I just played it cool, but I know that no smart gambler would have bet on me that night.

My driver's window had not worked since the day I got the car all those years ago, so I opened up the door and said hello. I don't have a crystal clear memory about what was said or happened between the that moment and when I was placed in the patrol car, but I remember trying to be completely cooperative with the state trooper, not saying no to the field sobriety test nor saying no to the field breathalyzer test because I knew that would be an automatic suspension of my driver's license, and I needed to have that for my job. I did tell them that I had thrown my back out the prior Friday (was not lying) and it hurt like hell, so I would have problems walking a straight line (I did). I failed every test I was subjected to and as he was reading me my rights and handcuffing my hands behind my back, I saw another trooper (when did he show up?) stand up after reaching in the passenger front of my car, holding up the empty bottle of vodka (I'm sure that wouldn't be in my favor) and showing it to the arresting officer. I was placed in the patrol car, just like they did on *COPS*, the officer held my head down gently so I would not bump it against the door frame. He closed the door and off we went back to the state patrol offices about 20 minutes away.

I was really tired, more just from resignation and defeat than from anything else, and I did just what they tell you not to do when you have been arrested for DUI. I blabbed up a storm, being stupid and also trying just to keep myself awake. I knew I was slurring, but I don't think I cared; I just wanted to keep some conversation going and show I was a nice guy. I remember asking the officer if he had everything ready for Christmas, stupid bullshit like that, and according to the police report, I said that I knew I was guilty and I shouldn't have been driving. They gave me another breath test at the station and I registered a .20 – something outrageous, and I asked him if that was high. He looked at me and asked me how many drinks I had had. I think I said maybe 2 or three. Yeah, right.

It came time to make my phone call, and right then, my cell phone rang and I saw by the caller ID it was Julie. The officer nodded that I could answer it, and when I told Julie where I was and that I had been arrested for DUI she just started screaming her head off, so loud that when I held the phone away from my ear the officer could hear her yelling. I looked at him with a very pathetic grin and said something like "you think I'm in trouble now? Wait until I get home. She is pissed!" He did look like he might actually feel sorry for me, and I tried to talk to Julie and let her know I was all right but she just kept going. Finally she calmed down enough to let me tell her where to come and get me, that they were not going to jail me overnight. That was a blessing, because I had no idea how I would ever explain my absence at work the next day. I had seen other people at dealerships lose their jobs after getting DUIs and if that happened to me I would be ruined. I pretty much thought my life was over with anyway, but I knew I had to salvage what I could. I handed the phone to the officer so he could tell Julie how to get to the station, then I signed some papers and was escorted to the front door. I longed desperately for a cigarette, but they were in my car. Julie finally got there and we drove back to my car. She did not say one single word during the entire ride back, she just looked straight ahead, her eyes red and wet from crying. She was still pissed (I really couldn't blame her) but at least she was not yelling anymore.

We got back to my car, and I told her we had to leave it there. If either one of us, especially myself, even attempted to drive the car home, we would be arrested on the spot and the car would be put into impound. I wanted to get a few things out of the car, specifically my smokes and my "water bottle" that they had not taken or dumped out. Funny the water bottle fooled someone after all! Before we left I went into the AM/PM and asked if they minded the car left overnight, and they said that was fine. When I got back into Julie's car I noticed the state trooper parked across the street in the vacant lot, watching us. As I got back into Julie's car and closed my door, his lights came on and he drove away. I knew he had been serious about making sure I wouldn't be stupid enough to try and drive home. I lit up a cigarette and looked at Julie and told her again I was sorry (I really was), and she just stared straight ahead and said softly, "I know." We got home and I saw it was only about 9:30, I was really surprised at how early it still was, as it seemed like I had just gone through a lifetime of events. I figured that considering what had just happened things were going to change things in my life, in more ways than one, but right then, I didn't want to think about those things, right then I didn't give a rat's ass—all I did want to do was drink more and forget. It was early enough still that knew I had plenty of time to get back that nice feeling that I had had before the state trooper pulled me over (I had lost any buzz I had had after that escapade), and I had more than enough left in the water bottle. Julie went into the computer room to do what it was she did and I went outside below the bedroom window and did what I did best: watch TV through the window and smoke cigarettes and drink my "water" while chasing it down with pop. I don't think I finished until I was numb enough to go to sleep.

At work the next day, Tuesday, things went on as usual, except that every time the phones rang, or my service manager was paged, I half expected it to be from the main store informing him that I had been popped for a DUI and would get fired. I was hung-over (not really unusual) and paranoid as hell. I remember rubbing my wrists, which were sore and I thought that I must have slept wrong or something during the night to make them that way. I then remembered it was because I rode hand-cuffed to the police station with my hands behind my back. That was what made them sore. I don't recall seeing any black marks under my fingernails to indicate I was fingerprinted though. It was a very long day, but there were no calls from the head office about me. It turned out there were never any calls about me from that day until the day I left there, so my worrying about that was for naught.

Wednesday evening the Christmas party was supposed to be filled with fun and frivolity, and Julie and I did the best we could to put up the façade of smiles and the pretense of enjoying the celebration, but inside I know I was just sick with guilt, frustration and knowing that I was living a lie hiding from work the fact that I had a DUI, and that my license was going to be gone in 30 days. Like I have said before, people had been fired from there for that, and I just could not afford to lose my job. I think the worst feelings that I was going through were that not only had I let myself down and embarrassed me, but not knowing what kind of damage I had I done to my relationship with Julie. I knew she might eventually forgive me, but I knew also that she would not forget, especially if it led to me losing my job and my income. She was not just the type of person who relied on a person solely for their income. I think the income of *both parties* is important in any relationship. I knew that if I fucked that up, we were in trouble.

I think that in situations where something major has happened, a couple should be able to rely on each other for comfort and support, gain strength from each other to help through the difficult times. I think that is certainly what I should have done with Julie. But instead of doing that, I went instead for the support of my other lover, my vodka. My fearless companion was always there for me, always helping me to soothe my stress, dull my pain. Instead of sitting down with Julie and telling her how I felt and share my thoughts of how scared I was, ask her what I should do, what could she do to help me, I instead retreated into my own space. I did not shut her out completely, but enough.

I knew now that Julie would be keeping an eagle eye on my drinking so now I had to be even more careful about how I drank around her, I needed to plan my purchases way more careful so that she did not know or could not monitor my consumption. I was pretty clever about that for quite some time. She would undoubtedly figure out that I drank more, but I didn't want to do anything to help her figure out how much more I drank..

There came an opportunity at work for me to attend a function out of state where we would be able to see and experience how one of the new models of one of the cars we sold drove. I would be flown to some exclusive testing grounds in Arizona and put up in a really fancy hotel with all the expenses to be paid by the dealership. All I would have to do is present my driver's license at check in because all the participants who would be driving the vehicles (I would be among them) had to have valid licenses in order to take part in the functions. At first I wasn't too concerned because I hadn't had to turn in my license to the Washington DOL yet, but a couple of days before I was to fly out, I noticed that my license had a hole punched right over the state seal. What the fuck? I hadn't noticed that before! After thinking about that, I realized the state trooper must have done that when I was arrested that night. Now I was starting to really sweat. I couldn't now tell my manager I could not go. There was not enough time to come up with a good enough excuse to allow me to bow out of the event. All I could do is go and hope they didn't notice the hole when they looked at my license when I checked in. If they did, and I was not allowed to participate, I would be liable for the round trip airfare, the hotel and any costs I incurred while I was there. Then I would be fired for sure. Julie was equally concerned, but she knew as well that there was nothing else I could do except keep my fingers crossed.

Luck was with me this time and I was checked in without any problems. I breathed a sigh of relief, knowing that I could relax and enjoy the weekend. I had packed two fifths of vodka with me, so I was set. It turned out to be a really nice time, I did learn a lot about the new vehicle and found out that there were a lot of partiers in dealerships from all over the country and enjoyed the alcohol flowed freely as I had heard at events like this. I did enjoy two other trips while working at that dealership, so I could never say my entire experience working there was all bad.

Either because I had not had any direct experience with DUI's to know exactly how to handle everything, or I can use the excuse of just plain procrastinating on taking care of things, I really screwed up and ended up missing the DOL hearing regarding my license. I received a letter in the mail telling me it was no longer valid and that I needed to remand it to the DOL. Julie told me I needed to take this a whole lot more serious than I had been and how come I hadn't thought about getting an attorney so I didn't fuck up and end up in jail. Julie was starting to get a lot more vocal with me, probably for the best...

Yeah, so here's what I can tell you about finding a DUI attorney: don't go out and get one just because you see him advertising on TV all the time saying he is the best and knows how to take care of you. I did just that and when it all came down to the wire, I was no better off than if I had gone to court and represented myself. Of course, I can't rightly blame *everything* on the attorney I had. In the end, it came down to the fact that I had blabbed in the patrol car that night and pretty much it was my own lips that had sealed the deal. I ended up pleading guilty and hope for the best. The nearly year and a half before my sentence was such a crazy time. I used up all of my available vacation days to attend all of the scheduled hearings; when I had to spend a night at the county fairgrounds for my "one day in jail" I told work that I had to help Julie's dad with the remodel of his basement so I needed two days off for personal time. With all the excuses and sweating and (to me) suspicious behavior I must have exhibited at work, I am really surprised that work never found out about my DUI and all that I had to go through just to take care of everything.

Also during that time, my car finally lost all of its oil and the engine seized and died. Consequently I had to take bus to work every day, which was really not a problem, since work paid for my bus pass, so transportation was covered. Riding the bus was a relief, actually, because I no longer had the stress of fighting traffic and I could literally sleep on the way downtown if I needed to (I did need to most of the time). I could also just sit back and unwind on the way home. The only bad thing was that Julie had to drive me down the hill to the bus stop every morning at 5:30 and make sure to pick me up on her way home from work at the end of the day. But for the most part, we adjusted to the schedule. I remember two times actually getting up, showering, shaving and getting dressed and waking Julie up to take me to work, only to be told it was 2 in the morning! I think that was caused by my booze. We laugh at that now.

I had my return trip planned perfectly so I was always be able to get my vodka before I got home. There were two routes I could take, each one with easy access to a liquor store (I had a problem with not wanting to be seen at the same store every day), and at some point after the purchase I would pour the vodka into my water bottles and then I could get a head start while waiting for the next bus. I would have an orange soda and chips to help mask my breath, and that became my daily on-the-way-home routine. I always would hide any extra bottles under newspapers or gloves or whatever else I had in my satchel that I carried to and from work every day, so Julie would not think to question me about things. I had her fooled pretty well or so I thought. There was no way with all of my "security" that she would ever figure that I started my "party" before she even picked me up. If I ended up taking the Express bus directly back to the stop at the bottom of the hill, there was a brand new liquor store that had opened up in that strip of stores that I used as a backup. I only had to hope that Julie did not beat me there, because if I ever got back home without my booze, my night was horrible. It was getting to the point where I really needed to have my vodka to help me relax and eventually get a good night's sleep.

One Saturday afternoon, I think it was, Julie and I were at the grocery store near the house shopping for things, and she was talking on her cell phone while maneuvering the cart around other shoppers. She stopped and started to hand me the phone, saying someone wanted to talk to me. It was "R," her old boyfriend, who she was still best friends with after all that time. He had been in and out of her life since before and after we had become a couple. I was never really jealous of their relationship because she had told me they were just friends and he had done a lot of good things for her. I trusted Julie and believed what she told me. Anyway, I asked her what he wanted and she told me just to take the phone. I did and he started telling me that he thought that I had a drinking problem, not specifically in those exact words (though he is a very abrupt person who says what he means, and has very little tact) and he had a book that he thought I should borrow from him and read. I remember the first think I did was deny it and no, I didn't. I said, sure, I drank more than some people, but I don't think that I was a crazy drinker, I never was obnoxious or overly aggressive, and I never got into trouble drinking, except for that "incident." I told him that I was not an alcoholic. He said that he really thought I should pay attention to him, that he knew all about drinking and what it can do, and how he had been to lots of meetings and that I should really read the "book" he had. I told him I was fine and gave the phone back to Julie and I think I went out to the car to have a smoke and take a swig from my "water bottle" to unwind. I felt offended by R's intrusion into my life right at that time. I felt it was none of his business, regardless of how much of a friend he was to Julie. I did not hurt her when I drank! I never laid a hand on her or caused us to lose money (except for all the money we were paying to my "attorney" for the DUI).

Of course, what I really felt was that maybe I *was* drinking a bit much, but I wasn't too bad, I knew friends and people who drank much more than I did! Besides, I always made it to work on time, never called in sick, always did my job. Sure I probably was never 100% and I always had to make sure to put cologne on before I got to work (so I didn't smell from the night before). I do remember quite a few afternoons around 4, I started getting the shakes a little, but that was all pretty normal, they were things I was used to. But I knew that I was in control of everything. Some days I purposefully did not drink, just to make sure that I was okay. Sleep was a little harder when I did that, but I didn't go into convulsions and die, so it was all good. Then the next afternoon I would get my vodka as usual and have my own party waiting for the next bus, and etc. etc. I think deep down though, I knew my drinking was probably more than just a "little" problem.

There started to be more than a few occasions that I would wake up and have no memory at all of what happened the last part of the night, that maybe I had done something but would not have a clue what I did. A few times I would be watching a movie laying on the bed in the bedroom and I had a pint or a water bottle in my hands thinking I would hide them under the pillow before I fell asleep and then I would all of the sudden sit up alert and they would be gone. That meant one of two things. I finished them off and threw them away or Julie came in when I had fallen asleep and confiscated the goods. Since I would never find the empties in the garbage, I always would assume the latter. I never asked her about it at the time because what if she hadn't done anything and it was me in a blackout mode hiding my own booze?

The funniest blackout story (not really "funny" but we'll just call it that) was when Julie asked me where the casserole dish with the lid was— that she wanted to return it to R's mom and she couldn't find it. We looked everywhere, and I mean *everywhere!!* Kitchen, living room, bedrooms even the carport and cars, but it was nowhere to be found. I even called my buddy Rob as he was over the prior weekend when he and I had our own little BBQ, and I asked if maybe he took home leftovers in the casserole dish. There was a pause on the phone and I heard him ask me if I was serious. I said yes, we had been looking for it all day, why? He asked me again if I really was serious, did I not remember what had happened. I thought Rob was messing with me. I had no idea what he was talking about. He told me that the dish was sitting on top of the little refrigerator that had gotten from the downtown Bellevue hotel and when he had closed the door after getting a soda, the dish came crashing to the floor and shattered into a million pieces, scaring the shit out of both of us. Rob told me he swept all the shards up for me because I was drunk and he didn't want me to hurt myself. Now it was my turn to ask, "Are you *serious*??" I actually thought it was kind of comical but when I told Julie, she was furious. So I told her that I would buy a new dish and lid, that there was no big deal. I couldn't understand why she was getting so bent out of shape! But she was more concerned that I didn't have any memory about the incident and also that she spent half the day looking for the dish and fretting.

It wasn't just the memory or blackouts that started bothering me, but there were a couple of times that by the end of the day, I would be shaking so badly that I could not hold a glass of beer or use a knife and fork to eat with. One of those times Rob and I were out eating Chinese and had to fake feeling sick so I didn't have to embarrass myself by knocking over the drink or dropping my silverware. But even with all that, it didn't really stop me from my drinking. I would just try to cut back on how much I drank and things seemed to get better and back to normal.

But what was normal? It was starting to get harder and harder to tell. I think all the alcohol had been waging war on my nerves, as I would be more jumpy than I can remember ever being. Someone could come up behind me and even though I could hear them getting closer, more often than not I would physically jump if they said something or touched me on the shoulder. I remember at the second office Christmas party, we had a surprise visit from a local charity group all dressed up as pirates and when they burst into the room singing a pirate song, I was so startled that I about shit my pants and almost dove under the table. Some people were more amused at my reaction than they were at the pirates. I don't ever remember reacting like that with such intensity before. That happened more and more as time went on, and that really started to bother me, but like usual, I kept on drinking.

Drinking was not only affecting my nerves, but I seemed to have gained much more weight during that past year than I could remember. I didn't think I was even close to what I thought was a good weight and the last time I had weighed myself I was well over 220 pounds. I have always felt that with my height and bone size, I should be no more than about 185 or so, but I was so much bigger than that. I remember walking to the store at lunch from work and seeing my reflection in the windows of stores I would be walking by and being repulsed at the size of my stomach. It was gross. I was embarrassed to be seen in public without a coat or something covering my stomach. For a while after that, I remember always using diet soda to chase my swigs of booze. No more of the regular high calorie sodas for me (like that was seriously going to help!).

The New Year, 2006 came and things were pretty much the same. Julie and I took one more road trip out to Lake Chelan in the spring and we were having a pretty good time, going to the little casino they had—I actually fared fairly well, though my winnings at the blackjack table seemed to end up in Julie's hands and then she would lose at the slot machines. But that was okay, she was having fun and that was a good thing. Later that afternoon, I finished the first fifth of vodka while we were watching TV in the motel room, talking and laughing and I had a nice buzz going. I am not sure what happened or what Julie said, but I remember all of the sudden getting angry and we started arguing about something, probably nothing of any importance and I got up and left the room. It was still very hot outside and I don't know where I thought I was going, but I just had to be away from her. Then I turned back around and went back to the room. I wasn't yelling or trying to cause a scene when I went back inside, but I think I apologized to her and said that she must have pushed one of my buttons. She had a knack of doing that (or at least that is what I always thought when I was drinking) and I told her that she needed to stop doing that. Julie told me she didn't know what I was talking about and I think I tried to drop the subject and told her I was sorry again. I opened up the second fifth and poured a stiff drink for myself and we went back to watching the TV. I think it was about an hour later when the bottle was half gone, Julie mentioned the bottle was going down rather fast and maybe I should slow down. I told her that maybe I should drink it faster so that it would be gone and she wouldn't have to worry about it anymore.

That is the last I really remember about that night. I woke up on the couch in different shorts than I had been wearing the night before. Julie said that I had passed out and peed myself because I couldn't get to the bathroom, so she put dry shorts on me after taking care of my mess. I had a severe hangover that day and drank a lot of fruit punch on the way home, neither of us talking too much. I remember thinking (I had a lot of time to think on that way home, traffic was terribly slow) that something had to change, I couldn't keep going on doing the same things, Julie didn't deserve it, I didn't deserve it, something had to change!

The last full week of July, 2006, Wednesday or Thursday, I don't remember which day it was, but work was work and I was hung-over pretty good. It was one of those times that I had the feeling I was still enduring the effects of the alcohol and it had not quite worn off yet, so I was still in that haze, things still not quite crystal clear... anyway, I was helping out with washing cars while our shuttle driver was out driving customers. As I had mentioned previously, the garage was small and cramped and maneuvering cars was tricky at best. The best way to put a car in the wash bay was to back it in. I was doing just this, backing a customer's vehicle from across the garage, moving in reverse slowly, being sure to watch carefully for any other moving vehicles. As I moved past another car, apparently I was too close and scraped against it, though I never felt or heard any noises that would occur in such an action. I saw my manager walking fast toward me and also noticed the customer he was talking to pointing at me shouting something. I rolled down the window and asked him what happened and he told me to get out and that he was going to send me out to get tested (meaning drug and alcohol tested). He told me to wait for the sales porter who would drive me. I got out and waited near the back of the garage, with butterflies swarming double time in my stomach. I think I knew at that point that I was in serious trouble. It wasn't necessarily the alcohol I knew that I had in my system that was worrying me, but two nights prior, I had found an old crack pipe somewhere in a drawer at the house and lit it, seeing if there was still any residue in it from way back when, so I was worried that I would test positive for cocaine as well. But either way, I knew that when the test was done, I would be done as well.

We got to the testing center and I remember having a very hard time blowing into the breath analyzer, I had to take three tries to register anything at all. Then I peed into the cup and they dipped the thing in (these days you know pretty much instantly) and the guy looked at me like I had just tested positive for some contagious disease and that told me pretty much everything I needed to know. All the way back to the dealership, I tried to think of something, anything I could say to my manager, but I think I knew that there was not going to be anything that would make a difference. Back in the service garage, I got out of the shuttle car and walked into the office as my manager was coming out. He said that by now "I'm sure you realize I have the results of your test." I looked at him and asked him if we could step out for a smoke and we could talk. He told me he didn't have time for that. The only other thing he told me was to go inside and get anything I needed from my desk and go home, I was no longer an employee of the company. That was it. I went in and grabbed a few things and my satchel and left, avoiding eye contact with my former co-workers. I was too ashamed to look directly at them. I remember being emotional, but not to the point where I was going to break out in tears. I walked out of the garage and made my way to a bus stop, not just any, but the one I knew that was closest to the liquor store; I had to get some medication.

I was feeling pretty numb as it was, but in a strange way, I felt free, I felt released from the constant fear of being found out that I no longer had a driver's license, free from working where I didn't like working, and I really wasn't bitter. I was not angry, not upset at what happened because I somehow knew it had been only a matter of time before something happened that would culminate in this. I just had not known when it would occur. But now it had and all I had to do was try to deal with the aftermath of it all. Facing Julie and telling her would be the worst of it. For that I needed my booze. It was still before noon, but the time of day did not mean anything to me at that point, and I went inside and bought a pint and a fifth of vodka and went in search of somewhere I could empty the pint into my water bottle. I caught a bus from Seattle to downtown Bellevue and called Julie, quite buzzed by then, and jokingly told her that I was taking the rest of the day off from work. She knew something else was going on, probably hearing something in my voice or in what I said, maybe hearing me slur or something, and asked what was wrong. I told her that something had happened at work and that I had been fired and was coming home... I don't remember exactly what I had said, but she said that she was going to have R call me. He did call and asked where I was and then he told me to wait for him to get there. I was feeling pretty detached and spaced out by that time, I suspect everything was starting to sink in as far as what happened and I was getting depressed. I went into the store I was waiting in front of and got some lunch, I was kind of hungry, not having had anything to eat since the night before. I drank more than I ate and probably stunk like booze by the time R got there because I remember him saying something like how much I must have had to drink so early. He didn't lecture me or chastise me on anything, he just told me about some of his past jobs he had had and lost due to things he had done. He was really cool about things and I opened up and told him everything that happened and though I didn't have a job anymore, I felt more relief than anything. I asked him what Julie had told him, and he said she was really concerned and just wanted me to go home and take it easy until she got home. I laughed and told him I wouldn't be going anywhere, I had all I needed.

I was in the computer room when Julie came home. She gave me a hug and told me that we really needed to do something about my problem. I knew what she was talking about and all I could say was that I agreed and I would. The look in her eyes was haunting and she said that she was serious, that I needed to get some help. I said that I know and I needed to just stop drinking and get another job and everything would be okay. I told her I would take care of things, for her not to worry. I would get things under control. I don't know that she believed anything that I had said, but she nodded and walked out of the room. I turned back to the computer and started playing Solitaire and took a swig of vodka.

I got drunk that Friday, Saturday and Sunday night and Monday R took me downtown Seattle where I went and turned in my work shirts and signed my release papers. I didn't talk to anyone in the service department but the sales people were really consoling and told me that if there was anything I needed, that I should be sure and call them. Then my manager came out and asked me if I wanted to get the extra Cobra insurance for while I was unemployed and I told him that was out of the question, how could I afford that when I was not making any money? I checked off the box that said I declined and left. That night Julie told me that she had been looking on the internet and checking into places where I could go to get help with my drinking problem. I told her that I didn't need to go anywhere, that I could just quit right at home where I was comfortable, that I knew I could quit on my own. She looked at me and shook her head and said that what she had read was that it would be too hard to quit drinking cold turkey and that I would be putting myself at serious risk if I tried, that my body would not be able to handle the withdrawals without medication. She was really worried and concerned and I could see the tears welling up in her eyes. This really touched me and I think I may have started to cry as well. I told her I knew I had a problem and I really wanted to try just quitting at home. Julie told me that I really needed to get professional help. She sounded very adamant about this, very convicted about it. I knew she wouldn't budge on this. I remember asking her "if I don't do this, are we over?" She didn't say yes or no, but she didn't have to. I didn't want to risk that right then, so I told her that I would do what she wanted. I trusted her and meant it.

I had to let my parents know what was going on, about my job, what had happened, about my problem and what I was going to do. I was just having a hard time trying to work myself up to actually doing that. I wanted so much just to call and talk to Mom on the phone, but just the thought of hearing how hurt she would sound, how disappointed that one of her sons was going in for treatment because of alcohol, I was sure that would shock and embarrass her because I don't know of anyone in the family who was at the point where I was. Of course, I had already given her cause for grief and stress with so many of the other things that I had done since leaving home, what more could this possibly do, I thought. But something about this seemed to me to be so different, so much more of a letdown, that I just couldn't bring myself to call. I wrote her an email instead and just said that I was taking some time off of work to go take care of a personal problem that had been escalating for some time. I wrote that I was worried about my drinking and wanted to take care of it before it took care of me and I hoped she understood. I sent it and then played Solitaire (I seemed to play that more and more on the computer) for an hour or so, waiting for what I assumed was going to be a brutal and scathing return reply from Mom.

About an hour or so later I received a reply from her that was more heartfelt and sincere than I ever thought I would get from her. She told me that I had 100% support from her and Dad, that they would *always* stand behind me no matter what, and that they were so very proud of the decision that I had made and what I was doing. She went on to say that she suspected that I might have had a problem, especially by the way I looked when she and Dad were last up visiting me when I introduced them to Julie a few months back. She said that my skin didn't look healthy and she thought that I seemed to be a lot pudgier than I should be... basically that I didn't seem quite right, though at the time she couldn't put a finger on it. She told me that I should not be ashamed of myself in the least and that I should feel good about what I was doing. They had close friends who had gone through the same thing. I think most people nowadays know or know of someone who has gone in for alcohol related illness or treatment. It is so much more common today, or maybe it is just more out in the open than in years past. I called Mom up later that evening and we had a really great talk, and she made me feel a lot better and surer of myself. I love my Mom!

It was now Tuesday and when Julie came home that night she told me that she had made arrangements for me to go to treatment. I asked her where she had planned for me to go and she showed me the website, which I have to admit looked pretty impressive, but also it looked like it would be expensive as hell. I asked her how we could ever afford something like that, and she told me she had arranged for me to have the Cobra insurance from the dealership. I reminded her that I had already declined that and how did she ever accomplish that? Julie said it wasn't easy, and it had taken more than a few phone calls and faxes and not so friendly words with the human resources department at the dealership, but that they finally relented and let her get my Cobra started. I have no idea what she said, but I know that when Julie puts her mind to something, she can be very persuasive. I know the thing she was pissed off about the most was that if that company really cared about their employees they would have offered to send them to treatment and have their job waiting for them when they were out. I told her that not all companies were that way and though I knew that had I been someone who had been there longer and more well liked, it's possible that might have been the case, but that sometimes life is life, and you just have to accept what comes and deal with it.

So it was all set and I would be entering treatment, but that was two days away, and that meant I had only two more nights that I could drink, so I didn't want waste them. R had told Julie that it might be wise to let me drink what I wanted so there would be less chance of having any withdrawal symptoms before I got to treatment. R was going to stay at the house with Julie while I was gone and since he had a good job selling cars, he agreed he would help out with the bills and keep things going until I got back and even until I got another job and started making money again. I trusted him with Julie, and I really was thankful that he was such a good friend of hers that he would offer to do that.

The day before I went in, Julie had told me she would bring me my last fifth of vodka on her way home from work and that was fine. I kept myself busy doing things around the house that afternoon, doing laundry, cleaning the kitchen, anything to keep me distracted and about 2 that afternoon I walked to the AM/PM and got a 6 pack of 16 ounce beers in the cans and drank them, thinking by the time I was done, she would be home. Then she called to tell me she was trading in her car for a newer used one and would be later than planned, which ordinarily would be fine, but this was my *last night drinking* and what the hell was she thinking? Did she have to pick this night of all nights to trade her car in? I was out of booze and didn't want to go out and get more *beer*! I wanted my *vodka*! By the time she got home it was after 9 and she didn't seem the least bit sorry or apologetic, it was like it was nothing to her, no big deal at all that it was my last night to drink! I really didn't want to get so late a start drinking that I would be up all night, though in retrospect, what matter did it make? Still, I was pissed off at Julie's obvious disrespect, lack of concern for me. Not that I thought she really did it on purpose, or out of any spite, she was just caught up in the excitement of her new purchase and wasn't thinking. As soon as she gave me the bottle, I was happy again, like a five year old when he finally gets that piece of candy he has been longing for. I drank my vodka that night, drank the whole fifth while smoking and watching TV and whatever else I did. After a certain point I didn't remember and I didn't care. Then it was morning.

TREATMENT

Julie had taken the morning off from her job so that she could take me in to the treatment center. She woke me up at around 7 and I certainly felt like I looked: like shit. But seriously, was I expecting to feel any different after consuming a whole fifth the previous night? Though I had done that before, something about that morning in particular felt different. I knew I was not going to be drinking again, or at least that was my heartfelt intention. I showered and shaved and still did not feel any better. This felt similar to when Julie dropped me off for my 24 hour "incarceration" at the state fairgrounds the year before as part of my 'sentence,' but this time it was going to be for a lot longer, 4 weeks longer. There was not much conversation in the car on the way there other than comments on how much nicer her newer car was than the one she had just traded in. Julie held my hand for a little bit, doing her best to keep my spirits up. She kept telling me it wasn't like I was going to be gone forever, or like I was going to jail, it was something I should be looking forward to. All I could think of was that I was going somewhere without her, totally unfamiliar, all by myself. I was not going to know anyone, and I was giving up something that I was not really sure I would be able to. In my heart though, I knew I was doing the right thing. There were so many emotions flowing through me during that ride, I didn't know whether to laugh, cry, or throw open the car door and start running at the next stop light!

It turned out the treatment center was the same place I used to live near when my ex-wife and I got our place, the one I always thought would be convenient in case she ever drove me to drink too much. Small world, I thought.

Julie parked in a stall marked "admitting only" and we got out, me carrying my duffel bag packed with clothes, books, puzzle magazines, toiletries and anything else I thought I might need for my stay. We went inside and were escorted to a waiting room that had several chairs in it and a fish tank; it looked like a typical doctor's office waiting room, but when the door was closed while we waited for whoever was going to talk to us, I felt imprisoned already. Julie sat across from me and she had tears in her eyes as she looked at me. I had to look away before I started crying. It was very hard, I just wanted to hug her and not let go. I just wanted to have her take me back to the car and take us both home. The door opened and a woman came in and started explaining to us about what was going to happen and that she needed Julie to sign some forms. We were told that during the first week there would be no be visitors allowed and no phone calls for the first 72 hours. Then she gave us a brief overview of the rules and regulations, and then asked us if we had any questions. I was so nervous I couldn't think of any, I just didn't want Julie to leave. Then I did remember one: was there going to be a huge push of Alcoholics Anonymous? I didn't want that crammed down my throat; I just wanted to stop drinking. We were told that AA was included in the treatment program, but it wasn't forced. I thought for a moment, and decided as long as it wasn't going to be "the Law!" Then after we had signed and initialed everything we needed to, we were given a few minutes alone before I was admitted. We hugged and kissed and then I told her I wanted her to go, I needed her to leave, right then, before it got any harder. Julie hugged me one last time and kissed me on the cheek and then left, I know she was crying when the door closed behind her. I sat down in the chair, alone, feeling so very alone. I felt like my dog Luke must have felt when I dropped him off at the Humane Society all those years ago, abandoned.

I was taken to an office and given the initial indoctrination, filled out some more forms and my duffel bag was searched, to make certain there were no hidden supplies of alcohol, drugs and other things that weren't allowed in the center. Those things I understood, but then my cologne was taken away (it had alcohol in it and patients had been known to drink colognes) and my mouthwash (alcohol free right on the label) was confiscated as well. I said something at that, pointing out that it was purchased especially for coming in here. They also kept my books and puzzle magazines. They said I would get them back when I left. There was no TV, newspapers or radios to be had. They wanted all the patients to have complete concentration, no distractions from treatment—because that's what they were in there for.

I was taken into the nurse's office and given a blood test, abreathalyzer test and then I had to give a urine sample. The alcohol breath test registered a .30, the same as I had registered when I got fired from the dealership. Now, according to what I read later, when one blows that high, they should technically be in a coma, but there I was, coherent and walking around. I might have made a joke about that, but it was brief and I just wanted to get to wherever I was supposed to go and curl up in a ball and go to sleep. I was given a physical exam and then medication to help ease the physical withdrawals of alcohol, so that I would not go into seizures. When that was done, they informed me they had taken my OTC heartburn pills that I had brought in and said if I needed them I had to come to the nurse's station and request them, that was just procedure. I had been taking those pills pretty much every other day for the last year and was scared that I wouldn't have control over them, but they said once I stopped drinking I probably would not need them. I was then given the choice to dig in and sit in on the afternoon seminar or go to my room and rest. I chose my room.

The room was like an old hospital ward room, very cold and clinical, right down to the tracks in the ceiling where the bed curtains used to be. If I got really bored, I could count the little perforated holes in the ceiling tiles. There was no view outside the barred windows except for a fence that concealed whatever yard was next door. There were two other beds in the room, both of them were currently unoccupied for which I was grateful. The person who showed me to my room helped me unpack my duffel bag and put things in the little nightstand drawers next to the bed. When he saw my carton of cigarettes (those were allowed there), he suggested that I keep them behind the counselors counter where many other patients did. I asked why, and was told that cigarettes were a precious commodity and sometimes patients' smokes were known to go missing. I said I wanted to keep mine with me; after all, almost every other personal item I had had been taken away from me. I was then left alone and I lay down on the bed. The mattress was like a hard plastic mattress-wannabe and the pillow felt like it was filled with Styrofoam popcorn, both were as uncomfortable as anyone could imagine. I probably could have slept better on the floor. I was tired, but all I could do was just stare up at the ceiling. I closed my eyes, but I could not fall asleep. I felt like an alien on a foreign planet, like a fish out of water, not knowing what to do or what to think. I had never felt so alone before. At some point, probably due to exhaustion and the help of the medication, I did fall asleep.

I woke up later, still depressed and groggy and saw it must have been late afternoon, as the light from the window was not as bright as it was before. There was a knock at the door and a younger guy came in and asked if I was Steve, and when I nodded he told me that he was my new "treatment buddy" and he was there to show me around the place. He seemed friendly and shook my hand and asked me if I felt up to coming with him or if I wanted to rest some more. I told him I was tired but thought I might be up to seeing what he had to show me. He was a very talkative guy, and as he was showing me where everything was, the lecture halls, the dining room, the lounge area with the ping pong table, the outside area with picnic tables and a sand-filled volley ball, court he was telling me about himself a little bit. This was his third week in treatment but it was his second time there. He seemed pretty vocal and opinionated, but I liked him. There were so many people he introduced me to and so many names, I knew I would never remember them all, so I just said hello and nodded a lot. By that time it was time to head to dinner.

I had been assigned to the same "color group" my treatment buddy was in. Every group was assigned their own table in the dining room where we sat and ate our meals. When I first saw all the people in the dining room, I thought at first it was odd that there were so many staff members working at the place, and then I realized they were all patients. I had no idea there were so many people there were who were just like me with the same problem. For some reason it was a major eye-opener. I sat at the end of our table and I think because I was new, everyone gave me space and did not pester me with lots of questions and respected my silence; they had all been where I was and knew I would come around in a day or so.

I spent two days in the "detox" wing of what I will hereafter call "The Resort," and then was moved to a regular room with two other roommates. Each regular room was more like a dormitory than anything else. There were three beds to a room, each room sharing a common bathroom that was located in between the bedrooms, just like my dorm when I was at the U of Idaho. The beds were not a lot better than the detox beds, though they were a little more comfortable. The guys I roomed with seemed pretty normal. Just looking at them, you wouldn't really suspect that they had any problems, but we all shared some addiction of one kind or another, be it alcohol or some other chemical or herbal drug. I found most of the younger patients were in for OxyContin abuse, which I was surprised was so prevalent among the youth of today.

251

I got to call Julie the third day I was there and I was so overjoyed just to hear her voice. I told her I missed her so much, and I really meant it. She told me the following weekend she would be able to come for lunch and spend a couple of hours visiting me and I wanted to talk more about that, but there was a long line of people who were waiting and only two phones available, so I had to cut out conversation short. We could only talk for five minutes at a time and it was like they zipped by before I could even say hello!! It seemed now that I had so little time I could talk to her that suddenly I had so much to talk about! Then my phone time was almost used up. I told her I would call her again the next day. It was so good to have talked to her, I almost cried when I hung up the phone and I remember going outside and sat by myself and smoked a couple of cigs.

Each day was regimented so we always had something to do things to keep us focused on recovery. The day started with group meetings, breakfast, a lecture of some kind, group meetings, lunch, another lecture or film, group meetings, afternoon recreation time, lecture, dinner, AA meeting, then free time with a snack if we wanted to eat and then finally it would be bed time. There was always coffee and tea (both decaf and free) available and pop (diet/decaf and not free) available for sale in machines. All the food served in the cafeteria was sugar free and nutritious and the menus for each meal varied from day to day. There was a seafood dinner each week, but thank god they had the salad bar, which was well stocked and fresh, so I never went hungry (I am allergic to seafood). I actually lost about 30 pounds during the time I was there and never left a meal hungry, so I knew that most of the fat that I had gained during my drinking period was from the alcohol.

During the color group meetings, I was able to spend more personal time with my group members and with our counselor, and as a group, we learned a great deal about each other and about our individual addictions. We were able to openly discuss our emotions, fears, ideas and we were able to build trust between each other, more than would be possible if we tried to do things on our own. It was during my first group sessions that I was able to admit out loud that I was an alcoholic, which I had been adamant that I wasn't for so long. That was a *huge* step for me.

Our group counselor had given each of us our own goals and projects to work on to accomplish during our stay, so that we would be better prepared when we got back into the "real world" and live our lives without returning to our old habits. The group leader in charge of our group when I got there was a substitute because the regular guy was on vacation, and I really liked him and was able to make a more personal connection with him. I am thankful he was the one who set up my goals with me than had the regular counselor had been there. I had heard that David was tough, like the old fashioned drill instructors you would see in war movies on late night TV. When David returned, I was able to see firsthand that what I had heard was true, but luckily I had only one and a half weeks remaining by that time. David was still able to make my life difficult though in that short period.

Julie came to see me on the first weekend I was able to have visitors and she had lunch with me and then we attended a lecture for family and couples. Julie was given some excellent information on what to expect when I came home, things she should watch out for, how to make sure the house was safe for me to go back to, all sorts of knowledge on how to help make my transition back into life as normal as possible. After the lecture, we went outside and sat on the grass together and talked. I told Julie that I felt so much better about myself and what I was doing. I said that I knew that I had hurt her with my drinking and had neglected her and I just wanted her to know how sorry I was for everything I had put her through. I was holding her hand and smiling and I could see tears welling up in her eyes and then I just pulled her to me and gave her a big reassuring hug. Julie didn't say anything, but she hugged me back and I could feel her trembling a little as she cried. We hugged each other for a few minutes more and then we just sat in silence for a while, enjoying the beautiful day. We walked around the grounds and made small talk for a while and then it was getting close to the time she had to go. I walked her back to the parking lot and we hugged once more. I told her I was going to be different when I got out, and I promised her life would be better. As she walked to her car, I told her I loved her, something I had never said before, and it just came out without me really thinking. She turned around and said she loved me too.

One afternoon during the group meeting, someone came in and delivered a message to me. I read it and was happily surprised to find out that my mom was in town; apparently my older brother had fallen down some stairs, so she came to make sure he was okay and to see if she could help in his recuperation. She wanted to be able to see me as well and left her cell phone number for me to call when I could. I remember asking David if I could use his phone to call her and he told me that I had to use the pay phones like everyone else during the scheduled times. Although I had seen him grant others special privileges, it seemed that I was not going to get the same treatment. I had mentioned during group sessions that I felt family plays an integral part in one's recovery which seemed to be in opposition to what he felt. What I got from him was that while in recovery, one must rely on himself and what was taught there at The Resort, there should be no outside distractions of any kind, family or not, which would take away from what we were learning. There is some truth to what he was saying, I did understand that, but I also felt that God was sending her to see me as *support* of my recovery and I was going to make sure I saw her no matter what! She did end up coming on family visitation day that following Saturday and it was so good to see her.

One of the things I learned as part of recovery was that we had to be completely honest with ourselves and others. No more lies as we had done in our past to further whatever it was we were addicted to. I was not going to lie to my mom about anything anymore, and if she asked me any questions, I wanted to tell her how it was. She did ask me some tough questions. The first one was did I have a job to go back to when I got out. I told her no, and when I told her why she did not come down on me or show any disapproval whatsoever, which somewhat surprised me. She asked me if I still smoked, and I told her I did. I then told her not to ask me anything more right then, I didn't want to shock her too much in one visit. We walked around the grounds and I introduced her to some of my new friends in my group. It was really a very special time being with her, I could never tell her how much it meant to me to have her come and see me, especially at The Resort... and it went by way too quickly. I walked her to her car and hugged her before she left, thanking her profusely for taking the time to come and see me. I wanted to ask her if she really came to see my brother or if she used that as an excuse to come and see me, but I did not. I didn't want to put her on the spot and I was content that she had come to me at all.

One of the last things we had to do for our individual treatment plan was to write and present to our group a history of our drinking life, or drug life if that was a person's addiction and our progression was analyzed by the group as a whole to try to pinpoint what our weaknesses and low points were so as to help us in our future, to come up with ideas and defense plans and employ tools we could use to enable us to maintain our sobriety in life after we left The Resort. It's hard to explain, but I think it was a good program, a good method that was used. However, after hearing that our counselor was prone to recommend further treatment or intensive outpatient treatment programs for people who he deemed highly addicted I felt it necessary to edit certain things out of my story regarding parts of my drinking history that I thought he might use against me (had the substitute counselor still been there, I doubt I would have done that) though I included pretty much everything in this book.

One of the things I didn't mention was that I really enjoyed drinking in the morning while watching cartoons. It was thought to be extremely bad to drink in the morning. Though I don't disagree or condone alcohol consumption for breakfast, I often on the weekends would take one or two healthy swigs of my vodka when I would wake up on early around 6 or so. I would then turn on the TV and then relax and fall back to sleep for a couple more hours. I would not do that on mornings I worked of course. I never thought that was a bad thing, at least for me. It was just another weekend perk that I enjoyed. I also didn't mention all of the blackouts that I had experienced over my drinking history, either. I didn't want to mention anything that would cause me more time in treatment; when I got out, I wanted to stay out. Not that I wasn't completely unhappy there, I was learning quite a bit at The Resort, and I was also taking everything seriously. My own personal goal was to leave sober and stay sober. I had a lot riding on what I was doing. Not just for my own personal well-being, but for my future with Julie as well

Though we were told that AA was not heavily toted at The Resort, it was in fact a large part of the treatment program. I never really fought the concepts and ideas of AA; I do think that the 12 Steps are a valuable tool in the recovery process of anyone's recovery. The Steps are a good, solid foundation on which to build one's sobriety and a process that everyone who is serious about becoming sober should try to utilize. By the time I left The Resort, I think I was getting close to the fourth step. Have I completed all the steps? Answering honestly I will say no. Will I complete all the steps? Time will tell.

I made a lot of friends during my time at The Resort, and I saw over half my group leave before I did. But then my 28 days were up and it was my time and trust me, I was ready to go. I was very glad to be going home, but at the same time, I was sad to be leaving because I had become very close to some of my group members. But I realized that in a few weeks or less, they would be going home as well.

We all had been given copies of the big blue book of AA and just like we did in high school, we all passed them around like yearbooks for people to sign. I got some phone numbers from some people so that I could be sure to stay in touch with them and everyone wrote words of encouragement and insight. One of the guys in my group wrote in my book that I was always welcome to visit Alaska and stay with him and his family, but unfortunately, he died shortly after going home, so I will always treasure his words in my book. His death will always be an inspiration for me and my sobriety.

My friend Rob was there to pick me up from The Resort on Friday, September 1. It was 29 days since I had left home and it felt very strange feeling to be leaving there, like I was leaving prison and was now a free man. For almost a month I had not left the grounds except for one AA meeting at a local church, and even then it felt odd to venture out into the world (we were forbidden to leave The Resort during the treatment or face eviction). But as we drove off, I felt like a totally different person. I had been sober for a longer period time than I could ever recall, and I truly did not miss alcohol. I never really had any urges to drink the entire time I was there, and I hoped that I would not develop them now that I was gone. Rob said that I looked like a completely different person, and I told him that was the way I felt, too. He drove me home and dropped me off and I went inside the mobile and it felt so good just to be home. I found my cats and they just looked at me like life was normal and kept doing what cats do.

Julie had told me that she would have a surprise waiting for me when I got home and I found it when I went into the bedroom. She had gotten a new bed and had rearranged things a bit, and it really was nice. New bed, new comforter, everything was clean and organized; it was just a wonderful change to find. I wondered if this meant that we were going to start sleeping together again. I had told her about the beds at The Resort, how awful and uncomfortable they had been and I was looking forward to sleeping in a normal bed. I turned on the fan that was sitting on top of the dresser facing the bed, turned on the TV and lay down and watched my first television in a month. Not much had changed. I think I fell asleep shortly after that and slept until Julie got home.

A NEW BEGINNING

I knew that life wasn't going to be the same anymore now that I was back at home to a normal life. But hell, I had no idea what normal was like, so I had no clue as to how life should be. The only thing that I did know was that drinking alcohol was no longer a part of my life, and I was fine with that.

I don't remember what we did that first night, if Julie and I did anything special, to celebrate my return, if we went out to dinner. R was living there and would be staying with us to help out financially until I got a job and started making money again. We had sort of planned for me to take it easy for a few weeks, or as long as I needed, so that I would not feel rushed to get back into a life of stress, or anything that might cause me to want to pick up a drink again. That was what they told us at The Resort, not to dive right back in and put ourselves immediately back at risk. I was fine with that, it was like a little vacation, but I had a lot of things that I had to think about.

I had caused a lot of damage during my drinking years, not only affecting my relationship with Julie, but I had completely lost track of the value of money and the importance of bills (thank god for Julie, keeping us afloat as she had done), but a lot of my personal bills, such as old credit cards, the payday loans I had skipped out on, my student loan that I had forgotten about completely, numerous other debts were still waiting for some kind of attention. They were not going to go away just because I had gone to treatment and bettered myself. But Julie told me that we could deal with those issues in a few weeks. For now I just needed to concentrate on moving ahead with my new life. The bills would be dealt with; we would make sure of that.

Before going in for treatment, Julie had made sure that I had filled out all the necessary forms for applying for unemployment, and she had sent everything in, and after I was back home, we were informed that our application was contested by the dealership and we were subsequently denied the benefits. When I looked over the paperwork and looked at the details of why they denied me, I figured that I should not even bother to fight. There was just too much against me with damage to customer's vehicles, alcohol and cocaine in my system, and I figured I was pretty much screwed if I went forward with the dispute. Julie was furious and she felt that I was being treated unfairly and she wanted to rip that dealership a hole where none had ever been before. I just looked at things and told her that I screwed up, and the dealership was just doing what it does to cover themselves, right or wrong. If I hadn't fucked up, things might have been different, but it was what it was.

The day after I got home, Julie and I drove out to see some ice caves that were near where we lived and made a day out of it. It was a great drive, a beautiful afternoon, and we had the convertible top down. I hadn't been on a road trip in such a long time without any booze with me or in me, at first it was kind of strange, but then I just sucked on real water and enjoyed the drive and thought about all the good things in life that I could think about. Once we got to the ice caves themselves, it didn't seem as spectacular as we thought they would be, so we walked back to the car somewhat disappointed, but I tried to be goofy and get Julie to laugh and she did, but I could tell that something was bothering her.

I tried to make conversation by talking about all the things we could look forward to, our future together, what things would be like after I got a job and R moved out, maybe we could move into a house somewhere else if the opportunity came up, but it seemed the more I talked about those things, the quieter Julie became, and it was obvious she was getting more and more uncomfortable. That was really frustrating to me, and I became moody and no matter how hard I tried to get myself out of that feeling, the deeper I sank until I was almost crying. I didn't know what to say or do. Anything Julie said after that, I would almost bark a reply back at her, which didn't make things any better. When we were almost home, I asked her if she was scared of me. I don't know what made me ask that, but that was what came out. She looked at me for a moment and then back at the road in front of her, not saying anything. Julie finally said that she was not, but from her hesitation I knew that I was on to something. I then asked her if she was afraid that I was going to start drinking again. Was she afraid that I was going to fall off the wagon and return to the way I was. To that, she just nodded her head. For some reason, that acknowledgment crushed me. I felt in a way betrayed and took it that she didn't trust me. I don't think we spoke anymore to each other the rest of the day.

As part of the rehab program, it was recommended that everyone who comes out should attend 90 AA meetings in the first 90 days, and though I didn't think I was going to do that, I thought it might be good to go to at least a few. I remembered that I had seen a sign by the church about a half a mile from our place that advertised AA meetings every Monday night, so I thought it would be good idea to check that out. I had Julie drive me there that first Monday and when I asked her if she wanted to come in with me, she just shook her head and told me that it might be good for me to check it out myself. It was clear that things were so different between us than before I was at The Resort. It was sad to me because Julie was so heads up about getting me help and I now felt she was bailing out with the moral support in my continuing recovery. I didn't make things any easier when I told her as I got out of the car, that maybe it was better that she wasn't coming in. Maybe I would feel better being around my "own kind" anyway (poor choice of words to use Julie told me later). Julie peeled out of the parking lot after I got out and had closed the car door.

My first AA meeting outside of treatment was different. Now I was attending because it was *my choice* and not a requirement, which was a whole different feeling. Also, I was going in without anyone I knew, feeling like a total outsider. The cool thing about AA however, is that when you attend any meeting (and I have been to many different ones), you are most always made to feel welcome the moment you enter. What I really liked about that particular meeting was that it was a smaller group, with only about 10 people, so I never felt like I was lost in the crowd. I felt like a part of the group immediately, and I felt wanted. Everyone who was there really seemed to care about everyone else and wanted to know how everyone was doing. We all got time to talk about whatever we wanted to talk about, however most of the times there were specific topics that we geared our conversations towards. I left the meeting filled with a new hope, a sense of purpose, and a much better mood. I was actually looking forward to being with Julie and sharing my experience with her. R picked me up and brought me back home, and he asked me questions about the meeting and seemed more interested in how I was than Julie had been the last few days. R sensed my frustration with how things were between Julie and me and told me that I just needed to give it some time. He said that Julie was just trying to cope with how things were now, how things had changed. It bothered me because it seemed at that she was talking more to R than to me about how things were.

I kept myself busy at home for the most part, getting up early and having my coffee and smokes outside with either the newspaper or my crossword puzzle books. The weather was still nice and I would just sit and enjoy the time, doing my puzzles, I think in a couple of days I had pretty much done all them in both magazines Julie had gotten for me. I made a list of all the chores and things that needed to be done in the house. I fixed kitchen drawers, cleaned the fans, reorganized the kitchen cabinets and made them more user friendly, completely cleaned the house; I did all the things in that first week and more that Julie had been wanting me to do for the last year and a half or so that we had lived there. I know she was really impressed with my enthusiasm and what I had done, because I heard her bragging to R what I had accomplished. Some of the tasks I had done I felt were things R could have taken care of while I was gone, but I realized a long time ago that he just likes to work at selling cars and then come home and be lazy. That is just him, and some people you just can't change, no matter how hard you try.

There was an aftercare part of The Resort's treatment that patients who were there due to court orders or wanting to keep their jobs had to comply with which was a 26-week outpatient program. It wasn't mandatory that I had to do that, but I felt that I should do everything I could so that when it came time to get my driver's license back, everything would be in order. I felt it would make things look better to the DOL that I had gone through treatment and had all the documents that were necessary, so I started to attend. They were once a week for 90 minutes and they really weren't as bad as I had thought they might be. I was more concerned that it would be a waste of my time and that it would be a burden to get to and from the meeting when I lived so far away, but it turned out to be a great diversion from staying at home and doing nothing. I did find that one of the members from new class was also one of the regulars from my Monday AA meeting, so we were able to carpool (well, she would always drive and I tried to give her gas money, I swear!), so that made transportation much easier. By that time, I was pretty adept with the bus system, so I would catch a ride with Julie to her work and take the bus to downtown Seattle. I would play tourist for the early part of the day and then catch the bus to Bellevue and go to the class, and then get a ride from my friend back home. I ended up looking forward to attending the meetings.

After a while I started getting bored just hanging around the house and doing nothing. There was nothing more that I could think of doing as far as home improvement that wouldn't have called for a lot of monetary outlay. Then when R was laid off from where he was working and decided to take time off from selling cars, I felt it was time for me to start looking for a job. It was one thing to take a few days off when you get laid off, but the deal that we had made was that he was going to help out financially while he was there seemed to have been forgotten. That really pissed me off, but when I mentioned how I felt to Julie, she just told me it was okay, he will get another job, that I shouldn't worry. I told her that I didn't want to feel that I *had* to get a job because of him—I wanted to start working again because I *wanted* to. Julie just told me to stop making such a big deal about things, that I was just over-reacting. Now I never had thought that I should feel special or be given preferential treatment just because I had changed around my whole way of life and quit drinking, but at that point I felt that Julie had changed her whole opinion of me and didn't give a shit anymore how I felt. This was not the way I felt the person who had been my lifeline, my whole backbone when I was at The Resort should be treating me now. I told her that and she just kind of brushed me off, like I was making too big of a deal out of nothing. I was beginning to feel overwhelmed with emotions... and I was used to drowning them out with booze, but thankfully it was Monday again and I went to the AA meeting at the church and then I again realized the benefits of the meetings. I felt so much better after I got back home.

I didn't think I wanted to get back into the automotive business, especially after my last job, I thought that might be too close to something that might trigger me back to my old habits, so I tried to think of anything else that I might be good at. I had never really used the computer to job search before, and found it a very interesting tool, so full of information and websites that were designed to help one finding a job solutions. I thought about the hotel industry and remembered that though I thought I had gotten burned out in working in that field, maybe I had just been using that as an excuse because I didn't like where I was. Maybe I wasn't burned out after all. Maybe I just needed some time to get away from the property I was at and do something different. The more I thought about it the better it and I became confident that I could do it. Even though it had been more than ten years since I had worked at a hotel, I didn't think it would be all that hard to get right back in the stream of things. It should be just like getting back on a horse, you don't forget how to ride after learning the first time. It would be just getting used to a new saddle.

I had been using a computer in the home for quite a number of years, but in all that time, I had never put it to serious use, I had just mainly used it for surfing the web or playing solitaire. Now I found it fascinating that I could conduct an entire job search completely on-line. I discovered a local job-search website where I entered all of my skills and job types that I was interested in, and I could even specify the mile radius from my house where I would like to work. I chose the hospitality industry, specifying front desk positions and let the website locate available companies that were hiring. In a few days of checking the prospects, I had several hotels that I found had open positions and I was able to apply right on-line and even link my resume directly to the application. This was so cool, not having to spend time and gas when I could apply from the comfort of my own home! Technology, what a blessing!

I got a call from the first hotel I applied at in Bellevue and went in for an interview. I was told it was for the part time night audit position 3 nights per week, Friday, Saturday and Sunday nights, which I thought would be fine, after all, those used to be the nights that I tended to party more often during my drinking days. I thought it might be a perfect schedule to keep me, the former drinker occupied.

As was part of my new way of thinking, I was very open and honest during my interview with the front office manager and the hotel assistant manager about my past and my having been in treatment for alcoholism. I just felt it was better to be up front right at that time, rather than to have things from my past come out for whatever reason after I had been employed for a time and then face the consequences for lying. I felt it was a very positive interview and they told me that they would be in touch in a few days one way or the other if they wanted to hire me. When I got home and told Julie about my day, she surprisingly seemed pleased and optimistic, considering how she had been acting towards me the past month. She told me to keep my spirits up, that she was sure I would get the job.

I was heading to my Wednesday alcohol class two days after my interview when I got the call that they wanted me to come and work at the hotel. I wondered if Julie had some kind of sixth sense, as she had sounded so sure I would get the job, and she had been right. I told them I accepted and that I would start as soon as they wanted me to, which was that Friday night.

Friday October 13, 2006, I returned to the work force, totally sober and worked for 13 hours. If I hadn't been falling asleep by the end, I probably would have worked the last three hours I was scheduled, but I just couldn't keep the eyes open. It wasn't all that different from the night audit responsibilities that I had when I worked at the smaller hotel over 10 years prior, so making the transition back into the hospitality field was not so bad. I knew that I was starting over and that I had to start out at the bottom of the ladder again. I knew I was starting out at a much lower pay than I had been accustomed to. I figured that I would give it a year, work hard and then see where I was after that, see what my opportunities for advancement would be. I thought that was a very positive goal.

I had made the deal with Julie that my paychecks would go toward the house bills and that I would get my spending money with the understanding that she give me rides to and from work. It actually worked out pretty well, because she was off of her job well in time to take me to work, and when I got off in the mornings it was early enough that she had time to pick me up and then get to her own job.

Since I worked at night, I didn't have as much interaction with all the employees at the hotel, but those that I had met were all nice and very helpful, and it was refreshing to be back with a group of co-workers who worked as a team, unlike the last dealership I had last worked at.

It was almost two months before I actually met our general manager, as I usually was gone from the property well before the management team arrived in the mornings.

I kept going to the Monday AA meetings, usually every week, and eventually fulfilled my obligation with the classes on Wednesdays. I felt that I had gotten a lot of useful knowledge from the meetings, and I also felt as if I had graduated into a new level of personal growth when I left that last night. I received a certificate and paperwork for the department of licensing for whenever I elected to get my driver's license back. That in itself wasn't a huge priority in my life right then, as I didn't have a car, and thanks to Julie, I was having no problems getting to and from work.

I said earlier that I had a lot of damages I cad created during my years of drinking that I needed to face when I got back into the real world. My finances had gotten seriously out of control and I was in trouble with bill collectors and one debt had even gone into litigation, and I had been served with papers again. I had been through bankruptcy back in 1990 and the thought of going through that process yet once again didn't please me to any degree, but I really had no other choice. It was either do it and get things behind me for the last time or forever be in debt. I contacted an attorney and found out I could not go for the complete bankruptcy as I had done before, but instead file for Chapter 13 and make payments monthly. That appealed to me more; after all, since I did incur the bills, I should make some kind of restitution. So when everything was filed and the motion was approved, I was paying $50 out of my paycheck every two weeks and the program would last for three years, but even then, the student loan would still be owing since that was a government loan, but I would just deal with that when the time came.

As far as my personal life and my relationship with Julie, things were not getting any better, but at the same time, things were not getting any worse. She and I had not slept together since long before I went into rehab (not even with the new bed), and I didn't see any signs of us resuming any kind of a sex life. I don't know if Julie had just lost interest in me sexually, or romantically, or what was really going on. We had not said "I love you" to each other since I had gotten back home (well for a few days she only said it after I did first, but never on her own). I knew she still liked me to some extent, since her relationship status on her Myspace page had never changed from "in a relationship" but it just never seemed like we did anything together anymore. But it was not for lack of my trying.

She had taken me out for dinner on my birthday the November after I got out of The Resort and we had a really nice time, and the chocolate cake I got for dessert was the best that I had ever had! But that was the last time I can remember us even doing *anything* alone together. The following February, I had set up a reservation at a nice hotel downtown Bellevue for Valentine's Day and I wanted to take her out to a romantic dinner and spend the night alone together. She met me at the hotel that night and we did go to dinner, though conversation was very awkward and I could tell she was distracted and not really into things the way I had hoped. When we got back to the hotel, she spent most of the time on the computer in the business center and then came up to the room for a few minutes and then told me she needed to go to take care of the dogs at home, but she could come back. I was really hurt, because after all, R was there and he could easily tend to the dogs for her, since he still hadn't gotten a job (he had been collecting unemployment for at least three months or so), so I became very irritated with her and told her to just go home, if that's what she really wanted. She looked at me like she didn't understand what was going on and wondered why I was getting so upset. I walked her to her car and after she got in, I told her that I thought the whole night had been a bad idea. She left and I spent the night alone.

Over the next few months, it just seemed to me that there was no reason to even be labeled as "boyfriend/girlfriend" and I told her that one night on the phone from work while I was on my break. I told her that we might as well break up and just be friends. Julie actually protested and said we were doing just fine, and I pointed out that she spent more quality time with R than she did with me. I understood that they were best friends and had a longer history together than she and I did, and though at times that had made me extremely jealous, I had come to accept that. But I told her that *I* was supposed to be her boyfriend, but it just didn't seem that way anymore. I then said that it would just be easier for me and my feelings if we broke up. She told me she didn't want to do that, but I was persistent and I just knew in my heart that it was the right thing to do. I told Julie it was not like things would change, really, we hadn't acted in any way remotely romantic with each other in a long time, why should we keep up the charade. This was hard for me to talk like that, this kind of conversation was one that I had usually gone out of my way to avoid in the past, but I have found that since I have stopped drinking, I seem to have become better able to stand up for myself and confront things that I used to be afraid of. I think that surprised Julie. She finally seemed to agree with me, or at least she stopped protesting against what I thought was the inevitable and we broke up. I know breaking up over the phone is not the coolest way to do that sort of thing, but hey, it was a big step for me just to have even been the instigator of the conversation to begin with.

Julie's father signed the mobile home over into her name and then once she became the owner, she decided she wanted to sell it and buy a home in another park, or maybe just get into a smaller house with a yard so she could take care of the dogs better. I didn't think she would be able to sell the mobile as easily as she thought. I told her I felt we should stay there because the rent was so low and it was in a nice park, but I could not convince her to give up her idea of the change. She and R had been looking for other places on the weekends when I had to sleep (R was pretty much there to stay, as I had subconsciously feared would happen when I agreed to him moving in during my absence) and they found a place much further north of where we lived. It was a small three bedroom house with a nice yard, but the third "bedroom" was really too small for a third person, and I felt that I was being nudged out of the picture. I thought about looking on the internet for rooms in Bellevue that I could rent near the hotel. I felt I had time, not thinking I would need to rush, after all, she still had to sell the mobile.

I was actually surprised when I woke up one Saturday afternoon to see a real estate sign in the front lawn of the house. Julie had gotten an agent and the house had been listed. That was much quicker than I had anticipated. That was when I realized how serious Julie was about getting out of the mobile. I knew I had to step up my own plans. I needed to make sure I had a place of my own to live at when the time came to move, as I had told Julie that I wasn't planning on moving with her and R. It wasn't just the fact that "my room" would be too small, it was just plain too far away to be feasible for Julie to drive me to and from work every day, hell, the amount of gas used would be outrageous not to mention the extra time out of her day. I just couldn't see it happening.

I got on the computer and started looking *seriously* for rooms and found a couple of prospects near the hotel that I was interested in. I called the first number and talked to the owner of the house and asked him about the place, and he told me it would be better if I just came out and saw it in person, that way he could meet me and we could both be sure we were on the same page, me with the room and him with me as a tenant. Julie drove me early to work one afternoon and we stopped so I could meet the owner and check out the room. It was not far from work and I could easily take the bus. I liked the fact that I would not have to walk too far in either direction and it was only a couple of blocks from a mall and grocery stores, so realistically, the place would be ideal for me. After looking at the house and the room, I had a feeling that it would work, and I told the owner, Andy, that I would love to be considered. I then e-mailed him a thank you message that night from work. He called me the next day and told me he had talked to his two brothers who also lived with him in the house and they like what they heard. Andy told me that if I was still interested, I could move in. I said of course I was. Andy told me later that he had had several applicants for the room, but I was the only one who had thanked him for showing it to me, and that actually swayed his decision in my favor. My mom always told me it paid to give thanks, and I do believe that.

ON MY OWN

I moved in to the room in that house in the middle of July 2007 and got settled. I paid a monthly rent for the room (fully furnished—bed, dresser, desk, and a free standing closet) which included all utilities and satellite TV. There was wireless internet available, a hot tub in the back yard, and I got to use the kitchen if I wanted. It was a small room, but I was very comfortable with my TV (I recently purchased a flat screen TV from one of the brothers upstairs and I had a microwave and a coffee maker in my room, so I really had everything I needed. My needs those days were pretty simple for the most part. Ever since I lived at the house, I re-discovered books and in the first year, I probably read over 30 books, mostly Stephen King and Dean Koontz, though there were some non-fiction titles and inspirational books I read as well. I don't think I had read that many books in all the years prior. Yet I still found time to watch DVDs and my TV shows plus work and still do lots of other activities, though I *should* also have started going to the gym.

Julie and R still lived together up north, she has since moved to a bigger dealership with better pay and hours, but still is pretty much living paycheck to paycheck to keep her head above water with all of her bills, but I am very proud of her. I don't have a lot of friends who own their own house. R worked for a smaller privately owned used car lot, and when he was selling cars, he did well, though he did fall back into his own bad habits frequently (I didn't go into a lot of detail about that, because that is another book in itself, but it wouldn't have been a bad thing for him to deal with his own demons sometime). He and Julie would probably live together forever, and that would all right for them. She really does still love him in her own way, and she would do everything she can to keep him on the straight and narrow, and I truly think that if it weren't for her, R would have likely been somewhere in a bad place.

Julie and I are better friends now than before, and maybe it just took us living apart to have that happen for us. R told me that the night I moved out and into my room in the house in Bellevue that Julie had cried all night and didn't get any sleep at all. I will admit that the first couple of nights were quite a difficult adjustment for me as well. Hearing of her reaction to our separation and knowing mine as well, I thought maybe we both were taking each other for granted for the longest time, and it took physical separation to make us see that. But I do believe that everything happens for a reason, and if being apart made us appreciate each other more, than I have to respect that.

As of the first publication of this book, I had lived at that residence for almost a year, but I saw Julie every couple of weeks or so. She would drive down on the weekend and we would get together for a couple of hours and have coffee or go do any shopping if she needed to while she was in town. We talked to each other on the phone or texted each other almost every day (all free and built into the phone bill). I never thought I would end up having a friend like her, and truth be told, I thought after I moved and she and R had moved that we would have never gotten as close to each other as we did, emotionally speaking. I love Julie as my best friend and I owe her so much, really. I do believe that she saved my life by getting me into treatment when she did. If I had continued down the road I was on, I am pretty sure I was headed for more serious health problems and quite possibly an early death.

For the longest time I still worked at that hotel front desk. I moved to full time shortly after I started working there. I transitioned from night audit to daytime and after the first year, I dabbled in the housekeeping department for a brief period, but I found that just wasn't my cup of tea, so I stayed at the front desk. My feet problems, being such as they are, make it difficult to work a job that requires me to stand the entire time, the entire shift, after that long I start to limp because the feet cramp up and begin to hurt like hell and it becomes impossible to walk normally. I then went back to full time night audit, where I was not on my feet the entire time, making life much easier. I had thought about maybe getting some kind of an office job that would have career potential, something that I would not have to worry about being on my feet all day, or maybe if I won the lottery then I could get the foot surgery that would take care of *that* situation. But that is wishful thinking at its finest.

My friend Jeff became my sponsor and we saw each other every couple of weeks or so or at least kept in touch by phone if not in person. He was the one of the first I would call if I ever got any kind of urge to take a drink and I know he would be there to help. He has been one of my best friends for a long time and I am grateful for the fact that he has stuck around for as long as he has. I like to think that I have been as good a friend for him as well.

Rob has since divorced the girl he married when we were roommates and has since married the woman he will be with most likely for the rest of his life. I am very proud of him and he will always be my Brother! Rob has helped me out in more ways than he knows, and I will be forever embarrassed by things that I have done and how I deceived him in the past. I know that he would understand and look past those indiscretions because that is just the type of person that he is. Rob really seen the best in me and now has seen the worst in me, but I think that he can be proud to know that perhaps my strong will and perseverance that has gotten me through almost two years of sobriety—I know I got a lot of that from him.

I still keep in touch with a few of my group members from The Resort, and I will always cherish their friendship. Two of them live up in Alaska, and that will give me an excuse to one day get out of Dodge and go somewhere I haven't been before, take a road trip up north and see them. One lives on the Olympic Peninsula, and I have already been there for a visit to see him and his family. Good times.

Have my older brother and I reconciled and moved past the things that happened? Not as of this writing. I am optimistic though. One day, hopefully, things will be more normal between us.

Do I have any regrets about my life? If I said no, I probably would not be completely honest, because I don't think there is anyone alive (or dead) who never ever thought that their lives have been perfect. I probably would change some things about my life if I had to do it over again, but I am not totally disappointed with where I am now. I do not have a job where I make millions each year, I don't own a house, I am not famous. But I am alive and a lot healthier than I used to be or would have been. I still have goals and I feel now they are a lot more attainable than they ever were now that I have better control over my life.

I have made a lot of mistakes in my life, and it took me a long time to realize how foolish and carefree I have been and have seen the consequences of my recklessness, and maybe that was all destined for me to have experienced it all. If my life had been different, I would not have had the opportunity to write this book. If someone laughs while reading this, then I have made a difference. If someone thinks maybe their life is as out of control as mine was and makes a positive change because of reading this, then just maybe I have made a difference. I am no better or worse than anyone else and do not claim to be. I am just human.

I recently talked to Julie and asked her if she was still totally into me and in love with me when we moved in to the mobile home together, and she told me she was. I then asked her if I had not gotten so caught up in my alcoholism, would things have been different between us. She told me again yes. So if I have any great regrets, that may be one. I had a shot at love and I threw it away, that's what can happen when one gives in to their addiction, you can lose out on something really good. But in the end, I haven't lost out, and maybe it wasn't in the cards for Julie and me to be anything more than the best friends we are now.

I had not had any alcohol pass my lips for almost two years as of the time when this book was first published, not even a night-time cold medicine that contains booze, not even mouthwash that contains booze. I used the tame stuff and it works just fine for me.

Bottom line is I am happy now and things are getting better every day.

The End? Hardly.... Just the Beginning.
July, 2008

Note: I re-edited this book during March of 2015 and re-published it as an eBook on Amazon.com under the new title "Steve's Story – Unraveled and Reconstructed, since legally I felt I probably should change the title. A few years ago, I separated from the original publisher since I have had more success self-publishing eBooks. I do plan on publishing a follow up to "Steve's Story" very soon, as a lot has happened since. Mostly good I can happily report. But I shouldn't give away too many spoilers!
I hope you also enjoy my works of fiction I have written.

Life is good.
Steve Wilhelm, May, 2015.

ABOUT THE AUTHOR

Steve Wilhelm is a freelance writer, author, and holds a Bachelor's Degree in Telecommunications. Steve has enjoyed writing journals and short stories since his early childhood days in rural Idaho. His passions include movies, writing, social media, photography, and the outdoors. He currently lives in the Boise area. You can find him on Facebook at:

https://www.facebook.com/stevedu

bb - message him if you have any questions or anything, he loves to interact with any and all readers!